DOUBLE GUNS
and
CUSTOM GUNSMITHING

❧

STEVEN DODD HUGHES

DOUBLE GUNS
and
CUSTOM GUNSMITHING

STEVEN DODD HUGHES

From the publishers of

SHOOTING
SPORTSMAN

Camden, Maine

Also by Steven Dodd Hughes

Fine Gunmaking: Double Shotguns

Custom Rifles in Black & White

ISBN 978-0-89272-735-3

Book and dust-jacket design by Lynda H. Mills

Printed at Versa Press Inc., East Peoria, Illinois

5   4   3   2   1

Shooting Sportsman Books
A division of Down East Enterprise, Inc.
publishers of *Shooting Sportsman* magazine
Book orders: 800-685-7962
www.downeast.com

Library of Congress Control Number: 2007932098

Dedication

For Skeeter, and Tim Crawford,
two of the best kinds of friends a man could have.

Table of Contents

Dedication   5
Table of Contents   7
Acknowledgements   9
Foreword   11
Introduction   13

Section 1—Case Histories of Used Double Guns
    Chapter 1: A Good Gun, But . . .   17

Section 2—Custom Shotguns
    Chapter 2: A Custom L.C. Smith   29
    Chapter 3: A Custom Model 21 Pigeon Gun   34
    Chapter 4: Custom Fox Shotguns   37
    Chapter 5: F.lli Rizzini, Gardone, Italy   43
    Chapter 6: Perugini & Visini, Brescia, Italy   49

Section 3—Evolution of the Sidelock
    Chapter 7: Understanding Sidelocks   61

Section 4—Custom Gunsmithing
    Chapter 8: Refinishing Gunstocks   79
    Chapter 9: Stock Bending   91
    Chapter 10: Stock Machining   98
    Chapter 11: Balancing a Double Gun   102
    Chapter 12: Arcaded Fences   109
    Chapter 13: Double Gun Metalwork   116
    Chapter 14: TIG Welding For Shotgun Repair   119
    Chapter 15: Gunsmithing Screwdrivers   126
    Chapter 16: Machine Screws and Gun Screws   132
    Chapter 17: Metal Finishes for Fine Guns   136
    Chapter 18: Hallmark: Signed in Gold   143

Section 5—A Stockmaker's View
    Chapter 19: Evaluating Shotgun Stock Blanks   149

Section 6—Shotgun Engraving
    Chapter 20: Custom Shotguns and American Engraving   159
    Chapter 21: Firearms Engravers Guild of America   163

Acknowledgements

When people equate "talent" with my gun-work, I surely appreciate the notion, but, I'm here to tell you, I didn't have much when it comes to any in-born, God-given, natural ability to make custom guns. My father, now gone almost fifteen years, always made things. But due to circumstances, he never had the opportunity to teach me much. I'm sure some of it is in the genes, but much more of it comes from desire. I've said this before: when I found out someone could actually make a custom gun, there was nothing else in the world I wanted to do. Having done it for more than thirty years, I can say that I was fortunate to have had this career at a time when it could be appreciated and financially supported.

My clients—fellows like Ian Shein, Jim Flack, Randi Hart, Pete Treboldi, Bill Heaney, James Jay Baker, and many others—have been far more responsible for my accomplishments than any innate talent. They have instigated multiple commissions, trusted that their ideas and my desires would in time become unique custom guns, waited oh so patiently, and kept a few bucks flowing at the end of each month when the mortgage was due.

Of my "best" friends—people such as Penny McAvoy, Alyssa and Brian Francis, the late David Joyce, Tim Crawford and Kathy Hanson, Ed Kaltreider, Kurt von Nieda, Ross Bruner, Bill McDonald, Daryl Hallquist, Jack Heckles, George Kelly, professional bartender Glen Godward, and many others—some of whom are gun folks, some not. These people almost never seemed to tire of hearing about my desires and have stuck with me when my work or writing didn't seem to be going anywhere; each gave me their talent—friendship.

My comrades in the trade—such as gunmakers James Tucker, Dennis Potter, Pete Mazur, Ed Webber, Jerry Fisher, Martin Hagn, Ralf Martini, Dave Wesbrook (my photography mentor), Italian friends Vicenzo Perugini and Agustino, Morris Hallowell (a fine firearms dealer), and many others—are more responsible for what is seen as talent than anything instilled at birth. I've learned more from them during phone conversations, visits to their workshops, or photographing their custom guns than I have by any other means.

My engraver friends—such as Michael Dubber, Sam Welch, Bob Swartley, Eric Gold, Ron Smith, Winston Churchill, Bill Gamradt, Larry Peters, and many others—who have either made my guns look spectacular or taught me what would help make them look that way.

And finally there are the authors of the more than three hundred volumes of gun-related books in my library which have been my "talent bank," a place I could go when I was in need of inspiration or instruction, and the place most of my gunmaking dreams and desires originated. I am fortunate to have studied custom guns from every era since the seventeenth century and, with my love of history, have always respected the tradition of fine gunmaking. I have known that when I needed a "new" idea, I could find it in something that had already been done, and done well.

As for the specifics of this book's coming to fruition, without my editors at *Shooting Sportsman* magazine—Ralph Stuart (especially), Vic Venters, Ed Carroll, the truly talented art director and designer of this book, Lynda Mills—and the book's editor Joe Arnette, it never would have happened. Each of them has played a large part in my appearing to be "talented."

When someone remarks about my talent and I look over my shoulder to see who they are referring to, it is all of these folks that I am looking for.

Thanks!

Foreword

It doesn't surprise me that Steve Hughes sees the same analogy that I do between creating this book and undertaking the long, complex process of making a custom gun. Each has so many layers and so many interdependent sub-processes that the hundreds of hours of concentrated effort in each can seem overwhelming at the start. One must learn in gunmaking and in writing—as in any craft—to break the whole into achievable steps, to research and plan each as thoroughly as makes sense, and then to begin one task, whether with a blank sheet of paper or the plain curves at the fences of a Belgian Britte double in the white. Done well, each craft is the culmination of years of learning and practice, each project informed by all those that came before.

Working with Steve and his *Fine Gunmaking* column has been one of the great pleasures in my years as an editor at *Shooting Sportsman*. Steve's detailed, workmanlike approach offers simple and direct explanations of some arcane topics, presenting both the fundamentals and the minutiae that fine-gun enthusiasts are looking for. In crafting *Double Guns and Custom Gunsmithing*, Steve had an advantage as a writer that he may seldom—if ever—experience as a gunsmith or custom gunmaker: In their original form as *Fine Gunmaking* columns, the parts of this book could be completed and sent off, all of worth on their own, utterly unlike the parts of a gun. An American custom gunmaker's life would be simpler by far if he could send out finished parts and an invoice every week or so. With this book, then, Steve has polished the parts considerably and come up with a finished product far greater than a simple assemblage of parts. It's been a joy to read these columns again and to see where a few file strokes here and some 320-grit there have brought up a fresh shine on the originals that I'm uniquely familiar with.

I visited Steve's workshop in Livingston with my family during an autumn Montana vacation, as much to get a sense of the physical space and the tools—for the brief glimpse of the work in progress, the tools, and the layout of the workbench—as anything else. Whatever my expectations, the modest shop behind his home fit perfectly with my impressions formed of Steve as a writer. It's neither antiseptically well organized nor a chaos of clutter, with a clear and naturally lighted core that holds the drawings and tools centered on the bench and the gun bits of the current work. The old things pile up toward the margins in shadow—wood and metal pieces set aside from past guns or for future projects, hulking industrial machinery used infrequently, and a small room in which he's purpose-built the fully functional photo studio he illustrates his columns with. In gunmaking, as in writing, there's nothing here too fancy; there is plenty that is not needed for the task at hand but has accumulated with experience and can't be discarded. In building guns or writing about them, Steve brings a craftsman's focus on just what is needed and nothing more.

Steve's daily business as a successful custom gunmaker does not require that he know the history of every metal finish used on guns or the evolution of the sidelock or the state-of-the-art techniques of contemporary Italian makers. His writing offers that path toward exploration. What lies within this book—as within his shop—is the result of a wonderful intellectual curiosity, made plain for the reader, for the same joy that makes a well-made gun a pleasure to carry afield. What lies within is an exceptional expression of his benchcraft brought to letters.

- Ed Carroll

Introduction

As one journeys through life, goals either become accomplishments or get left behind. Sometimes goals change and become something greater than one could have ever imagined. Such is the case with *Double Guns and Custom Gunsmithing*.

I have to admit that I didn't set out to write this book. It came about through the startling fact that I've been writing the "Fine Gunmaking" column for *Shooting Sportsman* magazine for more than fifteen years. My first book, *Fine Gunmaking: Double Shotguns*, is a compilation of early columns and has served as a primer for readers seeking a greater understanding of double shotguns.

Double Guns and Custom Gunsmithing contains material from my later *Shooting Sportsman* pieces. After I had written numerous further columns, it became clear that a second, more advanced, book could be compiled from them. When readers started asking me when my next book would appear, I began thinking about specific workshop procedures people had asked about and some of the techniques that simply aren't being practiced in this country and that folks would be interested in learning about and seeing in process. I continued shooting photos of in-progress gun work rather than only the finished results. Thus, in the past couple of years, some of these columns were planned and written with this book in mind.

When I started writing about gunsmithing and custom gunmaking, I chose the how-to-do-it format because there was such interest in that approach. Many people were genuinely interested in the subjects, but had no intention of doing the work. But those interested in the how-to approach are often sharp enough to apply this style of writing at their own workbenches and for personal gun projects.

Accordingly, most of this book's chapters were written from a how-it-was-done point of view. If you've ever wondered how the sculpting of your shotgun's action took place, you will find out here. If you've been thinking about having a stock bent to fit your physique, I'll help you with the relevant considerations. The chapters about chiseling side-by-side actions are definitely not how-to material, and the reader proceeds at his own peril if he attempts this work. I'll take this moment to declare that I'm not responsible for your screwing up your gun.

The "Refinishing Gunstocks" and "Gunsmithing Screwdrivers" chapters especially employ the how-to approach and are meant to convey procedures the hobbyist can readily put to use. Refinishing stocks is probably the most common home gunsmithing done by those who seek to improve the appearance and durability of their own guns. I relate five different refinishing methods that cover a wide spectrum of techniques used by professionals. These how-to subjects will open doors to other arenas of gunsmithing for those who have an interest in getting inside shotguns to further understand the fascinating mechanisms that—joined with rich walnut—unite us with the sporting life.

Three chapters in particular—"Stock Bending," "Balancing a Double Gun," and "Evaluating Shotgun Stock Blanks"—speak directly to frequently asked questions about double shotguns and gunsmithing. "Stock Bending" serves to replace some of the subject's "black magic" with professional procedure, although there still may be some "smoke" involved. "Balancing a Double Gun" is about understanding why one gun feels like "I could hit with it," while another handles like an oak post. Gun balance is a subject of great interest to many gunners, though one that is seldom visited. Conversely, "Evaluating Shotgun Stock Blanks" is a common topic of discussion and advice; often, these days, consumers buy wood for its exquisite beauty rather than for its soundness, strength, and stability. I approach the subject as if I want your new shotgun stock to last as long as I would my own.

America has a splendid tradition of customizing, of taking that which was mass manufactured and tuning, refining, or re-creating, until an object of better function, finer handling, and higher esthetics results. I review three popular American-made guns with the hope that more readers will feel compelled to have a unique shotgun created for themselves.

As mentioned in the "Custom Fox Shotguns" chapter, I'm amazed and humbled when I see a Fox gun that has obviously been remodeled following the information in my first book. In the future, I hope to see examples of and to hear readers relate how this current book has helped them—as clients, gunsmiths, and hobbyists—by stimulating their curiosity and encouraging them to take on more sophisticated custom gun projects.

You will read about my visits to the workshops of Italian gunmakers—visits that were enlightening and frustrating as I witnessed sophisticated craftsmen working alongside youthful apprentices. It was enlightening for me to see their techniques for myself, knowing someone was being trained to do this work; frustrating in the realization that I had to return to my shop and try those techniques with no one around to coach me.

Reading about the "Evolution of the Sidelock" may help you understand the context of the historical continuum and how the advanced geometry of these intricate mechanisms amounts to no more than a few moving parts. It is a wonderment that most gunlocks haven't advanced, or needed to, since the late nineteenth century.

I've been told that my writing is straightforward and clear, and for that I am thankful and humbled because I have no background as a writer. All my words come from the desire to share my experiences with those who are interested. Note that several levels of professional editing have made these chapters more than I am capable of presenting alone.

As for my gunsmithing, that is another matter altogether. I am tremendously proud of my accomplishments in that arena. They were hard won, every step of the way. A fellow recently wrote to me about the preparations, incantations, moon phase, and elaborate rituals he would have to undertake before he could begin to think about shaping a gun's action as I do. I wrote back: "The truth is, I did a full-scale gun drawing, several action drawings and sketches, Sharpie lines on the metalwork, fitted and rough-shaped a pattern stock, set the project aside for two weeks, compiled the dozen or so photos of similar guns torn from magazines, consulted four books and looked at three more, talked with a couple of other gunsmiths, and only then, about a month after starting the project, finally took a file to the metal. I did most of the initial shaping one evening, and then there was no turning back." The point is that although this stuff may look easy, rest assured that it isn't.

It is my fondest hope that each of you will enjoy reading *Double Guns and Custom Gunsmithing* as much as I have enjoyed making it. For me it was much like a sophisticated custom sidelock shotgun project, requiring much planning, many years of work, a multitude of pieces and parts, detailed finishing with the help of other professionals, hopefully resulting in a useful, worthy, and enduring accomplishment.

Steven Dodd Hughes
Livingston, Montana

SECTION 1
Case Histories of
Used Double Guns

CHAPTER 1
A Good Gun, But . . .

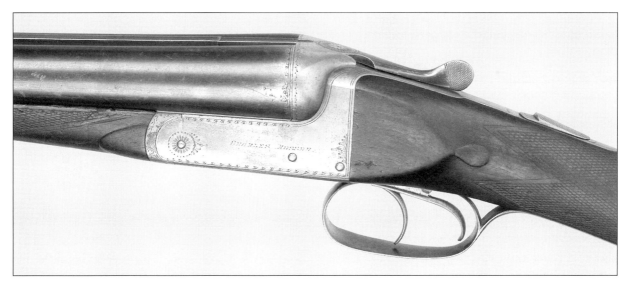

A generic Anson & Deeley boxlock. This gun is a Rosson, but it was probably made from the same forgings used on Birmingham shotguns.

It happened again a couple of weeks ago. A client came by the shop to show me his new pride-and-joy Birmingham boxlock, which was was loose as a goose. He wasn't surprised to find out it was off-face, but the estimated repair costs were a big surprise.

My friend Jim Flack calls this type of firearm "a good gun, but . . . ." Virtually every used gun on the market has one form of "but" or another. In this chapter I present case histories of good and bad gun purchases. Each of these guns needed some kind of work. I've read and written stories about what to look for in a used double and consider these examples valuable. Here I'll take the slightly different approach of examining actual guns rather than presenting hypothetical problems.

It's almost as safe to speak of Birmingham boxlocks as a class of gun as one would Parkers, because so many of them were made at about the same time, with similar manufacturing methods, based on the Anson & Deeley system. The guns do vary in quality of fit, finish, and embellishment, but just as Parker doubles have ejector problems and Fox guns often have worn locking bolts, most Birmingham doubles share their own common virtues and faults.

The boxlock I mentioned was from a little-known Birmingham gunmaker and probably of 1920s or '30s vintage. The fellow bought it from a local sporting goods store, where it had sat behind the counter on consignment. It was a 12-bore with a straight grip, 30-inch barrels, extractors, and twin triggers. It balanced well, felt good in the hands, and cost $900. Of course, the clerk had known nothing about the gun's choking and chamber length.

The first thing I did was remove the forend, hold the gun by the barrels, and shake it. I saw and heard a noticeable rattle. Further inspection revealed that the bores looked good, the barrels and furniture had been competently reblacked, and the stock dimensions at the comb were reasonable. The straight grip—amateurishly converted from a pistol grip—had an obvious dip where the guard tang ended, and the tang itself had been cut off and rounded in the middle of an engraved scroll. The recut checkering was hashed. Measuring instruments showed $2^{1}/_{2}$-inch chambers, bores oversized by a few thousandths of an inch, no choke in the right barrel, and just a few points in the left. Overall it was a decent gun, but . . .

The client had shown it to another gunsmith who had pronounced it "loose but safe to shoot." (There's that "but" again.) I explained to the owner how a gun gets off-face and that, though it might be safe, it would only get looser if it were shot in that condition. When the owner asked the cost of refitting the barrels and breech, I said "at least $600."

Now we're looking at a $1,500 gun with obvious cosmetic problems at the grip. I also noted that the 14-inch length of pull was a bit short for the new owner's tall, lanky, long-armed build and that the reasonable solution would be to add a recoil pad and bore the butt to counter the additional weight. If it were my gun, I said, I'd have the barrels slightly back-bored—providing there was sufficient wall thickness—to restore a bit of choke, and I'd have the chambers lengthened to $2^{3}/_{4}$ inches.

My estimate for installing a recoil pad, back-boring the barrels, and lengthening the chambers added several hundred dollars to the cost. Along with the purchase price and off-face repair, we're looking at investing a couple grand

into a gun that couldn't be sold for that amount.

I empathized with the client's tight budget, but I realized he'd let emotion enter into his decision-making process. The fact is, he had wanted an English gun so badly that when he saw one within his budget he'd snapped it up without having a gunsmith inspect it.

The next two gun stories involve my friend John Barsness, a gun writer of some note. John has gun savvy, is rarely swayed by emotion, and has stocked and checkered enough guns to know how he might contribute to getting a gun "right."

John wanted an American double primarily for waterfowling. He also had a weakness for Ithaca shotguns because of an emotional attachment to Elmer Keith, who had liked and shot them. John had stocked an Ithaca NID a few years before, so he was familiar with that model's works and stocking requirements.

At a gun show, John found a Lewis Model Ithaca with steel barrels, good bores, and tight ribs; a gun that appeared to lock up soundly. He correctly identified small dents, blemishes in the bores, short chambers, and one broken firing pin. This work would have to be farmed out, but he decided that the few-hundred-dollar price, plus some hobby stockmaking, would get him into a reasonable double that would fit his budget and satisfy his desires.

His gunsmith confirmed his evaluation, agreed to do the work, and gave him an estimate of $300. Once into the project, however, the gunsmith discovered that, although the gun appeared to lock up tight, it was off-face and the top fastener (an arm projecting forward from the lever) had broken off and was missing. Rejointing alone, with a new hinge pin, would bring the cost of repairs to $600. Also, the three-position safety didn't function properly.

In the meantime, John and I had struck a deal in which I would weld, recut the slots, and refit eleven buggered screws. When I saw the Ithaca, I warned John he was getting in deep, but

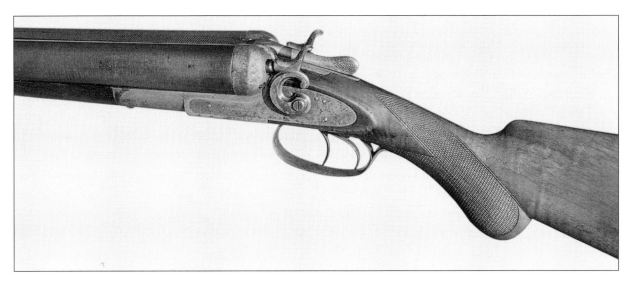

An 1889 Remington 10-gauge twist-barreled hammergun—a lovely wall-hanger.

we agreed to go ahead and that I would also take a stab at fixing the safety. My work came out to our mutual satisfaction, but I wasted hours making no headway on the safety, and I couldn't find a replacement toplever with the fastener arm.

The gun sat in a repair specialist's shop waiting for safety work, and John realized the mistake he made: "I'll probably hang it on the wall to remind me of an emotional attachment and a bad experience." With close to serious money into the gun, he'd already lost several hundred dollars (without being any nearer to shooting it) and all enthusiasm for restocking the piece.

The point to remember is that American guns all changed, for better or worse, during the course of their production; thus, it behooves buyers to study individual models before making a selection. (John, being more familiar with later-model Ithacas, had been unaware of the potential problems with the older gun he purchased.) In addition, regardless of model, the better the gun's condition when you see it, the less likely it is to have problems.

John's second go-round had much happier results. When dropping off the Ithaca at the gunsmith's shop, he found a Fox Sterlingworth 12-gauge that had been restocked with shootable

dimensions. It sported an attractive piece of American walnut, a few case colors, and about 80 percent of the original bluing. The gun was reasonably priced, so he bought it from the smith who'd done the work and knew what it looked like inside.

The gun had moderately light 28-inch barrels, double triggers and extractors, and was tight as a drum. Although it had a few barrel dents and needed its chambers lengthened, barrels honed, and trigger pulls lightened, the cost of the work was acceptable. John had already pared down the comb to give it more drop, slimmed the buttstock to suit his tastes, and refinished the wood for aesthetics and durability. He added a recoil pad to lengthen the stock and bored holes in the butt to shift the balance point. He's now looking forward to checkering the stock.

With a bit more into the Fox project than he put into the Ithaca, John has a 7-pound gun that balances, fits, and functions as it should—with the added bonus of personal time invested to make it his own. If he ever decides to sell the Fox, he's confident he can get his money back and probably something for his time.

Where John really came out on this project was in the low cost of stock adjustments. I can't stress enough the importance of shootable dimensions in double guns, old American guns in particular. I've yet to see an original Fox Sterlingworth with a comb high enough to suit me. Years ago I sold a near-mint Fox 20-gauge that I loved but couldn't shoot because of its 1³/4-by-3-inch comb. Adding spacers or bending stocks often only adds to the "but" considerations and may ruin a perfectly collectable gun.

Here is a story about what I call a grandad's gun—old guns that belonged to dad's dad and have spent years in a closet, gathering dust. I bought this particular Remington Model 1889 10-gauge hammergun for $100, mostly as a favor to a waitress who always had a smile and gave good service. It was wrapped in a bedsheet, and I hardly gave it a look before plunking down the money.

Back at my shop, I unwrapped the gun to find it a uniform brown from the bead at the end of its 32-inch Damascus barrels to the refitted buttplate. Let's just say this one didn't look like a shooter. Months later, I took another look and realized the gun was in quite good condition and all original, except for the shortened stock (a 13-inch length of pull) and a replacement brass hammer screw. Curious about how the Model 1889 looked inside, I completely disassembled the gun, then decided to give it a thorough cleaning inside and out.

Several hours later I was looking at the firearm I wish people would bring me when they ask about restoring grandad's old shotgun. The wood was sound and handsome with good checkering, the metal had an appealing patina, and, although the twist barrels were freckled inside, they were quite attractive outside. It was a lovely wall-hanger that I wished I could say had been in my family for generations. (Note that for some folks, restoring a family heirloom is important, and that is the only time I can justify putting more money into a gun than it would bring at resale.)

A rough experience can also happen with high-dollar imported double guns. A few years ago I scored my own "good, but" gun. The 16-bore Anson & Deeley-style boxlock was built in Ferlach, Austria, around 1910 and had all the features I was looking for. This just might be the gun of my dreams! Or so I thought.

Weighing six pounds, the gun had 30-inch Krupp steel barrels that were dent- and flaw-free, measured .028 inches minimum wall thickness, had 98 percent rust bluing, and were ideally (for me) choked open and nearly full. The gun had been recently reproved in Birmingham, although the chambers had been lengthened to 2³/4 inches since. It also had numerous Continental features, such as Southgate ejectors, sideclips, cocking indicators, and an Anson-type, push-button forend latch.

The gun locked up like an armored car, with a Purdey double underbolt, hidden toplever fastener, and square crossbolt hidden in the doll's-head barrel extension. And all were well fitted. Adding charm to the M. Ogris-signed gun were fancy-back scalloping, arcaded fences, and nearly full-coverage engraving with attractive small scroll and a gold-inlaid "SAFE" to boot.

Heavily marbled, high-contrast walnut was the first thing I noticed about the gun, and, though its open-curved, horn-capped pistol grip and European cheekpiece were not currently in vogue, I found them pleasing in appearance and comfortable when mounting. The gun was 90 percent of what I wanted in a lightweight game gun. Sure, there were some stylistic features I could live without, but that's the nature of any used gun. Add the fact that I got the gun in trade for labor on a friend's custom single-shot rifle, and I'd say it was a sweetheart deal.

From the first time I picked up the gun, it was apparent the length of pull was too short and the gold oval monogram plate (that at one time covered the hole in the stock where the sling swivel had been) was missing. These problems could easily be remedied by replacing the hard-

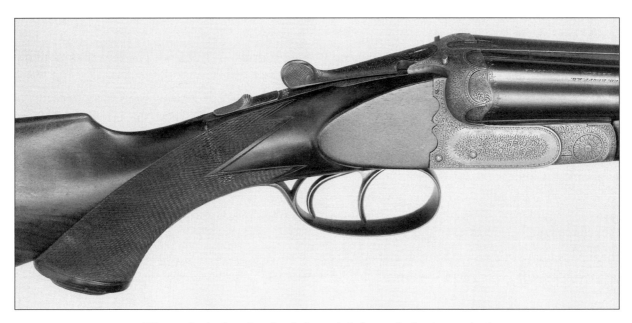

The author's Austrian boxlock needed the cracked grip repaired.

rubber buttplate with a recoil pad and installing a new oval plate. A potentially more difficult problem was the grain flow through the stock wrist, which, although exceedingly attractive, would make the wrist somewhat fragile.

Back in my shop I inspected the gun closely and realized I'd made the error I most often warn clients about: I hadn't measured the stock dimensions. There was simply too much drop at heel to suit me. Also, under magnification, I spotted a minute crack from the top tang down through the checkering to the guard tang. I was afraid to attempt bending the stock for fear of breaking it through the cracked and squirrelly wrist grain. I realized I might be over my head with this "nearly perfect" shotgun.

I sent it off to gunmaker Jack Rowe, who has probably bent more stocks than I've even handled. I told him about the wrist grain and the crack, then asked him for a half inch up at the heel.

Jack's letter concerning the boxlock was a gunsmith's classic: "I cannot risk bending this stock; that crack on the right side goes top to bottom. Steve, my old mate, it won't stand up; it will break. Just like the Austrians to use a piece of firewood or a piece with a badly grained head. It is a

well-made A&D with unnecessary lock-ups."

Ideally, the Austrian gun needed a new stock—if I ever hoped to shoot it well. It sat for a year before I reevaluated the project. I decided to keep the gun, repaired the cracked stock, and installed a recoil pad to lengthen the pull. I found a fellow who (at my risk) successfully bent the repaired stock upward at the heel. I love the gun, and it will probably never get a new stock.

How about the following for a nightmare gun story that involves the wrong approach and poor decisions? It makes me cringe every time I think of the gun.

In a gunsmith's shop a few years back, I was shown a restocked Cogswell & Harrison boxlock. The proprietor told me it looked as if the gun had been "stocked by a rifle guy" before any mechanical problems had been addressed. As I recall, the owner bought the gun for $700, spent $1,600 for the new stock, then put another $1,700 into having virtually every internal part rebuilt or replaced. (This included replacing the hinge pin and five springs, which at one point had been broken and brazed together so the gun functioned marginally.) When I saw the Cogswell it was on its third journey to a gunsmith, this time for cosmetic metalwork, including nine or ten new screws, engraving touch-up, and reblacking, at a cost of another $500.

Lest you think buying new will preclude problems, let me tell you about the Italian hammergun currently in my vault. It's from a moderately prestigious maker and has been a long, bad trip for its owner.

The fellow purchased the gun, new, from an American dealer's inventory. He then hopped and skipped his way over to a stockmaker friend, to whom he raved about the beautiful wood. "It's got terrible wrist grain and will probably break" was not the response he was expecting. Sure enough, a couple hundred rounds later the stock broke from top to bottom through the grip.

There having been no guarantee on the wood, it took much haranguing and implied legal action to convince the dealer and maker to restock the gun at no cost. The owner was offered, and agreed to, an upgraded conversion to a self-cocking ejector mechanism.

Nearly three years after its initial purchase, the gun was sent to me for lightening and balancing. It seems the gun had gained a half pound during restocking—a 7 3/4-pound 12-gauge was a bit much for the owner's liking.

The updated mechanism was also a potential problem that required resolution. While hunting, it seemed natural for the owner to open the breech, insert shells, close the gun, then lower the now-cocked rebounding hammers. But when he wanted to unload the gun without firing, he had to recock the hammers or the ejectors would fling out the loaded shells—lowering the hammers activated the ejector trips. The ejectors were slightly out of time already, from flinging out loaded shells that were heavier than they were designed to handle. This man has now invested $10,000 in the gun, and I'm still trying to figure out how to remove weight and balance the piece.

The next fellow—we'll call him Robert—did everything right. He purchased a turn-of-the-century Joseph Lang sidelock from a reputable dealer in England. The buyer asked all the right questions, and the seller answered them honestly; the side-by-side was fairly priced, and a few months later the gun arrived, much to Robert's delight.

The seller had altered one choke and bent the stock to suit Robert's tastes at no cost (an advantage when buying from an English dealer with in-house gunsmithing). Robert had made a study of English doubles and, seeing as he knew how to remove and inspect the locks, went over the gun completely, making a list of questions in the process. He brought the gun to me; together, we disassembled it, and I answered his questions one by one.

We found four items worth further evaluation. One was a striker-retaining screw that had a broken head; I told Robert that if it was easy to remove, it would be easy to repair. The second was an interceptor safety spring on one lock that didn't function. This was not a big problem, but it demanded attention. The third was an old but sound-looking repair to a crack in the horn of the stock above one of the lockplates. (Sidelocks have four "horns," or fingers of wood, one above and one below each sideplate, where the stock meets the action. These are the weak spots on sidelock stocks.) The fourth was that the stock head and forend were oil-soaked—a common problem in older doubles.

Robert loved the gun and agreed to send it to a gunsmith of the seller's choosing. The gun was fixed and returned in a timely and professional manner. Robert figured he now had the gun of his dreams, but after just three boxes of 1-ounce shells, cracks showed in both the upper stock horns.

A call to the seller brought the immediate (and respectable) reply: "Why don't you just return the gun? I'm sure you've lost confidence in it." This is an extraordinarily rare occurrence and, in my opinion, the dealer acted above and beyond what was ethically required.

According to Robert, "Whenever you order a gun over the phone, you have incredible expectations. This gun met mine. If the stock hadn't cracked, I would have shot that gun forever. I returned it because of accumulated disappointment. I just lost confidence in it, although I now have even more confidence in that dealer." He then added: "The only sensible thing to do is take your new purchase to a professional gunsmith for evaluation." In this case neither I nor the repair gunsmith was able to foresee the action's setting back and cracking the stock. In retrospect, I could have stressed the importance of rebedding or glass-bedding the stock-head after removing the oil from the wood.

*   *   *

Clearly, my examples aren't all stories with happy endings, but they are true and serve as cautionary tales. To summarize and close this chapter, I'll offer a bit of advice on preparing for the best and avoiding the worst when purchasing double guns.

I described the purchase of a "loose" Birmingham boxlock in need of costly work. The buyer had been so set on finding an affordable English gun that his only criteria had been origin and price. To avoid disappointment, the buyer should have had a gunsmith inspect the gun before the deal was consummated.

Similar circumstances surrounded John Barsness's purchase of an old Ithaca. An honest gunsmith would have told him to keep looking. But Barsness's second go-round, with the restocked Fox Sterlingworth, turned out to be a good buy—he knew at the outset that the gun would require an investment of money as well as his own time to get it "right."

The restoration of grandad's gun—my example of an old Remington hammergun—is another fairly common situation. Through the

years, I've had many folks bring me family heirlooms, and many times I've been able to convince them the guns don't need to be shot to be appreciated and that full restorations would eliminate the character left from honest use. Thorough cleaning and conservation, as opposed to restoration (such as repairing cracked or broken stocks and getting oil into the bottom of rust pitting), are often in order. When clients insist on a complete overhaul, I warn that it will entail more work than I can quote on and probably cost far more than the gun is worth.

I described one of my own purchases, the Anson & Deely-style boxlock, and how I fooled myself by not checking stock dimensions or closely examining the stock for cracks or damage. Taking some time away from the project gave me a new point of view and all came out well. An important lesson here is that not all stocks can be bent to modify dimensions. Also remember that cracks or repairs to the wrist can be camouflaged by checkering. I've seen guns with shattered grips pieced back together and recheckered so the repairs were nearly undetectable without examination under magnification.

Remember the nightmare story about the Cogswell & Harrison boxlock that after a few thousand dollars of rebuilding wound up functional? A competent gunsmith would have told the buyer to stay away from it in the first place—a reputable smith would have never started the sinkhole repair project. Still, the anecdote points out the importance of a logical order of progression in having a gun rebuilt or restored. The fellow who had restocked the gun before it was repaired proved his amateur status with poor judgment and mediocre workmanship.

When things are done properly, an older gun first gets an overall evaluation and the client gets written notes so he has an idea of what he is getting into. If necessary, barrel repair or alteration is done next, because if the barrels can't be brought up to snuff, there's no point in going further. Mechanical repairs follow; the gun should be functioning perfectly before stockwork is even considered. Then stock dimensions can be altered by bending, shortening, or installing spacers or a recoil pad. The stock can then be refinished. Restocking should be considered a last alternative, as it is the most drastic and expensive alteration.

Metal polishing follows stockwork so dings or scratches can be addressed. Picking up, or recutting, the engraving and repairing the screwheads are the final steps before finishing such as bluing, blacking, or case coloring. Departing from this order will create problems for the gunsmith and cost the client more money in the long run.

As for new doubles, I described an Italian hammergun that broke through the wrist. I'm seeing more new guns with poorly laid-out stocks, often with gorgeous wood. When buying new, find out if there is any guaranty against stock breakage. I'll bet there isn't. When inspecting any gun—not only the new ones—look at the wrist grain carefully and remember that the stock is nearly hollow between the tangs. I'd much rather have straight and sound grain through the wrist than the fanciest stick of the rarest walnut poorly laid out.

When it comes to older American doubles, each presents its own problems. L.C. Smiths, for example, frequently have cracked stocks; graded Parkers and Foxes have gotten expensive; all Lefevers are old; and, at least to me, most Ithacas aren't inspiring. Prices are all over the map, and many of the guns don't have shootable dimensions. For sound mechanics and good dimensions, Winchester Model 21s are probably the best of the bunch, but they have achieved cult status and require a moderately large investment.

There are still good buys in Continental guns, both boxlocks and sidelocks. French, Belgian, German, and Austrian guns represent some of the best values for shooting and hunting guns. Most are of good design, are well made

with fine steel barrels, and have shootable dimensions. They can be evaluated in the same manner as British guns; but remember, you're likely to find cheekpieces, horn trigger guards, or sling swivels.

When I peruse used-gun ads, I look at the following in order of personal importance: gauge, barrel length, weight, chokes, then stock dimensions—drop at comb and heel, length of pull, and cast, if any. How the butt is finished-off is less important because it is the easiest thing to alter. For example, if you need a 14⅝-inch length of pull and the gun is 14¼ inches with a one-inch pad, you're going to mess up the gun's looks with spacers or a wood extension. If the length of pull is 15 inches and the wood butt is checkered, the stock can be shortened and still look appropriate.

Triggers, grips, and forend styles are personal preferences, but don't buy a pistol-grip gun and expect to alter it to a straight grip; sometimes it works, sometimes it doesn't. By the same token, if you want a single trigger, don't alter one that has two. In my experience, if a used gun sounds perfect in an advertisement (mirror bores, 98 percent bluing, original stock finish), either the ad is false or the gun has been cosmetically restored.

Before talking to a seller on the phone, make a list of questions and ask them in the following order: Do you have any room to move on the price? How long is the inspection period? Do you mind sending the gun to my gunsmith? Are the screws buggered? How do the barrels (bores, chokes, ribs, and dents) look? Does everything work—does it fire and eject? Do the triggers and safety function? Does the gun lock up tight? What are the stock dimensions—length of pull, drop at comb and heel, cast? How is the butt finished-off? What is the condition (dings, cracks, repairs, checkering, finish) of the wood?

What if you've asked the right questions and the price is right, but the gun needs repairs? Have your gunsmith make a list of the needed repairs and their prices, then ask the seller if he would be willing to split the cost.

Remember the story of Robert, who bought a Joseph Lang sidelock and brought it to me for inspection? The seller agreed to repair the problems, but then the stock cracked when Robert shot the gun. Fortunately, the seller had a clear sense of ethics, and Robert's money was returned in full. Not all dealers are that straightforward when it comes to used shotguns. Finding a dealer and a gunsmith you can trust is second only to educating yourself.

To stack the odds in your favor, research the details of a gun before you buy. Also remember that guns are generally sold as is, with you paying the shipping. When buying sight unseen, you will almost always have higher expectations than are warranted. Always get a gun to a qualified smith before the inspection period (at least five days) is up. Never be afraid to return a gun if you are not satisfied. And most important, don't bank on a bargain when searching for a good gun; look for quality at a fair price.

SECTION 2
Custom Shotguns

CHAPTER 2
A Custom L.C. Smith

L.C. Smiths are the darlings of many collectors of American shotguns, and for good reason. Several hundred thousand hammerless guns were manufactured, representing the sole American sidelock made in any quantity, with numerous grades and manufacturing changes that currently fascinate collectors. As with all American double guns, L.C. Smiths were made in every gauge from .410 to 10, with barrel lengths from 26 inches to 32 inches, with straight stocks, half and full pistol grips, splinters, beavertails, vent ribs, single or double triggers; you name it, the variety of examples seems endless.

Smith collectors have suffered the caste system of firearms snobbery since the first DHE Parker was compared to a No. 4 Smith at some long-forgotten trap club. It continues to this day; I've even seen a custom gunmaker's advertisement that said, "No Elsies."

L.C. Smiths have gotten a bad rap. Collectors will point out how the stocks crack behind the lockplates. Gunsmiths don't like them because they are difficult to reassemble and because their single triggers can be a nightmare. But one Smith fancier's retort puts things in perspective: "Shot for shot, year for year of shooting, I'll put an Elsie up against any English sidelock. These guns weren't made to go back to the gunsmith's shop every other season. They were made to endure." Anyone who has seen an eighty-year-old L.C. Smith that has never been in a gunsmith's shop would be hard pressed to argue the point.

L.C. Smiths as custom gun projects are scarce. Over the years I've only seen a couple of custom Smiths. One was the #10 American Custom Gunmakers Guild raffle gun. Doug Turnbull Restoration has been responsible for upgrades including a Field Grade to Monogram styling. And the following description is another example of American custom gunmaking that elevates an also-ran to a level of distinction.

In the custom gun trade, projects often evolve beyond their initial conception. In this case, gunmaker Mark Silver's client wanted his old L.C. Smith 16-bore restored. As with many old American guns, whether gifted or inherited or purchased, folks like to see them brought back to their original level of appearance and shootability. Silver agreed to evaluate the project. The more he considered the scope of the restoration and its expense, the more he imagined a new gun rising, Phoenix-like, from its own ashes.

As he conceived the project, visions of London sidelocks danced in his head. Photos of representative turn-of-the-century J. Purdey & Sons and Holland & Holland guns collected on Silver's desk. Although the Elsie could never be the same as the old English doubles, there were enough possibilities to make the undertaking worthwhile. The challenge, as Silver viewed it, was to subtract weight to improve the balance and handling properties while adding a degree of elegance not normally associated with American shotguns. It was clear that he must treat the Smith's metal as if it were a rough forging presented to an action-filer.

When the gun came into Silver's shop, it

was in sad shape, "a basket case," he called it. The stock was broken, the metal had no finish, the gun was unshootable. Although this Field Grade L.C. Smith had the so-called lightweight frame, what was left of the gun weighed a clunky $7^1/4$ pounds. Silver knew it wouldn't handle well without loosing weight.

With the gun stripped to its pieces and parts, I can imagine Mark sitting at his workbench, holding the heavy action in his hands, knowing a great deal of hand-filing would be required to resurrect the Smith. I'm sure he imagined that, while removing metal to achieve a significant weight reduction, he could make a good-looking and fine-handling gun for his client.

To fully appreciate the amount of forethought and work invested in this project, Smith fans should compare a factory gun to the photos of this custom Elsie (see page 33).

Mark Silver's twenty-plus-year gunmaking career has focused on two very different paths. His early work involved creating American flintlock long rifles, pistols, and fowlers exclusively. Later on, Silver built a number of high-end, 1920s-era, British-styled bolt-action rifles. These days he moves between extremes and occasionally takes on specialized projects, such as English single-shot and double rifles or this Smith. Silver's gunmaking skills are highly developed, and his work is esteemed by his peers. I've long admired Mark's custom guns and consider him one of an elite group of professional American gunmakers. His client with the L.C. Smith 16 did, too. When Silver suggested giving this Smith the full custom treatment, making it into the gun it could have been, he got an enthusiastic go-ahead.

The project began with the most obvious alteration to the action body, which also removed the greatest amount of weight. Taking a cue from the London gun photos, Mark creatively shaped the action bars closely following the arc of the front of the lockplates. A finely chiseled ridge and concave molding starts at the fences, loops around the action bars, and follows the hard edge of the action panels back along the bottom to the wood. As compared to the original L.C. Smith's massive and blunt action bar, this touch of Londonesque elegance removed ounces from the frame.

The shape of the barrel bars (the exposed flat edge along the barrel flats) was changed as well. After carefully filing the bars to a rounded bead, thus removing the obvious ledge, the bars now flow harmoniously into the bottom of the fences. The front of the action was rounded in cross section, and the forend iron's front edge was curved to match the knuckle.

Originally, the top of the action was nearly flat across the barrel breeches, with just a hint of file work where the action meets the top rib. Removing the surrounding metal effectively raised a panel around the barrel extension, as the shape of the action blended to match the contours of the barrel and top rib. A considerable amount of iron was removed while streamlining the look of the action.

Just behind the point where the action meets the wood on top, judicious filing visually raises the metal above the stock. This looks more British in style than the gentle slope of the factory metal. At the same time, Silver squared the metal where the stock meets the action, providing a better recoil abutment and reducing the chance of a cracked stock (the stocks on factory Elsies are prone to cracking).

The lockplates were also subtly reshaped. Although this change is hard to distinguish, the refinement is more evident in the pleasing shape of the stock panels that surround the them. These panels are quite unlike those on factory guns.

If you examine the toplever and safety button separately, they more closely resemble Holland & Holland features than those of an Elsie. After the triggers were filed and contoured, the trigger guard bow was forged to a

A custom L.C. Smith by gunmaker Mark Silver, with engraving by Lynton McKenzie.

genuinely delightful oval. This came after a six-inch extension was welded to the tang in converting the grip from pistol to straight.

Besides removing metal—and therefore weight—and adding a significant amount of grace to the gun, the action modifications set up new lines for the stock. It is clear that, from the start, Silver visualized the changes and how they would improve and complement the stock lines.

An early L.C. Smith catalog describes the stock of an A3 Grade (Monogram) gun as: "The very finest of Circassian walnut, especially selected from the roots of the oldest trees; the color is wonderfully rich and the figure beautiful. We choose these stocks from thousands and hence have an opportunity to select the best."

This promotional quotation aptly describes the wood chosen for this custom Smith. I can't image it having a richer color or more beautiful figure. In any era, this stock would be one of the chosen few. It has that dense-cell look, great wrist grain, plenty of swirling black marbling, and strong feather-crotch on both sides. Silver has added a red toning agent to the stock finish, adding English richness while slightly subduing flamboyant feather-crotch.

The stock's lines are clean and smooth—so smooth that they are difficult to describe, and one must look for the details. In the photos, note how the wrist flows well back into the stock below the comb. Forward, the oval wrist transitions into the crisp lock panels so naturally that it is almost unnoticeable. This is accomplished by removing just the right amount of wood above and below the lock panels, a place where many gunstocks appear heavy.

The bottom line of the forend has a similar look. With a rounded bottom and nearly flat sides at the iron, the forward taper increases, then flattens out to the tip. The line of the barrel bar continues onto the forend, disappearing up front where it meets the border of the checkering pattern. The grip checkering, taken directly from an English gun, meets in a V on top, has a V forward on each side, and is as uncluttered a pattern as is possible. Grooved (or mullered) borders and sharp diamonds are the only enhancement. The wood butt is finished off with the same 24 lines-per-inch checkering.

Connect the lines between each of these details and one finds a lovely shotgun stock. It is also matched to the client's dimensions, including 3/16 inches of cast-off. And well executed drop points are the sole embellishment, as they should be.

The metal was engraved by Lynton McKenzie with his signature scrollwork. Leaf-chiseled fences and sharply foliate scroll lend a fiery look to the engraving. Note how the rosette-engraved hinge pin is mirrored in the fine-slot screw heads. Negative space complements the design, and bold banners on each sidelock proclaim "L.C. SMITH." Mark Silver's 24-karat touchmark at the breech end of the top rib identifies the craftsman.

Silver's investment of better than two hundred fifty bench hours brought this Elsie to a degree of sophistication seldom seen in an American-made double gun. Did Silver achieve his goals of dropping the weight, improving the handling characteristics, and adding a healthy dose of elegance? The answers are an unqualified yes. I have seen and handled this gun, which now weights 6 pounds 6 ounces, and I can tell you I'd love to shoot it. As for the gun's elegance, you can see for yourself. The owner shoots clays and hunts grouse with the 16, and is no doubt delighted with Mark Silver's custom work.

Those of you thinking about a similar project would do well to add up the numbers first. At the $70 to $100 per hour that today's top craftsman charge, plus even a modest engraving fee, the price of high-grade walnut, and the initial cost of the gun, a similar project would be *very* expensive. Thankfully, there are a few enthusiasts who can appreciate, justify, and afford such an

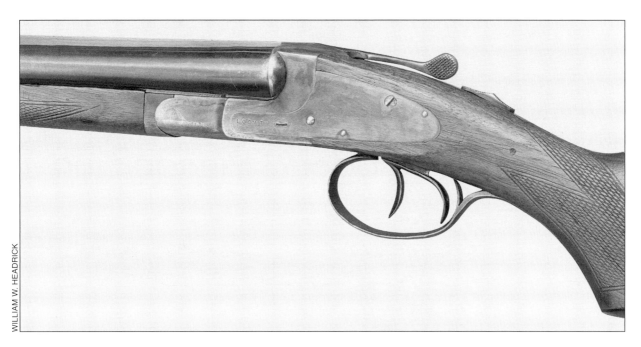

WILLIAM W. HEADRICK

A factory L.C. Smith (above) serves as a comparison to show the amount of work that gunmaker Mark Silver and engraver Lynton McKenzie put into the custom 16-gauge project (below).

TURK'S HEAD PRODUCTIONS, INC.

investment in one-of-a-kind custom American shotguns.

Mark Silver has moved onto other projects and says he probably wouldn't want to do another custom Elsie. I, for one, hope this project inspires other craftsmen and clients to embark on custom projects to make workhorse American guns into unique and shootable masterpieces.

CHAPTER 3
A Custom Model 21 Pigeon Gun

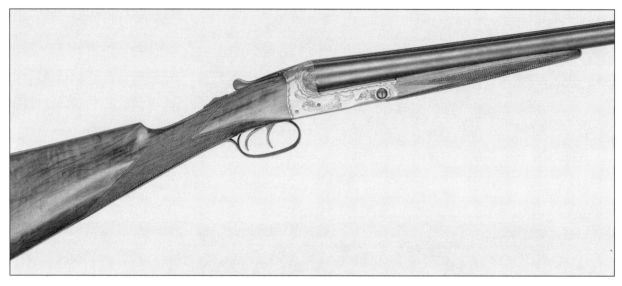

Much thought and preparation went into the creation of this Model 21 Winchester "pigeon gun."

Several years ago I showed my recently completed custom Fox gun to a very knowledgeable English-shotgun aficionado. Because my goal was to emulate the looks and handling qualities of a high-grade English boxlock, I was interested in this shooter's opinions of the results.

His comment was, "I don't know what to make of it. It reminds me of a chopped and channeled Chevy coupe. There's simply no way to compare it to an English shotgun. It has no history, no heritage."

Frankly, that hurt.

Since then, I've come to realize that cultures outside the United States don't share our penchant for altering, modifying, or customizing. The Anglophiles in this country don't get it either. From the Little Deuce Coupe to the Dodge PT Cruiser, or the military Mauser to the custom .270 sporter, Americans always strive to make their sporting toys into something better, faster, more efficient, and, always, more stylish. We borrow style from wherever seems appropriate and oftentimes create new entities, such as Harley Davidson choppers or thumbhole riflestocks. (The Harleys wound up in the most popular show ever held at the Guggenheim Art Museum. The thumbhole stock? Well, a few companies still do them, but . . . .)

I'd like to think that some American custom shotgun jobs dish up a bit more history, a bit more heritage, and end up a bit more purposeful than the original items. There's no doubt about what purpose they do serve: the functional demands of the individual, his notions of aesthetics, and certainly his personal dimensions.

Gunsmith and stockmaker Scott King, of

Wenatchee, Washington, loves to shoot varmints, and his chosen birds are barn pigeons. He shoots scores of them every year. One of his clients, named Donnie, shares a passion for this sport, and during the course of several years the two developed the notion of a custom pigeon gun. I'll bet you've done it yourself: talked about the "ideal ruffed grouse gun." Substitute woodcock, pheasant, pronghorn, or Cape buffalo and the possibilities become almost endless. But did you ever actually follow through and find it, buy it, or build it? Did that "ideal gun" ever shoot a ruff, a buff, a rooster, or even a barn pigeon?

An awful lot of shots were fired at forty-plus-yard rock doves while King and Donnie's concept was being developed. Much of the action was pass-shooting high, fast birds from stationary positions. The shooters had settled on 1^1/$_4$-ounce loads of No. 5 or 6 shot and developed handloads to match commercial pigeon loads. In between flights, they determined the functional and pragmatic aspects of the gun.

The criteria were settled: The gun would be a side-by-side with long barrels, ejectors, double triggers, and substantially different chokes. It would have some heft and be a bit weight-forward in balance. Most important, it would be capable of sustaining a regular diet of heavy 1^1/$_4$-ounce loads.

Sound like a pigeon gun? You bet. But this was to be a project gun, and unlike the typical box-pigeon gun, this one would have a straight-grip stock with a smallish forend.

A couple of years passed before King and Donnie found a 30-inch-barrel, double-trigger, ejector Winchester Model 21 that was long in the tooth and short on collectibility—the perfect project gun.

The Model 21 has achieved genuine cult status in this country, and that popularity is not without reason. Critics will say the guns are heavy and awkwardly balanced. The crux of the situation is that they are comparing them to light game guns, not wildfowl or pigeon guns. Almost every high-end gunmaker in the world has built pigeon guns for competitive shooting. This "feed-lot pigeon gun" would approximate the weight, balance, and durability of a "race gun" without the pedigree or fragility of an English sidelock or the expense or service issues of a high-end Italian piece. It was to be a by-golly durable American shooter.

Much of the Model 21's weight comes from the mass of the action and stout barrel tubes. Cultists will cite the gun's durability and ability to absorb heavy, hard-kicking loads. Anyone familiar with 21s knows of Winchester's own comparison testing against a London gun and how the 21 kept on ticking after firing 2,000 proof loads (whereas its well-heeled rival did not).

Altering the Model 21's metal for functional and aesthetic requirements was gunsmith Scott King's first order of business. The gun's bores were honed and the chokes let out to .010 inches right and .025 inches left: an improved cylinder and improved modified combination would provide a meaningful difference for double-trigger use. With No. 6 shot and tailored handloads, the right barrel would be good to thirty-five yards and the left effective at longer ranges.

During Scott and Donnie's barnyard discussions, some cosmetic metalwork features had been determined. The first and foremost was to mimic the more recent 21s from the factory Custom Shop. The arrowhead-shaped action panels were removed, leaving the action sides flat and true. This was accomplished by surface-grinding in a special jig, removing just a few thousandths of an inch at a pass.

The action body of the Model 21 is arguably the longest of the 12-gauges. Although most notice this unique proportion, few recognize that the vertical back is not perpendicular to the action flat. In my opinion, this rear line gives the action an odd look.

King shortened the action slightly and

shaped the back with a curved line. This reshaping, coupled with the removal of the action panels, helped set up nicer lines for the stock.

Details from Parker Bros. guns were borrowed in dishing the hinge-pin recesses and filing the flutes behind the fences. A couple of other modifications included lengthening the trigger-guard tang for the straight-grip stock and altering the forend latch to increase the taper of the forend from knuckle to tip.

King previously had altered and built custom stocks for Donnie, so a set of working stock dimensions had already been determined. King has long been a purveyor of fine walnut blanks, and a modest stick of Turkish walnut was chosen from his inventory. The blank was quarter-sawn, with plenty of wavy black streaking and a good portion of fiddleback figure. This was to be a working gun, and I can't imagine a stronger or more structurally sound and handsome choice.

Donnie's 5-foot, 10-inch, 170-pound physique meant rather normal stock dimensions: drops of $1^7/16$ inches at the comb and $2^1/4$ inches at the heel, a length of pull of $14^1/2$ inches, and casts of about $3/8$ inch at the heel and $1/2$ inch at the toe. With the stock nearing completion, the pair took the gun out to shoot and to rasp in the final comb height.

King shaped the straight grip with a modified diamond cross section. His thinking was that more diamond on the right side would fit the hand better and help prevent Donnie from canting the gun. A half-inch-thick black rubber recoil pad was fitted to cap the butt. The stock was finished with a commercial modified teak oil. Initially, the head of the stock and all the inlets were doused with sealer until the wood wouldn't take any more. Many professionals consider this a vital step in quality stock finishing.

Stock filling involved the sanded-in method, progressively wet-sanding with 320-, 400-, and 600-grit paper using stock finish as the lubricant. Several more coats of finish were hand-rubbed on for a built-up top coat. The resulting finish is uniform, with some shine, and looks very durable.

Ron Collings, of California, engraved the gun in a style I'd describe as lively. An unusually flamboyant border treatment combines with a medium-sized American-style scroll for very visual decoration. A large banner reads "Winchester," declaring the gun's original manufacturer.

The action was French-grayed by Collings. The barrels, toplever, and other appointments were rust-blued with a light graininess that I find attractive and that is probably quite durable.

King checkered the stock at 24 lines per inch. The point pattern has mullered, or grooved, borders at the points and single-line borders elsewhere.

Anyone criticizing the handling qualities of a Model 21 should try this one on for size. At 7 pounds 10 ounces, it is no lightweight, but that wasn't the idea in the first place. It handles wonderfully and feels like a seven-pounder. With its very shootable dimensions, I'd love to take this prize out to the feedlots. I've shot enough $1^1/4$-ounce loads through a gun weighing a pound less to realize the benefits of a heavier piece. With this Model 21, there'd be no concern about abusing the shooter or the gun.

The best part of this story is that King and Donnie have taken the American custom double out to the barnyard and shot the blazes out of the rock dove population. It took six years of dreaming, thinking, and planning, then another nine months in process, but the pair have created and are shooting an ideal gun for its intended purpose.

CHAPTER 4
Custom Fox Shotguns

In 1991, when I set out to make myself a custom shotgun, I really had no idea where it would lead me nor of the impact it would have on the custom gunmaking trade. I didn't even know for certain what kind of a shotgun I would start with. The notion came up in a conversation while sitting at the Lion Fish Bar in a Reno, Nevada, casino during the 1991 Firearms Engravers & Gunmakers Exhibition. Michael McIntosh and my good friend Jim Flack pretty much determined that I ought to start with a Fox.

What I did know was that I wanted to transform an existing American shotgun into an emulation of the best British boxlocks in function, handling qualities, and aesthetics. I had notions of metalworking techniques I wanted to try, and I was particularly interested in experimenting with weight and balance and how they could be altered to rescue an American 12-bore from the "clunker" status such guns typically were given when compared to imported side-by-sides.

At that time, Parkers and Winchester Model 21s were the darlings of the side-by-sides built in this country. Fox guns were just starting to become interesting to collectors, and the subsequent publication of McIntosh's book, *A.H. Fox*, in 1992, brought that interest to a peak. For me, the timing couldn't have been better, and my copy of Mac's book is now dog-eared, smudged with oily fingerprints, sprinkled with sawdust, and still has more than a dozen page markers citing photos of particular importance to my project. But before you get the notion that I believe I started all this custom Fox enthusiasm, I'll tell you who really started it—Burt Becker.

To quote McIntosh: "Becker became a gunsmith in the best European tradition. By the end of his long career, he was an engineer, a machinist, a barrelmaker, an actioner, a stockmaker, and even a competent engraver." He was associated with the Fox company in Philadelphia and was known to have built some of the firm's highest-grade guns. His own custom Fox guns show the frame rebates and the fancy-back scalloping and were the inspiration for me to do the same to my gun.

Whenever I want to try something new at my workbench, I research what already has been done, which in this case led me to the XE-, DE-, and FE-Grade Foxes—the so-called Specials—and Burt Becker's work for the factory and from his own shop. Not that I duplicated any of them, but the obvious quality of these American-made guns set the standard—and a high one at that.

My goal was to build a custom gun that didn't look like a Fox; rather, I wanted something that might be confused with the English guns I was so taken with. The first gun I built was the only one like that; the origins of the others were all readily identifiable. But by studying and researching high-grade Foxes, I came to appreciate a new benchmark for the superb craftsmanship available from a few American gun factories. Today's custom shops could learn something from this.

McIntosh's *Shooting Sportsman* review of the original Hughes/Fox shotgun, along with his *A.H. Fox* book, my two-part *Shooting Sportsman* article on the making of the gun, and the expanded version of the process in my book *Fine Gunmaking: Double Shotguns*, presented a lot of ideas about Fox shotguns in a relatively short period. Less than a year after the publication of my book, I saw another custom Fox: it wasn't a restock, and it was apparent that my writing and photography had been of help to the maker. At the 2004 Safari Club International Convention, I saw two custom Fox guns. At the joint Firearms Engravers & Gunmakers Exhibition the same year, I saw three custom Foxes. One had been so radically altered with round-body reshaping that I didn't recognize it as a Fox.

Then, during 2004, I received an e-mail from a fellow informing me that a dealer was advertising a Fox gun as my work. A phone call verified that the gun wasn't from my shop, but the dealer commented, "It sure looks like the guns in your book."

In the decade since I completed my project, I've seen nearly a score of custom Foxes—in photos or in the flesh—that were obviously influenced by my research, writing, and photos. Initially, I was a bit miffed, but I came around to being flattered, then humbled by the attention.

Which brings me to the subject of this chapter: a fine custom Fox finished in 2004. The reasons I chose to describe this gun are threefold. First, it's a truly fine shotgun. Second, it shows innovative and challenging detailing. And third, one craftsman did almost all of the work, including the engraving.

Larry Peters has been quietly plying the gun trade in various forms for more than twenty years. Peters was born in Victoria, British Columbia, in 1954, and he began hobby gunsmithing in his teens. With the encouragement of a high school machine-shop instructor, he built a muzzleloader as he learned machine-tool operation. After working as a welder for several years, Peters began helping British-trained gunsmith Kerry Jenkinson. Jenkinson needed some-

one to touch up the engraving of older English guns, and Peters, who had been building custom bolt-action rifles, had been teaching himself to do this work. With a good eye, he carefully examined the existing engraving; and with a deft hand, he chose and sharpened the correct tools to match the fresher cuts on the older guns. Peters worked as a full-time engraver in Canada for more than a decade. He joined the Firearms Engravers Guild of America, and in 1986 he attained Professional Member status.

In the mid-1980s, Peters struck a deal with Kimber of Oregon to engrave the firm's high-end guns. For several years the guns were shuttled back and forth between the Kimber shops, near Portland, and Peters's shop in Vancouver. In 1987 Peters moved to Portland to work full-time for Kimber. By 1991 and the company's demise (Kimber was subsequently reborn as Kimber of America), Peters was doing all of the engraving as well as running the engineering department.

Finding himself out of a job, he did what he does best and contracted engraving from various factories such as Colt, Parker Reproductions, Dakota Arms, and Cascade Arms. Peters also did commission work for many individuals, engraving a wide variety of guns in a wide variety of styles. He prefers English-style scrollwork, but he also has done a lot of American-style engraving, having embellished many Colt single-action revolvers in period motifs.

Peters credits his versatility to his many years of experience "picking up" the engraving on British guns made from the late 1800s to WWII. "I can identify more than a dozen variations on English scroll," he said. "The Birmingham guns were quite different from the London guns; then you have the large scroll seen on Hollands and a medium-size scroll right down to the very small scroll often referred to as English. Each is cut a bit differently, sometimes the background forms the scroll, some isn't backgrounded, and some is more floral or European-looking."

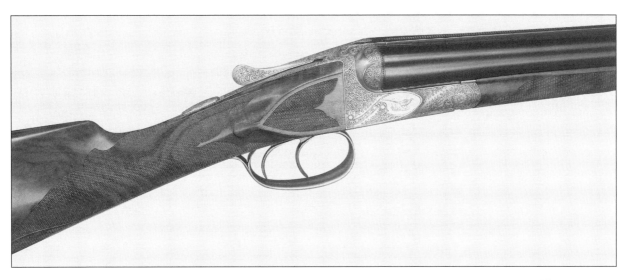

Larry Peters's custom Fox shows innovative detailing as well as excellent workmanship.

A couple of years ago one of his regular clients asked Peters to accompany him to the Firearms Engravers & Gunmakers Exhibition. There a custom Fox caught the client's eye. He had read my book, and he asked if Peters was interested in taking on a Fox project.

Back home, Peters located a high-condition Fox Sterlingworth 16-gauge. With 30-inch, No. 3-weight barrels sporting excellent bores, it seemed like a good start, except that the entire forend was missing. Peters found a rough forend-iron forging for a graded Fox and converted it to a snap-on-type Sterlingworth forend. The iron had to be lengthened and the attaching roller

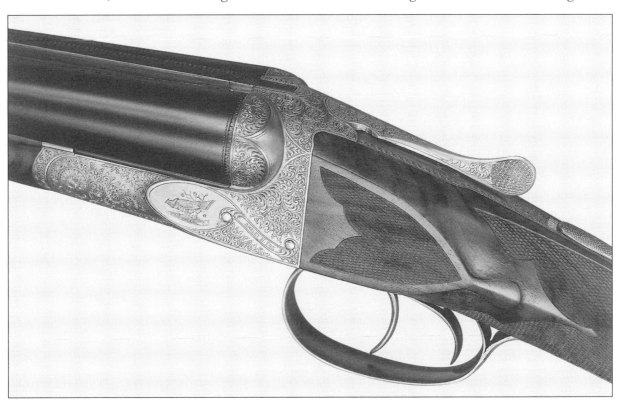

Peters's engraving includes his own version of arcaded fences, a game scene, and well-executed scroll.

assembly fabricated and mated to the keyhole. Once this was accomplished, he could fit it to the wood and action. This was a major task, but because this was an extractor gun, the process was simplified considerably.

Following that, the rest of the metalwork was completely refined and polished in preparation for stocking. Rebates were filed next to the top and bottom tangs, the top tang was straightened, and the triggers were filed up and repinned to remove lateral play. Starting with a strip of $^3/_{16}$-inch-by-$^3/_4$-inch steel, Peters fabricated a trigger guard. His approach differed from the procedure described in my book: he sliced the guard return (that pointed part curling back behind the triggers) from the bar with a jeweler's saw and filed away the rest. This method is similar to the one used by Fox and other gun companies to make trigger guards from forgings. He completed the guard by filing away enough metal to leave a rolled edge on the right-hand side. The guard is one piece of steel, except the mounting stud, which he welded in place.

Peters did his own barrelwork, lengthening the chambers and forcing cones and opening the choke of the right barrel but leaving the left tight. The bores themselves were in excellent condition, so they needed only light honing.

Then the fun started—the action sculpting. Using high-grade Fox guns as examples, Peters contoured the flat top of the action to follow the curvature of the barrels. He left a raised oval portion around the barrel extension on the action top. Differing entirely from my example—and long before my article about arcaded fences was published—he chiseled the ball fences in an abbreviated form of arcade. There are two semicircular petals on each of the balls. One petal starting at the top rib arcs around to the midpoint, then it arcs back around to join the barrel bar. Already an accomplished engraver, Peters had a leg up on me, but his methods were very similar to those I used. He first cut a light outline

of the petals, then, with a diesinker's chisel, he removed the bulk of the metal. He used scrapers and files to clean up and refine the chiselwork.

The gun was stocked from a blank of fancy Turkish walnut. Peters didn't own a bandsaw, so he used crosscut and rip saws to profile and thin the stock blank. All of the inletting was accomplished with hand tools, and much of the shaping was done with a spoke shave (Peters says he prefers using edge tools to using files and rasps). Of course, these tools were used for shaping the stock panels, but it was back to chisels and edge tools to form the drop points.

At the client's request, Peters created a buffalo-horn forend tip with a lip at the front and a scalloped point to the rear in the style of Lefever guns. Scalloped heel and toe plates also were made from horn. He also filed an elongated diamond escutcheon from steel to anchor the forend.

Rough-stocked, the gun was muzzle-heavy and light in the butt. The client had requested a weight of 6$^1/_2$ pounds. Because the gun was somewhat lighter than that, Peters worked with the client to perfect balance and handling. By taping weights to the off side of the butt, they arrived at a preferred balance point three inches in front of the breech face. To make this change, Peters drilled a deep hole in the buttstock and kept adding weight as far forward as possible until the balance was reached. He then closed the hole with a matching walnut plug.

He sealed and finished the stock with a blend of spar urethane and boiled linseed oil. He then mixed several coats mixed with walnut dust were built up to fill the pores. It was sanded back between coats and, when filled, several thin top coats were applied by hand and rubbed out to perfect the finish.

Engraving being his forté, Peters had plenty of ideas and, fortunately, a willing client. For years he had wanted to do a vignette of a Clumber spaniel hunting dead for a pheasant, a

The original Hughes/Fox 12-gauge action was shaped with beaded fences and a scalloped and rebated frame.

scene from a dog book published in the 1950s. Peters recreated it on the bottom of the action. The bottom also sports a circular rosette surrounding the triggerplate screw and medium-sized English scroll in a very well-laid-out, negative-space design.

In the photos, notice that the action panels are just a bit less pointed than on a factory Fox; this helped set up ovals bordering portraits of a ruffed grouse on the left side and a pheasant on the right. Chiseled scroll clusters enhance the lines of the metalwork, and several details enliven the overall look. These include rosettes for the hinge pin and guard screws, checkering on the left side of the lever, scrolls increasing in size on the right side of the lever, nick-and-dot borders at the breech, and the Ansley H. Fox banner

spanning the pins on the action sides. Perhaps my favorite element is the absence of engraving—save for thick and thin border lines—on the top of the fence sculpting, which gives the sculpting depth and showcases this difficult task.

Processes not completed by Peters were checkering, which was done by Kathy Forster; metal finishing with rust bluing, by George Komadima; and case hardening, by The Color Case Company.

Peters acknowledges his use of *Fine Gunmaking: Double Shotguns* as a guide for this project. I'm pleased with his use of my book, and I readily acknowledge that this is a fine Fox shotgun and that I admire the innovation, planning, and excellence of Peters's detail work.

Thanks to all of the attention Fox guns

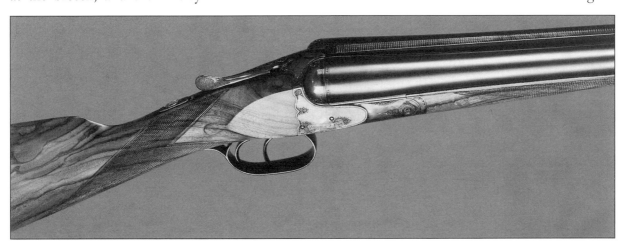

This is the original Hughes/Fox 12-gauge as it looked when new in 1993. The engraving is by Eric Gold.

have received in the past decade, there are more of us who believe that they are the finest shotguns ever created in America. I quote Michael McIntosh: "Even the lowest-grade Foxes show an intrinsic beauty in line and form . . . so it is easy to imagine what a lovely thing one could be if some master craftsman brought out its full potential."

I think Mac would agree that Larry Peters has rung the bell. So would Burt Becker.

CHAPTER 5
F.lli Rizzini, Gardone, Italy

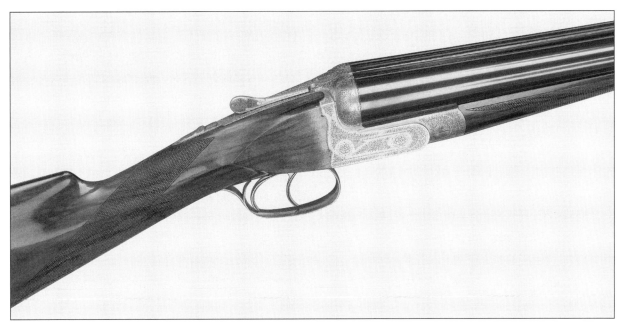

An example of Italian "best" quality gunmaking: a Rizzini R2 boxlock.

During the past three decades, I have visited the workshops of many custom gunmakers, mostly in the U.S. Throughout my career, I have continued to learn about new and old guns, manufacturing processes and techniques, mechanical design features, and stylistic considerations. Often this education has come through reading or inspecting guns as I've taken them apart in my workshop. I have also had the good fortune to visit some of Italy's most respected gunmakers, and I enjoyed the even rarer opportunities to disassemble these makers' guns at my workbench. The experiences of meeting the gunmakers and seeing the guns in-process, then inspecting the finished results at my leisure, have brought me a deeper knowledge and understanding of the work.

When I visited the workshop of F.lli Rizzini in Magno di Gardone, Italy, my first impression was that of walking into a laboratory. Not a sterile research lab, but more like an aeronautics design facility, with well-kept tools on the workers' benches, tile floors swept clean, and everything neat and organized. My initial impression of the guns was similar, in that they appeared orderly and extremely well executed.

My host for that March 2003 visit was Stefano Rizzini—son of the late Guido—who along with his brother, Amelio, make up the Brothers Rizzini. (*Fratelli* translates to brothers; "F.lli" is an abbreviation.) Looking younger than his thirty-five years, Stefano wore a lab jacket and spoke English fluently and articulately. It quickly became apparent that he'd been steeped in the tradition of fine gunmaking.

My introduction to this maker was through a *Shooting Sportsman* review by noted gun writer, Vic Venters, of a F.lli Rizzini R3 boxlock. Venters's review left no doubt that the model should be considered a "best" gun. F.lli Rizzini guns are renowned for excellent craftsmanship, superb finishing, and unique, innovative mechanisms. Incidentally, I had an R3 boxlock on my workbench as I was planning this chapter, a year after my Rizzini workshop visit. It was the personal gun of Montana resident Ed Kaltreider, of the Old Friends Hunting and Shooting Company, one of the U.S. agents for F.lli Rizzini. Kaltreider had ordered the gun specifically to be a heavier-than-normal field piece tightly choked for long-range dove and pigeon shooting in South America.

The day I visited F.lli Rizzini was not a workday, so I saw few operations taking place, and none of the machinery was being run; but I did see many different gun parts at various stages of manufacture. I saw enough parts, as well as disassembled finished guns, to acquire a sound understanding of the manufacturing steps and the finished products. But even having Stefano explaining things to me wasn't as special as putting an ultrafine-bladed screwdriver to the engraved surfaces of the tight screws of Kaltreider's gun, which was valued about the same as my home mortgage. I had to regrind a set of screwdrivers just to fit Rizzini's tiny slots, so I wouldn't recommend trying this at home. (Ed Kaltreider had put more than two thousand rounds through his 12-gauge before I examined it, and I'll refer to the R3 specifically in this chapter.)

F.lli Rizzini will build your gun however you want it for weight, balance, stock dimensions, rib type, engraving style, and so on. Unlike many makers of custom guns, Rizzini has few extra-cost options, allowing clients to choose from various offerings that fit within the param-

eters of the firm's notion of a fine double. Rather than describe my entire shop tour, I'll relate the most significant and brightest memories I have and note my observations of Kaltreider's boxlock.

Chopper-lump barrels. I have been looking at them for years, but had never seen a raw chopper-lump forging before visiting the workshop. F.lli Rizzini does all of its barrelwork in-house, starting with soot-black rough forgings from England (seeing them leaves no doubt where the descriptive name originated). The forgings are bored, reamed, and choked, then the external contouring is done concentric with the bore. One small room is devoted to a Computer Numerically Controlled, or CNC, lathe that does much of this work.

In my shop, I measured the wall thickness and concentricity of one tube of Kaltreider's R3 in three spots. Maximum variation was only .003 inches around the tube from rib to rib. I've measured many older English and Continental tubes with as much as .015 inches of variation in concentricity. As long as minimum wall thickness is sufficient, I don't consider such variances unusual, Rizzini's close tolerances are remarkable, at least in my experience. The minimum wall thickness of the R3's tube was .034 inches. One thing's for sure: seeing a rough-forged chopper-lump barrel beside a finished tube answers the question of why a garbage can full of lathe chips sits next to the CNC machine.

The breeches and lumps are then machined and the breeches joined by brazing in a small furnace. I had often seen the fine braze joint of such barrels at the lumps and underneath the extractors, but I'd never seen a pair of barrels prepared for joining or the small, modern, intensely hot furnace that performs this operation. The ribs are then laid and soldered. After fitting to the gun, the barrels are finish-polished. The polishing is to a very high degree, and F.lli Rizzini is known for its excellent rust-bluing. The bluing is accomplished by the same methods in general use and the same as I use in my shop, so I can testify that the lovely luster is the result of much preparation and detailed methodology in the process. The barrels of Kaltreider's gun had a concave, polished game rib and, although some might prefer a tall matte rib (a no-cost option), they looked very classy.

The author and Stefano Rizzini examine quality walnut stock blanks in the drying room.

Amilio Rizzini holds a newly CNC-machined trigger guard.

F.lli Rizzini craftsmen work at benches bathed in natural light.

R3 boxlock actions were in-process during my visit, and I remember a half-dozen initially machined (rough-machined doesn't accurately describe them) actions sitting next to the CNC machine. Again, there was a garbage can full of steel chips nearby. Many of the milling operations had been completed. Rectangular slots for the cocking rods and locking bolts, keyholes for the lumps, and round holes for the spindle and hinge pin were all in place. Tiny pieces of flashing, like pieces of shiny cigarette paper, were left where two machining operations had met each other. I wanted to measure the thicknesses, but not only were the slivers of flashing so sharp that I was afraid to touch them, the measuring tools were metric, which I couldn't compute.

The tangs had been left short, machined with wedge-shaped ends for welding on extensions later. This was a wise and innovative manufacturing decision and unlike the action forgings with bent-up integral tangs that I'd seen in the past. Examining the bottom of the R3 tang under powerful magnification, I barely was able to discern the weld; there was absolutely no trace of it on the top of the tang.

Precision machining is taken steps beyond my ken. For example, the triggerplates are machined very close to a finished state, as are the triggers and forend irons. Trigger guards with bows and tangs are milled from solid blocks of steel, and even forend tips, with complicated little finials, are almost ready to inlet into the stock as they come off of the machine. Other makers often file up these parts from forgings. Even as I looked at the same parts from Ed Kaltreider's disassembled gun on my bench, I had difficulty imagining them precisely whittled from solid blocks of steel. Because I have made each of these parts by hand, I marveled at the factory's advanced gunmaking technology.

But, don't think that there is a lack of handwork involved in creating F.lli Rizzini shotguns; they are far from wholly machine-made. Sculpting the fences and action shoulders is done with chisels, similar to the way I will describe the process later in this book. And all of the working parts of the mechanism must be hand-fitted to one another and timed to operate properly. All this is patiently done with hand tools. Sophisticated programming for the intricate machining simply brings the individual parts much closer to finished form, allowing time for dedicated handwork.

It was obvious, both inside and out, that no time is spared on any aspect of building an F.lli Rizzini shotgun. All of the internals appeared to be polished to the same degree of finish as the external surfaces. In other words, all of the working parts—the locking bolt, sears, tumblers, and so on—as well as the bottom of the tangs, the triggerplate recess, and the back of the action were polished as if they were to be engraved. There were no machine or file marks anywhere.

Indeed, what you can't see without disas-

sembling F.lli Rizzini guns is a hidden testament to quality. The price of these shotguns is beyond the reach of most of us, but it is nice to know that in this overpriced, underachieving world there continues to be a level of craftsmanship worth the extra money.

* * *

Let's take a close look at the functional aspects of the Rizzini R3 mechanism and my observations while disassembling one.

Even though Stefano Rizzini explained and demonstrated the mechanism to me, this was no substitute for operating it in my own hands. What I saw in Ed Kaltreider's gun would improve any boxlock. The interceptor works as Vic Venters related, but the sears themselves are different.

Major Sir Gerald Burrard, in his book *The Modern Shotgun*, criticized boxlocks for having harder trigger pulls than sidelocks, because the lengths of the sears on a sidelock provide more of the mechanical advantage of levers. The sear tails on the Rizzini gun—instead of jutting back along the sides of the triggerplate as on an Anson & Deeley gun—turn upward nearly ninety degrees along the back of the action. The triggers contact them about a half inch above their pivot points, adding mechanical advantage. Also, because of the vertical (versus horizontal) arrangement, the triggers actually push the sears forward rather than upward to disengage the notches at the hammers.

Using my Lyman digital gauge, I measured the trigger pulls at 4 pounds 4 ounces for the front and 4 pounds 13 ounces for the rear. (Ed Kaltreider is not enamored of superlight pulls and requested these weights.)

All of this trigger-pull measuring, with the stock removed, gave me a chance to examine the interceptors in action. As the hammer is cocked, the interceptor bar swings sideways, under coil-spring pressure, to effectively block the hammer fall. As the trigger is pulled, the upward movement pushes the block out of the way as it pushes the sear tail forward. Only the trigger can move the interceptor. In the unlikely event of the sear jarring off, the hammer fall would be blocked, but not in the manner of any other gun I've seen. The vertical sears leave more wood in the most fragile part of the stock: the grip. I'm always in favor of removing less internal wood from a gunstock.

All this "raccooning" added to my experience of the basic operation and function of the gun. I noted that Rizzini seems to know when a bit of looseness is appropriate in building a gun. There was just a "wink" of trigger movement to engage the sear. Some new high-end guns are fitted so closely that, without this minute play, if the stock swells or shrinks, the triggers may be forced against the sears, preventing full engagement. I've seen this more than once in abnormally dry and wet climates.

The safety was crisp but did not bind in any way; again, it had been fitted perfectly, and even though this gun had been broken in, there was a distinct lack of "shiny spots," which would have shown less-than-perfect initial fitting. The extractors had zero lateral play, yet they glided in and out under light finger pressure. Close examination showed no shiny spots here either, revealing high or low areas needing breaking-in. (Have you ever experienced sticky safeties or tough extraction with a new gun? Have you ever been told, "It just needs breaking-in?") Vic Venters's review described the R3 function as "silky," and I concur, with just the right resistance in the toplever to remind me that this was a relatively new gun, with only about two thousand rounds through it.

I was curious about the R3's bore dimensions, so out came my trusty bore micrometer. I measured both of the gun's bores at .724 inches, with a minuscule taper (.001 inches) toward the muzzles. The chokes were each about 1³/₈ inches long, with a parallel section about ³/₄ inches

long at the muzzles. The right barrel had .020 inches constriction and the left .034 inches. And I liked the ivory bead nestled between the muzzles as well.

With an overall weight of 7 pounds 4 ounces, this gun was not light by game-gun standards. That's the way Kaltreider likes them, and he'd ordered this gun for specialized shooting. The barrels' weight was marked 1.43 kilos. Rizzini will accommodate requests for balancing, and this gun balanced spot-on at the hinge pin. Although the overall weight may sound heavy, the gun handled dynamically.

As soon as I removed the buttstock, I knew something was up; it felt heavy. I have a pretty good feel for wood, and even though this stock was crafted from the heaviest, densest Turkish walnut, I hadn't expected it to feel that weighty. I removed the recoil pad and underneath, in the center of the stock, I found a round hole plugged with matching walnut. I surmise that weight had been added here—a sure sign of thoughtful and conscientious craftsmanship in the art of balancing.

I also was impressed with the quality of the wood. When I visited the Rizzini workshop, I spent some time in the walnut storage room, which is sealed to maintain a consistent atmosphere. Looking over the many Turkish walnut blanks, I was pleased to see that they'd been picked not only for flamboyant figure and color but for layout and strength as well. Stefano showed me blanks that had been purchased many years before and some that had been bought more recently. He remarked that the quality of the wood had improved over the years and that the company was getting the best walnut it had ever purchased. (I personally would have loved to have had even some of the older selections in my shop.) The Rizzini craftsmen are very conscientious about aging stock blanks, which are always stored for at least seven years.

The wood on Kaltreider's R3 buttstock was nearly quarter-sawn. The grain was dense, straight and strong through the grip, and turned down toward the toe, with some fine figure at the butt. It was far from exotic but had enough black marbling to make it very attractive. I would have proudly used that stick for any straight-grip shotgun. The wood had a distinct reddish tone, and though I don't remember seeing any stocks being stained during my visit, I'd be surprised if this one hadn't been.

The stockmaking corner of the Rizzini shop had the best natural lighting. A stock in the early stages of finishing was being hand-sanded with very fine paper. A row of stocks in various stages of oil-finishing was visible inside a dust-free cabinet. I saw a large jar of Tru-Oil finish on the workbench, and this was consistent with the well-filled, built-up finish of Kaltreider's gun. Although this is not my first choice of stock finishes—some clients might not like guns that shiny—I could not find fault with the results.

I noticed a couple of interesting details on the inside of the buttstock of Kaltreider's R3. The inletting was very clean: All of the surfaces showed signs of having been worked on with hand tools, and I was unable to determine whether any of the inletting had been machined. (Of course the hand-tooled look is preferred even if machining is involved.) More important, the wood underneath the metal had been sealed, unlike many other new guns. I suspect the tangs and action surfaces contacting the stock had been given a light coat of epoxy. I applaud the use of epoxy for sealer and not as a stopgap for shoddy inletting. I also noted the use of a steel tube, or sleeve, in the stock at the hand pin (rear tang screw). This vertical tube ensures that the proper distance is maintained between the tangs and, in my opinion, is a quality addition.

Rizzini offers a couple of "house" engraving styles, and Kaltreider's R3 had a very fine version of English rose and scroll. When I say "very fine," I mean some of the tiniest scrolls I've ever seen, with such light cutting that it might be described as *bulino* scroll. Negative space predominated, with lovely rosettes on all the screw heads. In the Rizzini office, I was shown various guns that had been embellished by some of the legendary names in Italian engraving. In this realm, imagination and styling is virtually unlimited.

Externally, the R3 boxlock follows the tradition and character of truly "best" guns from an earlier era. Rizzini's pinless action, flat-topped checkering, unique lever shaping, and action scalloping provide the company's singular stylistic character. Internally, the innovative sear, interceptor, and trigger mechanism is a decided improvement on the traditional Anson & Deeley mechanism.

I am not one who appreciates innovation for its own sake. I recently heard someone say, "How could the basic A&D boxlock be improved upon? It's been around for more than one hundred years; what could make it better? Different, yes, but better?"

Why does Rizzini continue to improve its guns' designs? The question is answered when one realizes the dedication and commitment of generations of family craftsmanship. As much as I enjoy the character that can come only with a century of acceptance, I now understand the Rizzini family's desire to innovate and improve. I can easily imagine Rizzini boxlocks being the company's—and family's—pride and joy a century from now. Rarely do we see tradition and innovation brought together with such a high degree of sophistication and quality.

CHAPTER 6

Perugini & Visini, Brescia, Italy

I've been doing benchwork for almost three decades, which has given me a lot of time to think. I've often pondered gunmakers in other countries working at their benches and wondered how similar or different they might be. I've wondered about their tools, techniques, and attitudes toward the work. I've been especially curious if, or how, I'd be able to communicate with craftsmen who speak a different language.

I recently returned from a visit to the workshop of Perugini & Visini in Brescia, Italy. I came home with answers to all my questions and a fresh outlook on my own work.

My friend Ed Kaltreider (owner of the F.lli Rizzini boxlock described in Chapter 5) is an importer of Italian shotguns, and we had talked several times about my visiting Italy to help him understand some of the gunmakers' production methods. So when he offered to send me to Brescia, I happily agreed to go.

Vincenzo Perugini and Darko Visini formed Armi Perugini & Visini in 1968. The two had met while working in the custom shop at Perazzi. They founded their company because they had ideas about creating guns outside the confines of the larger firm's production.

At that time almost no one in Italy was building custom double rifles. Perugini & Visini originally specialized in side-by-side rifles for affluent European sportsmen. The firm developed the only magnum Mauser bolt-action rifle built in Italy and also holds patents on a double-rifle ejector system for rimless cartridges and a self-compensating bolting system for single-shot rifles.

Through the years, the company grew steadily and began making side-by-side and over-and-under shotguns, which were enthusiastically accepted in England and Europe. Perugini & Visini has been in the same location for about thirty years, periodically expanding a former residence into the shop it has today. The company employs a dozen craftsmen, most of whom have worked there for at least five years.

The P&V shop was not in Brescia proper but around the mountain, about an hour to the east, in the small village of Nuvolera. I was traveling with Ryan Sones, a young and enthusiastic fellow I had known for a couple of years. Just prior to leaving Montana, we had discovered there would be no interpreter for the first several days and that we would have to rely on Ryan's "border Spanish" to communicate.

We reached Brescia in time for lunch at the hotel where we would be staying. We dined with Claudio Tomasoni, P&V's house engraver, and Giuseppe Aleo, former world champion and international box-bird shooter. Claudio knew a bit of English, and Giuseppe spoke Castilian Spanish with a Sicilian accent, but for the most part I didn't know what anyone was saying. Ryan did his best to interpret, but once in a while he would look at me and admit, "I haven't got a clue what he said."

Off to the shop. We entered a courtyard through wooden gates and were greeted by a small sign reading, "Perugini & Visini." The shop door was steel-barred and operated by an electronic lock. Claudio led us through the tiny—

and very cluttered—office into the main shop, then into his engraving room, which adjoined the gun storage room. I set my briefcase on the counter and stared across it at a couple of hundred shotguns, rifles, and barreled actions. These were an assortment of repair jobs, pieces and parts of future projects, finished guns, and custom guns in process. I was then introduced to Vincenzo Perugini and Darko Visini.

Vincenzo is a man of small physique but abundant enthusiasm. His wiry gray hair and tennis shoes suit his energetic personality. Like many Italians, he speaks rapidly and is quick to smile and laugh. Darko stands taller than six feet and is the reserved half of the duo. He speaks more slowly, and we hit it off the moment we met. The two men—both about sixty—have been working in the gun trade for most of their lives.

I had been determined to have no preconceptions about what I might find or who I might meet, but I had figured on establishing some measure of personal credibility as a gunmaker so that those I did meet would know that I understood what they were doing. I showed them my *Fine Gunmaking: Double Shotguns* book, pointing out the photos of me working in my shop and on different jobs. This was a good move, as both Vincenzo and Darko looked surprised, pointed at me, then pointed at the photos and said, "You?" As I turned the page to another photo, they exclaimed, "Si, si!" and again pointed from me to the pictures.

Ryan was chatting with Giuseppe in Spanish, the other fellows were rattling on in Italian, and I simply stood there grinning and nodding my head. Communication had been established, sort of.

Vincenzo took us into the main shop, with its bench-to-ceiling windows and six craftsmen wearing blue shop coats and plying their trade at waist-high workbenches. It was like walking into my dreams; although I had tried not to anticipate how things would look, the shop was much as I had imagined.

I then was introduced to Agustino, the Italian equivalent of a shop foreman. He is a dignified thirty-five-year-old fellow with a crew cut and one day's stubble. I was immediately drawn to the project on his bench: a boxlock double-rifle action roughly machined externally and milled for the internal parts. He was filing up a forend iron from a blank and hand-fitting it to the knuckle of the action. His bench was littered with files, many of them the same files I had on my workbench back home. I held one up and said, "Nicholson," the brand name. Then I pointed to myself, mimed a few filing strokes, and said, "Comprende?"

Agustino nodded and said, "Si, si," I pointed to the action and said, "Anson," for I had seen the word used in Italian gun books.

"Si, si," he replied, smiling. "Anson."

Next to Agustino, a young man—nineteen years old, I later learned—was in the process of rejointing an older double shotgun. The other apprentice was across the room, hand-polishing a new over-and-under shotgun barreled action. The grit paper he was using came off a roll similar to one I had and was marked "320," the same finish I use.

I continued working my way around the shop, establishing myself with each craftsman with more finger-pointing and pantomime and by speaking the few Italian and corrupt Spanish words I knew as well as the few English gun terms I thought they might know.

Perugini & Visini builds many types of shotguns and rifles, with an annual production of about fifty-five to sixty custom pieces. The side-by-side shotgun line includes Holland & Holland-style sidelocks, Anson & Deeley boxlocks, and a bar-action hammergun. All of these models are built with chopper-lump, or demiblock, barrels. The firm's Maestro Model over-and-under competition gun sports a removable trigger-lock group and an adjustable trigger, and it is available with sideplates for extra engraving, extra trigger groups and barrel sets, and any top- or side-rib configuration you might imagine.

All told, P&V produces ten different models of shotguns and rifles plus several different frame sizes. All of the shotgun and rifle actions are machined in-house entirely from bar stock.

Vincenzo Perugini and Darko Visini at their shop's entrance.

The barrel sets, whether for chopper-lump or mono-block guns, are custom bored and reamed, then joined and regulated in-house.

Vincenzo Perugini, whom I nicknamed, "Maestro," was working on a sidelock 20-bore while I was there. I watched him filing and fitting a safety button to the gun. These fellows work very rapidly. Starting from a machined

Agustino, the shop foreman, drilling an extractor-dog-screw hole with a special jig.

blank, Vincenzo chucked the piece in his lead-jawed leg vise and whaled away with a very coarse file. He then held up the piece for a moment, to check that both sides were the same, tossed the file on the bench, picked up a finer one, filed some more, and in five minutes had the button shaped and fit to its recess in the top tang. Slowing down only slightly, he spent another ten minutes perfecting the shaping and fitting. Finally, he cleaned it up with grit paper and tossed it in the parts box on the bench. Then on to the triggers, which were filed, fitted, and polished in the same manner and at the same speed. It might have taken mc a third more time to accomplish the same tasks.

Later that day, with all the action parts assembled, he began fitting a second set of barrels to the action. The lumps were carefully fitted to the action, and the forend iron fitted to the barrels, then Vincenzo began fitting the barrel breeches to the standing breech of the action. When he brushed on spotting blue, I asked, "Prussian blue?" thinking it looked like the same blue I use for fitting metal to wood.

Vincenzo laughed and nodded, and again we shared a commonality between our shops, continents apart.

Holding the barrels upside down in his left hand, he whacked the action shut with a leather-covered bag of lead, then whacked it open on the edge of his padded bench. He did this repeatedly with blinding speed—open/shut, open/shut, open/shut—until the barrels showed good contact at the breech. Removing the barrels, he showed me the Prussian blue, indicating the contact at the breech, then lightly filed the barrel breech only where the blue was showing. He reassembled the action and repeated the whack, whack, whack with the rhythm of a drummer. Then light strokes with the file, as if gently playing a violin; then speedy, forceful percussion. The Maestro making shotgun music was stunning!

The main shop was perhaps forty feet long and twenty feet wide. At the far end, down a short flight of stairs, was the CNC machine—a five-axis Ferrari. Another room contained the computers and special tooling for the automated machine. Behind that was the Electrical Discharge Machine, or EDM.

A very young man—Roberto—manipulated the buttons and watched the digital readout for the most sophisticated machine in the shop. Giancarlo, gray-haired and mustachioed, was working on a Bridgeport milling machine and the high-quality Italian lathe next to it. The men took turns with the EDM. Giancarlo is a retired machinist/gunmaker who hadn't been able to stay retired. He was sleeving shotgun barrels that day. The old barrels' mono-block was indexed on the Bridgeport and reamed to accept new tubes. The tubes were turned down at the breeches to

just fit into the mono-block.

Giancarlo advanced the lathe's cross-feed and engaged the carriage to cut long, heat-blue chips at high speed. The cut's smooth surface was indicative of work by an experienced and careful operator. Indexing the breeches and turning the tubes, Giancarlo worked with calipers that had seen many years of use. With half-glasses perched on the bridge of his nose, he would tilt his head down to look at the work, then tilt it up to read the calipers.

I looked to the opposite wall—at the picket fence of mono-block barrel sets awaiting soldering—and at that point discovered the rest of the work area.

With the last set machined, Giancarlo led me out the back door, under a fiberglass roof and to the soldering shop. Here he lit an ancient horizontal propane burner about twelve inches long that was sitting on fire bricks. He placed the mono-block and barrel breeches on the coarse screen above the flame and turned them as they heated. With sufficient heat, they were swabbed with flux and coated with solder. After a few more minutes of heating, the parts were "tinned" using steel wool and returned to the burner. When the solder ran shiny, he picked up the mono-block with tongs, slipped each barrel tube into place, dropped the hot breech end onto a wood block on the concrete floor, and struck each muzzle with a heavy brass mallet, driving the hot tubes into the mono-block in a process called, "knocking them down."

Giancarlo leaned the barrel set against the wall and returned to the shop for another. I began looking around and noticed that in the open air, under the plastic roof, was an old, stout reciprocating hacksaw slabbing off chunks of steel. On a table piled eight deep were more of these 2-by-3-by-4-inch blocks of steel.

When Giancarlo returned, I pointed to the pile and gave the universal shrug of the shoulders for "I don't understand." He replied, "Mono-block." I found it incredible that these were the basic blocks of steel from which the barrel breeches for Maestro shotguns would later be milled.

I got Roberto and Giancarlo together and, referring to Roberto as "bambino" and Giancarlo as "grande," asked why the older and younger men were doing the most sophisticated machining. Through few words and many gestures, I learned of the one's years of experience and of the other's trade school education to master the CNC machine.

"Maestro" Vincenzo Perugini hand-filing a safety button.

Shop foreman Agustino schooling an apprentice while working at a leg vise.

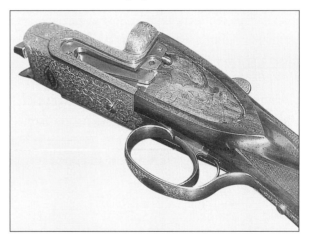

A highly finished Perugini & Visini sidelock ready for case hardening and bluing.

The EDM machine was used only for removing the trunnion raceways inside the Maestro over-and-under action, which was bolted to a jig in a steel tank. Copper conductors in the shape of the metal to be removed slowly descended into the tank of oil. The electric spark between the conductors and the action eats away the metal, cutting a recess that otherwise would be very difficult to machine.

The CNC machine was milling the barrel flats and lumps for Maestro barrel sets. This was an older machine that didn't automatically change cutters. On the bench next to it sat about ten different cutters, each in a collet holder ready

Giancarlo operating the EDM machine.

to be placed in the milling center for subsequent operations. After each operation, Roberto would clean the chips off the barrels, change cutters, reprogram the digital screen, and start everything running anew. He would check the EDM machine and the hacksaw to make sure they were running properly, then return to the main shop.

Upstairs, he was working on an ancient muzzleloading side-by-side, filing the pits out of the metal, and sanding the stock. At one point he stopped and asked Vincenzo a question, pointing to the barrel key in the forend that held the barrels to the stock. He didn't know how to remove it. I interrupted, took the stock in hand, showed him the tiny pin in the barrel channel securing the wedge, then picked up a pair of needle-nose pliers from the bench and showed him how to remove it. Both Roberto and Vincenzo were pleased.

Later, with the interpreter, I asked them why a fellow who was running the CNC machine also was restoring an old shotgun. Vincenzo explained that Roberto had been taught machinist skills but needed to know how guns were made, so he would learn by doing handwork on old guns. Fascinating and practical.

I noticed some other fascinating things about the Perugini & Visini shops. Vincenzo Perugini, the Maestro, used an old, simple caliper for measuring. Agustino, the foreman used a newer dial caliper, much like my own except metric. Roberto used a thoroughly modern digital readout caliper with the CNC. I had seen three separate measurements representing three generations.

All of the shop floors were concrete. Gunmakers often have foot trouble from years of standing on concrete. To avoid that problem, in front of each P&V bench was a wooden walkway that could be picked up and moved for cleaning. A closer look revealed that the walkways were of different thicknesses gauged to the height of the vise and the height of the worker.

All the workers had leg vises at their benches, the kind with a leg going down to the floor that you sometimes see at farm auctions. They are the most stable vises, but they can't have a swivel base like my Wilton. All the vises were equipped with heavy lead vise-jaws. They appeared to be castings, in an L-shape. The thickness of the lead allowed the worker to reef down on an action in the vise, even at an odd angle, as the steel will dig into the lead holding the work securely. Steel-framed work benches were covered with some type of heavy rubber matting that would not damage tools or gun parts.

There were seven leg vises in the main shop, and each of these work stations was equipped with a compressed-air nozzle. After filing on the gun actions, each worker would unconsciously grab the nozzle and spray the work blowing out the fine metal chips before proceeding. The air compressor was behind the shop so the noise was not a problem when it kicked in.

Many of the work stations were decorated with fine Italian artwork in the form of giveaway calendars depicting luscious nudes. Claudio Tomasoni, the house engraver at P&V, had several, but in his case it was research material as he showed me on voluptuously embellished sideplates. With a wink of his eye, he pointed to one of the calendar girls; she bore a remarkable resemblance to the engraved golden Circe. Claudio's nickname was "Romantico".

I watched him inlay a gold female form one day, all day, checking back about every hour. After chiseling out the perimeter, removing the background material that would be replaced with gold and casted-up little steel barbs to secure the gold, he began the old method of inlaying precious metal. Many modern engravers use a jeweler's saw to cut the figure out of sheet gold and inlay it as one piece. The way Claudio did it, tiny pieces of round wire gold—about the size of 0.7 mm pencil lead—were inlaid next to each other. Each wire was cut to cross the length of the recess, laid next to the previous wire, peined into place and into the neighboring wire until the entire cavity was filled with dozens of individual wires bonded together by hammering the soft metal.

This is time consuming, and the artisan must be careful not to let any steel particles, even dust, contaminate the inlay. After all is melded, the top surface is dressed down flush. One would never know the inlay was made up of a multitude of single gold wires. The background scene was completely cut in steel, but Claudio cut only a few definitive lines in the gold. The major engraving of the inlay would wait until after color case hardening so that no damage could occur to the delicate gold engraving during the hardening process.

Claudio worked standing up, as did all of the craftsmen in the shop. For the most part, he used just a few different hand-held burins (specialized engraving tools) to cut, and a hand-held folding loupe to view the work. No power chisel or any mechanical tool was used; Claudio engraves entirely by hand. He was doing *bulino*, what we call bank note engraving, while I was there. A well-rounded engraver, he is also quite adept at deep chisel work and tiny English scroll.

During my time in the shop, I saw several engraving projects come to form. A game scene, started in the morning on a sideplate, grew from bushes in the left corner to hedgerows and a harvested field. By evening a staunch setter and a covey of flushing quail had emerged from the shiny steel.

For the vignettes, Claudio used no particular layout method prior to engraving. He simply, and lightly, hand cut the major elements in place, then added all of the surrounding scene in detail. Lastly, he engraved the dogs and birds. He worked with a photo, book, photocopy, or from a "lifting" off a previous engraving. Watching the process told me the story of skill and years of experience, coupled with infinite patience, which

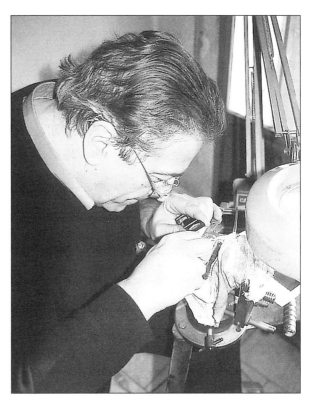

Engraver Claudio Tomasoni putting the final touches on a gold inlay.

begat a remarkable amount of work accomplished in a single day. Claudio was educated in art and, rightfully, was proud of his creations.

At the end of the day no one bothered to pick up and put away the tools on their benches. Each work station was as individual as the personality occupying it. Vincenzo's was probably the most cluttered, which I guess set a precedent for the others. But he rarely took more than a couple of seconds to dig through the heap to find the next tool for each operation. After I was accepted as a good fellow around the shop, I took the liberty of inspecting his tools. I found many Grobet needle files, also A.B. Dick brand, both Swiss made and the same as I use. At one point, when he was examining a very small screw, he picked up a set of Optivisors, or magnifiers. I pointed to them, then to my eyes, and we shared a laugh.

So many tools, techniques, supplies, and procedures were nearly identical to my own shop that by the third day I felt entirely at home and each of the workers was comfortable with my presence. I did little to interrupt their work but occasionally, at an appropriate moment, would stop them and ask a question. The struggle with words, hand gestures, and mime became a game, and almost every successful communication would bring laughter and a sense of accomplishment and camaraderie.

In one such event at day's end, I was trying to communicate to Vincenzo that, like my own shop, progress was measured in metal chips on the floor. (That's the way artisans think.) I took him behind the shop to the hacksaw and made reciprocating motions with my arm, then to the Bridgeport and the lathe pointing to the metal cuttings, then to Agustino's bench and his chiseling chips, and last to the floor in front of his bench, pointing to an impressive pile of filings. I gestured at the clock and gave him the universal thumbs up. "Si, si," he replied. It was a good day in the shop, with lots of metal chips on the floor.

I was intrigued with the apprenticeship and training going on around me. Agustino supervised the two nineteen-year-old apprentices at his end of the shop. The next bench was occupied by a twenty-eight-year-old man who had been there for a decade. Ricardo, a second generation stockmaker who was taught by his father, works with Max, in his thirties, who is a journeyman stocker himself. With the help of the interpreter, I spoke with Darko Visini and Vincenzo Perugini about the future.

They were both concerned about P&V continuing after they were no longer able to work. Encouraging the workers to stay and make a career in the shop was only half of the equation. The other half is knowing that young men in this age are less likely to spend a lifetime in gunmaking; the work is difficult and demanding and the apprentices may not develop or want to stay. Perugini and Visini apparently are setting up a sort of buy-in for the younger men to one day

own and run the company. I told them, through the interpreter, that in my experience the deciding factor was the love of guns and the satisfaction one gets from creating them. After translation, this brought bright smiles, nodding heads.

Foreman Agustino loves the work and is the heir apparent. At the end of a long day, I laughed and teased him about punching out at 7:00 p.m., holding my hands next to my tilted head. He grinned, grabbed a piece of paper and wrote the number 11, meaning he had clocked eleven hours that day. Agustino and Vincenzo were always the last to leave.

Vincenzo usually came to work very early in the morning, hours before the others arrived. This was his quiet work time, a chance to concentrate on difficult and special projects. During the day he was always available to answer questions, handle the phone, keep track of the various other projects, and still make headway at his bench work. He often works seven days a week, but only in the morning on Sunday.

I learned many workshop "trade secrets" by watching. All gunmakers use tall screw heads during the fitting and assembly. Nearing completion, one of the last steps is to dress down and fit the screw slots so they all align. Fitting a trigger plate screw, Vincenzo leaned on it getting it really tight. He took his chisel and aligning by eye, smacked it with a hammer, marking the new slot on the top-center of the screw head. He left the mark not quite perfectly turned up. Removing the screw, he clamped it in the vise and cut the new slot using the chisel mark to start the saw cut. Then he filed the head down to near finished height and put it back in the gun. The screw slot was left so that it would be perfectly aligned when final assembly took place.

I was most impressed with the overall sense of purpose, diligence, and respect for quality handwork. These fellows labor long and hard, together, with as many as seven different men working on different stages of the same firearm.

Each uses his own experience and special skills to create a masterwork of gunmaking. Although the shop is equipped with a Computer Numerically Controlled machining center and an Electrical Discharge Machine, the guns are as close to totally handmade as any I've ever seen. Most of the parts are machined as blanks, but they are all hand-fitted and function-tested through each stage of construction.

It was a great privilege to spend four full days in the Perugini & Visini shop, watching each of the projects progress and each of the craftsmen performing their daily operations. Most visitors get the standard hour-long tour and wouldn't want to hang around as I did. But each hour of every day I made a new discovery; something old, something familiar, something I had never seen, or something I had only imagined.

While Vincenzo is the Maestro of the workshops, Darko is the solder that bonds the whole shop together. He was in the office typing invoices or orders, answering the phone, and making sure the out-sourced projects were returned to the various jobs. He did the shop tours, dealt with the Russian and American distributors, relegated the hierarchy of the gunmaking, logged the repair jobs, and occasionally worked in the shop as well.

One afternoon a batch of rust bluing came in, I watched him put all the groups of parts away except for one barrel set. He took those barrels to a large blending wheel used for final polishing and proceeded to remove the bluing. He never said a word, but I knew the bluing wasn't good enough and would be redone.

In the showroom, across from the shop, Darko showed me finished guns. Although his English is better than his shy personality lets on, he didn't need words to express his pride and personal satisfaction with the guns bearing his name.

At his home the last night I was in Italy, he showed Ryan and me several guns he had made

Pieces and parts for a 20-gauge sidelock two-barrel set on Vincenzo's well-worn workbench.

Barrels and actions ready to become custom Perugini & Visini guns.

for himself over his thirty-five years in business. A couple of bolt-action rifles, a couple of double rifles, and a couple of lovely shotguns, each bearing the moniker, Perugini & Visini. Anyone would be proud to own these guns, but to say they had made them? No interpretation necessary.

SECTION 3
Evolution of the Sidelock

CHAPTER 7
Understanding Sidelocks

Have you ever been curious about all the little pins on the exterior of a sidelock? Why are they there, and what are they attached to? Perhaps you've heard of a "seven pin" or a "five pin" sidelock and wondered about the differences between them. There are many variations, and in this chapter I am going to take a step into the realm of understanding the basic, through the sophisticated, sidelock. I will clarify what can and what can't be identified by looking at the outside of a sidelock. Although most contemporary sidelock shotguns use basically the same mechanisms that were developed in the late 1800s, certain locks—most notably some Spanish and Italian versions—have evolved markedly since that time.

This chapter tells the sidelock story with photos, nomenclature, and explanation. I was lucky to have access to nine different locks from different eras and different origins to illustrate sidelock evolution and variation. They range from a percussion lock to a Remington 1889 hammer gun, from a Holland & Holland to an 1894 vintage Purdey, from the ubiquitous L.C. Smith to modern Spanish and Italian guns, all of which makes this evolution pertinent to most sidelock owners.

* * *

In the very early days of sidelocks, these firearms lacked bridles. The bridle of a sidelock is one of the singular identifying features and an indicator of the evolution of the mechanism. The bridle is a small nonmoving part normally attached with screws to the inside of the lockplate that supports the off-side axles of the tumbler and sear.

The earliest flintlocks did not have bridles, which left the tumbler and sear unsupported on the inside. I'm sure this caused the locks to wear out rapidly. As near as I can tell from my research, bridles were added to English flintlocks about 1700. (I've seen photos of unbridled locks from the 1690s and bridled locks as early as 1711.) This was one of the first major evolutionary changes to the sidelock, and it was an enormous improvement. Evidence of this betterment is that in an era short on communication—due in part to large bodies of water and political barriers—the bridle was universally adopted within a couple of decades. Whoever invented this revolutionary bit of technology has been lost to time, along with however the word was spread toward complete acceptance.

When discussing firearms development, we often take the vantage point of superiority, as if the earlier work were crude or underdeveloped. This is a mistake. Each generation of gunmaking has examples representing a peak of technological advancement. In the late 1600s, when Huguenot artisans and gunmakers were run out of France for their religious beliefs, many settled in England. It didn't take long for the local talent to adopt and replicate the French flintlock brought by the Huguenots. Why? Because it was the most technically advanced gunlock in the world. I suspect the French also brought the sidelock bridle to England at that time, but I don't have supporting evidence. It was this influx of firearms innovation that vitalized the English gun trade and eventually evolved into the sporting guns we prize today.

When studying archaic firearm mechanisms as an evolutionary process, it is important to respect the work of the period. It is also important to realize that new concepts and inventions—of both guns and the accessories necessary to shoot them—took time to become available. The invention of the percussion cap, for example, was a major improvement, but how long did it take for guns using caps to come into general usage? These periods of advancement overlapped considerably.

If one looks at the development of firearms as a technological continuum, it can be imagined that the advent of a hammerless lock was a frightful thought after two centuries of hammer guns. Who could tell if it was cocked or uncocked? Numerous safety features were invented and offered to the doubting public, but it took time for the truly useful and practical ones to sort themselves out. This transition was instituted by the gunmakers but consummated by the shooting public's acceptance.

In gunmaking, there have always been varying degrees of quality, but the "best" gun of any point in time was just that—even today it would be hard to beat a Joe Manton flintlock double or a James Purdey percussion side-by-side for bird hunting. When one knows how to operate them safely and handily, they remain purposeful and effective for wingshooting.

I've always found it easy to understand the parts, principals, and function of sidelocks because I learned to understand the simpler percussion locks first. And it is helpful that almost all sidelocks have the same parts; they are simply arranged differently in different locks. For the most part, the modern hammerless sidelock has the same components as a percussion lock, except that an interceptor, or safety sear, has replaced

the half-cock notch (or "bent" in England). Sometimes coil springs are used for the sear and interceptor instead of V-springs.

The way I see it, a percussion lock has only three moving parts—the tumbler, sear, and link (or swivel)—plus the two springs that power them. The hammer also moves, but because it is connected directly to the tumbler, I have a hard time thinking of it as a separate moving part.

A hammer gun is cocked manually by pulling back the hammer, which rotates the tumbler on the inside of the lockplate until the sear nose, powered by the sear spring, snaps into the notch. The sear holds the tumbler cocked. During the cocking process, the mainspring is compressed, putting downward pressure on the link and the front of the tumbler. Pulling the trigger lifts the sear arm, which disengages the sear nose from the tumbler notch and allows the mainspring to pull the tumbler/hammer downward to fire the gun.

A hammerless gun works in the same fashion, except that opening the action and dropping the barrels pushes the cocking rod (or lever), which rotates the tumbler and cocks the lock.

NOMENCLATURE

Shotgun-parts nomenclature is, at best, a transient and vague subject. The English have their own version, which often varies from maker to maker. American terminology is different from the original, and each maker has its own names for the bits and pieces. Add Italian and Spanish translations for components, and it is anybody's guess what to call them. Below, I have blended English and American nomenclature in an attempt to be clear and consistent.

Sidelock: The gun's lockwork is mounted on a sideplate. The earliest firearms (matchlocks and wheellocks) had the mechanism on a sideplate and evolved through the flintlock, percussion, and breechloading hammer gun to the cur-

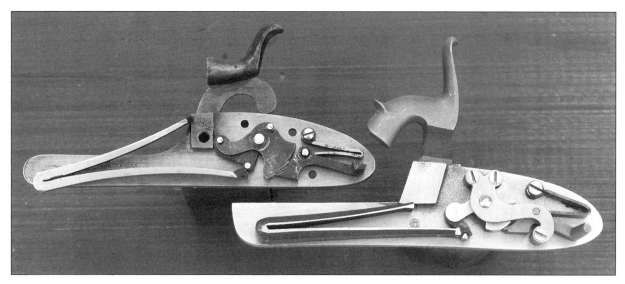

An original 1889 Remington hammer lock(left) with bridle removed, and a replica percussion lock (right).

rent hammerless sidelock. Little has changed since the beginning of the twentieth century.

Hammer/Tumbler: Sidelock hammer guns —flintlocks through breechloaders—have their hammers connected to the tumblers, which are located on the inside of the lockplates. The parts of the tumbler are the hammer, either external or internal and integral; the front arm, which connects the link to the mainspring; the notches; and the axles and the body. In the case of later hammerless locks, the tumbler also has a stop to engage the interceptor and a lobe to engage the cocking lever.

Sear: The sear is an L-shaped bar that pivots to engage or disengage the notches in the tumbler. At half rotation of the tumbler, the sear would engage a half-cock, or safety, notch; at full rotation, the full-cock notch. The sear is powered by the sear spring, which snaps it into the notches. The sear has four parts: the nose, or sear surface, which engages the notches; the body, which lays against the lockplate; the axles, which are either integral or a screw running through the body; and the sear arm or leg, which projects at ninety degrees from the body and is contacted by the trigger.

Notch (Bent): The notch is the angled cut in the lower rear of the body of the tumbler that engages the sear nose. This engagement holds the tumbler in the cocked position. Normally, the angle of the notch corresponds to a like angle of the sear nose. The angle and depth of the notch partially determine the weight of the trigger pull.

Interceptor (Interceptor Sear): The interceptor provides a safety feature for hammerless locks by catching, or intercepting, the tumbler or hammer should the sear be jarred out of the notch. The interceptor stops the tumbler or hammer from hitting the firing pin, or striker. Most often, the interceptor is shaped like the sear with a nose, body, axles, and a ninety-degree leg that contacts the trigger. The interceptor normally sits on top of the sear with the leg beside and parallel to the sear leg.

Link (Swivel): The link is an S-shaped part with T-shaped integral axles on both ends. It looks like the handle for a railroad handcart with an S-curve. One end contacts the claw of the mainspring and the other the front of the tumbler. The link connects the mainspring to the tumbler, allowing a swivel-action movement.

Springs: Sidelocks normally have just three springs: the mainspring, the sear spring, and the interceptor spring. Traditionally, the mainspring and sear spring are V-shaped and the interceptor is flat. Each of these has a small locating stud which fits into the lockplate. The mainspring stud normally protrudes through the lockplate and can be seen on its outside. Modern Spanish and Italian sidelocks often have coil springs to power the sear and interceptor.

The mainspring location determines whether a sidelock is a "back action" or "bar action." If the mainspring is in front of the tumbler, along the bar of the action, it is a bar-action lock. If the mainspring is to the rear of the tumbler, it is a back-action lock. Many conventional sidelocks have back-action mainsprings, as does the Fabbri shown in this chapter and most double rifles. The rearward location of the spring allows a solid, therefore stronger, action body.

Many hammer guns have true back-action locks with the entire lockplate inlet into the wrist of the stock behind the action. Mainsprings sometimes serve a second function as in rebounding locks and the Purdey self-opener.

PERCUSSION LOCKS

The percussion lock is the simplest form of sidelock. Without the external parts necessary for a flintlock and with none of the later improvements of the hammerless lock, the percussion lock might be called the essential sidelock.

The illustration shows a modern commercial lock supplied to builders of replica percussion guns. It is an English-style lock, circa 1870, the most advanced mechanism prior to breechloading guns. Except for the screws and sear spring, it was made entirely from casting, and some of the parts are in "as cast" condition.

The cast mainspring is easy to identify and connects to the link, which is pinned to a leg on the front of the tumbler. The three-screw bridle adds support to the tumbler and sear axles, which can be seen protruding through the bridle. The delicate sear nose rests against the bottom of the tumbler in the fired position. At the rear of the lockplate, the V-shaped sear spring applies tension to the sear.

An 1889 Remington Hammergun

The next lock shown is from an 1889 Remington 10-gauge hammer gun with the bridle removed and the mainspring in a relaxed state. The three bridle screw-holes can be seen in the plate. This also shows the disadvantage of the early unbridled flintlocks: without the support of a bridle, the force of the mainspring and hammer on the tumbler would wear an oblong hole in the lockplate in short order.

Both springs, the sear, and the tumbler are nearly identical to the percussion lock, including half- and full-cock notches. The only differences are the shape of the hammer and the addition of its rebounding mechanism. The link has been modified with the addition of a third T-arm just above and behind the tumbler axle. (The three link axles are polished bright, as are the larger tumbler and sear axles.)

When the gun is cocked, the mainspring pulls down on the front of the tumbler via the link. After the lock is fired, the mainspring pulls down on the rear of the tumbler, behind its axle, pulling the hammer back to half cock. The lock is shown in the half-cock position.

The rebounding hammer provides a measure of safety by pulling the hammer off the firing pin. Rebounding locks were an early improvement to cartridge-gun sidelocks, and there are many types. This one is simple and ingenious.

Note how small these lockplates are in comparison to the hammerless guns, which must have their plates enlarged to cover the internal hammers.

EARLY HAMMERLESS SIDELOCKS

The biggest evolutionary change to the sidelock was the internal hammer, in which the striking surface was moved to the inside of the lockplate. This required a much larger tumbler and, therefore, a much larger lockplate. The

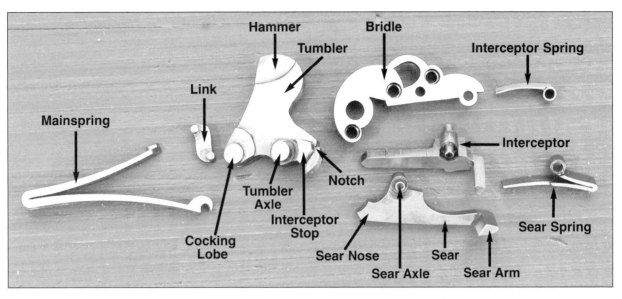

The oft-copied Holland & Holland-type sidelock exploded into its integral parts.

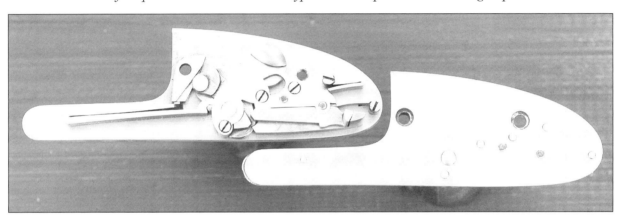

Holland & Holland-type sidelocks.

internal hammer also needed a self-cocking mechanism and an external safety. The tumbler was enlarged by the addition of a lump to engage the cocking mechanism. Four improvements—internal hammers, self-cocking mechanism, external safety, and interceptors—were necessary for the transition and were in nearly universal usage by 1900. The two most accepted lock mechanisms, the Holland & Holland and the Purdey, apparently remained unchanged until the later twentieth century. And then it was Spanish and Italian gunmakers that carried on the evolution of the sidelock; H&H and Purdey locks from those firms remain close to unchanged today.

Holland & Holland Type Sidelocks

Because of its reliable operation, relative simplicity, and ease of manufacture, the H&H sidelock is the style most copied by the world's gunmakers. Belgian makers Marcel Thys, LeBeau Courally, and August Francotte built H&H-type sidelocks. All of the Spanish and many of the Italian sidelocks I've seen are the H&H type or derivatives thereof.

The pair of H&H-type sidelocks shown here are from 1930s-vintage, in-the-white Belgian metalwork made by the Britte Company. (Note the exploded view of the parts of one of these locks.) They were used in one of my custom shotgun projects.

"Holland's Patent Safety Lock," the firm's first hammerless lock, was introduced in 1878. The "Safety" is one of the earliest successful forms of interceptor, or safety sear. This type had its bar above and behind the sear but caught the tumbler in front of the hammer. This early style H&H hammerless sidelock had the "dipped edge" sideplate later associated with Rigby guns. The dipped-edge style was a carry over from percussion lockplates, with the fat upper portion just covering the hammer.

According to Donald Dallas's book *Holland & Holland, "The Royal" Gunmaker*, the firm's transition from hammer to hammerless was anything but abrupt. Starting in 1878 with six hammerless guns, it wasn't until the 1890s that they reigned supreme. Hammerless guns were a hard sell; the advent of the interceptor sear apparently didn't convince everyone that the new patented lock was truly safe.

About 1894, the interceptor was moved under the sear to catch a lobe on the bottom of the tumbler (as shown here). At the same time, the lockplate shape was changed to the current ovate form and the action refined so the stock came forward "to the fences," eliminating the earlier square back. The H&H sidelock has remained virtually unchanged since.

From its outward appearance, this could be called a "seven pin" lock. The sear and the interceptor sear axles appear as a darker shade of gray than the plates. The pin in the front bar of the lockplate is the mainspring mounting stud. This identifies it as a true bar-action lock. The two large counter-bored holes are for the screws that mount the lock to the gun. In the front, a machine screw attaches the lock to the action. In the rear, a through-screw threads into the opposite lockplate.

As with many locks, the tumbler axle has a gold line serving as a cocking indicator. When the gold line is in an angled position, it indicates that the tumbler is cocked; when parallel to the bottom of the lock plate, it indicates the fired position.

The pin just below the tumbler and the two pins immediately above and right of the tumbler are the bridle screws. The pins showing at the upper right and the most rearward are the sear spring and interceptor sear-spring mounting screws.

Comparing the inside of the lock to the external-hammer locks, there are three additions to the H&H-type tumbler: the internal hammer/tumbler, with its large lobe to strike the firing pin; the circular lobe at the front, which contacts the cocking lever; and the lump at the bottom of the tumbler, to engage the interceptor.

The sear and interceptor axles are darker gray where they show through the bridle. The interceptor, with the rearward axle, lies on top and forward of the sear bar. The sear pivots quite a way forward of the sear bar (where the trigger contacts it), offering a good mechanical advantage (leverage) and allowing a good trigger pull. Note that the front of the sear is in the full-cock notch. The front nose of the interceptor is V-shaped and is in place to block the projecting lump on the tumbler just in front of it. Pulling the trigger lifts the interceptor away from the tumbler, but if the sear were to be jarred off of the tumbler by recoil or a hard blow, the interceptor would catch on the tumbler projection and stop the hammer fall.

At the rear of the lockplate are the V-shaped sear spring, the flat interceptor spring, and the screws attaching them. The three bridle-mounting screws are easily identified, as is the large tumbler axle, which shows through the bridle. Note that this is a "pierced" bridle with a horseshoe-shaped hole in it. The piercing is simply for style, and when it is inlet into the stock, a post of wood will be left for the hole.

With its relative simplicity, good functional geometry, and robust parts, it's no wonder the H&H-type sidelock has remained so popular.

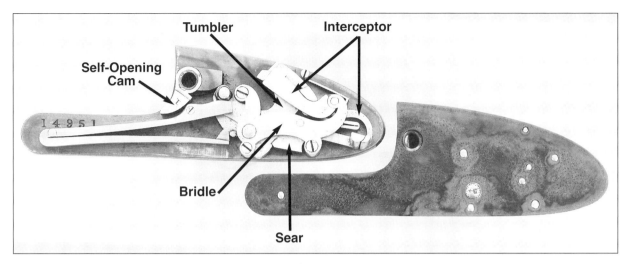

J. Purdey & Sons sidelocks.

Purdey Sidelocks

The James Purdey sidelock was invented by Frederick Beesley and patented in 1880. Purdey locks are singular in form (the Henry Atkin lock is somewhat similar) and quite a bit more complicated than the Holland & Holland type. A major part of the patent is the self-opener system, which incorporates the mainspring to assist the opening of the action. Few gunmakers still produce Beesley-patent guns, but those that do—Purdey, Peter Nelson, Hartmann & Weiss —make some of the most exquisite guns on the planet. This speaks highly of the design, if not its popularity.

Researching this material brought a couple of interesting historical notes to light. In 1861, at the age of fifteen, Frederick Beesley apprenticed with the firm, Moore and Grey. He later worked in James Purdey's shop and was thirty-three years old at the time of his invention. According to Richard Beaumont's book *Purdey's*, "he [Beesley] had risen to be one of the most respected gun-makers in London" later in life.

The rights to the Beesley-action patent were assigned to James Purdey in January of 1880, with a down payment of £20 at the time of the signing. The contract called for a royalty payment of five shillings per gun for a total quantity of two hundred guns. Or the patent could be bought out for an additional sum of £35 payable within four months. In October, 1880, nine months after the agreement, Beesley accepted Purdey's check for £35 and released all rights to his patent lasting fourteen years. James Purdey went on to become very wealthy building Beesley-actioned guns.

The Beesley-patent, Purdey self-opening gun was introduced in 1884 and has been in production by the firm ever since. Just a glance at the outside of a Purdey sidelock gives an indication that it is unique and more complicated than other locks. It has eight pins rearward and the mainspring stud forward. Except for the tumbler axle, engraved with a tiny horizontal arrow in the cocked position, who could know what all of the other pins are connected to? The pair of sidelocks pictured is from a gun that was built about 1894.

A view of the inside reveals a very different arrangement from other sidelocks. The three-screw bridle is an elaborate, serpentine-looking affair. If you can imagine the two bridle screws as the feet, the upper screw would be the head of the serpent. The interceptor pivot would be at the tail.

The interceptor bar is behind the sear bar and arcs upward underneath the bridle. It has an L-shaped extension in front of its pivot, which is flush with the bridle. If jarred off, the hook on the upper front of the interceptor will catch the tumbler projection nestled in the leg of the L. The interceptor's right-angled spring is at the top of the lockplate. The sear V-spring is underneath the bridle in the arc of the interceptor. The tumbler notch and the sear nose can be seen at the bottom of the lock between the lower bridle screws.

The mainspring is very different as well, because it provides extra functions that the others do not. The lower leg of the mainspring is connected to the link, and the link to the tumbler, to fire the lock in the conventional manner. The upper leg of the mainspring contacts the forward part of the tumbler rather than bearing on the lockplate. This leg cocks and rebounds the tumbler as well as acts as a self-opener in conjunction with the rotating cam above it. The tiny screw in the upper mainspring holds a roller that contacts the self-opener cam to reduce friction between the parts.

When the action is opened, the upper leg of the mainspring pushes on the rotating cam, which pushes on a rod through the action body to assist in opening the action. (The gun feels like it is "springing" open.) This is popularly known as a "self-opener" action. If the locks have been fired, some tension remains on the self-opener system, but the forend iron also pushes back on the rods, rotating the shoe, and the upper mainspring leg cocks the lock. (The extra effort required to cock the locks has led some to refer to the mechanism as a "hard-closer.")

The design of the mainspring allows it to be at rest, without compression, whenever the gun is broken down. Unlike those of other locks, the mainspring is under no tension, as shown.

Certainly ingenious, if complicated, the locks shown are one hundred and ten years old and function perfectly. Purdey locks are sophisticated mechanisms, and this makes them the most difficult to describe and more difficult to work on. Although I've made many mainsprings in my career, I surely wouldn't want to have to reproduce one of these.

L.C. Smith Sidelocks

Although several American gunmakers flourished in the glory days of side-by-side manufacture, there was only one true hammerless sidelock that enjoyed any success. And was the L.C. Smith ever a success! Even today, I run into more "Elsie" guns than Parkers, Foxes, and Ithacas combined.

The L.C. Smith hammerless lock no doubt evolved from the earlier Smith hammergun lock, which was generic in form except for the mainspring. Instead of the spring having a forged integral stud locating it to the lockplate, the Smith spring was fitted into a solid lug that was part of the lockplate, so both the upper and lower legs flexed. Otherwise, this lock was similar to the Remington lock shown earlier, although it had a different rebounding function using the dual flexing legs of the mainspring. The lower leg powered the hammer for firing, then the upper leg would contact the front of the tumbler to rebound the hammer off the firing pin. As early as 1884, L.C. Smith advertised its lugless mainsprings as being totally interchangeable, right or left side. The later back-action mainsprings also were interchangeable throughout the gauges. These features speak to the American notion of mass production and a very different attitude than that of English and European makers.

Lyman Cornelius Smith was more interested in manufacturing typewriters, so he sold the company to John Hunter in 1888, about the time of the introduction of the hammerless gun. The Hunter Arms Co. of Fulton, New York, continued to manufacture the guns—some 260,000 of them—until 1945. The guns are divided into pre-1913 and later guns. Connoisseurs prefer the earlier guns, which are said to have been better fit and finished, both the wood and metal.

The Elsie sidelocks shown here are from a

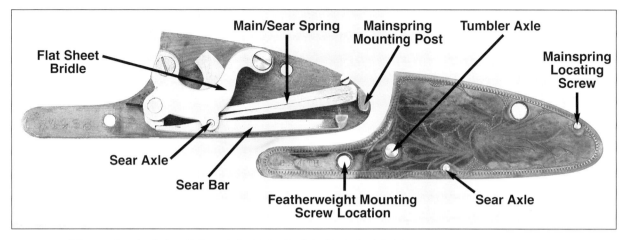

The mechanical simplicity of the L.C. Smith sidelock aided its mass-produced popularity.

20-gauge Lightweight frame. It is an Ideal-Grade gun from 1925 in 99-percent original condition. Standard-frame locks can be identified by the rounded lobe shapes of the upper corners of the locks versus the sharp, angled corners of Lightweights. Standard-frame guns lack the forward mounting screws of these locks, as their locks are held in place by single through-screws at the upper rear of the plates.

The L.C. Smith sidelock is absolutely the simplest I know of. With a total of eight parts, including the plate, it is a genuine marvel. The outside shows three pins—the farthest forward (and largest) is the tumbler axle; the middle, the sear axle; and the rearward, a screw for mounting the spring. Part of the simplicity of the Elsie is the lack of an interceptor, which also draws its greatest criticisms.

The bridle is a flat piece of sheet steel, sitting on top of two posts integral with the lockplate and held in place by two screws. It has only one spring and no swivel between it and the tumbler. The spring has no mounting stud, so both arms flex; the upper arm provides mainspring tension, the lower arm acts on the sear. The springs are interchangeable among all gauges and right- or left-side locks.

The tumblers are cocked by a unique, rotating cocking rod. It contacts the foot of the tumbler, visible just in front of the bridle. Note the length of the sear bar behind its pivot; it provides a leverage advantage that enhances a good trigger pull.

Elsies were mass-produced, which is evident in the lack of polishing seen here. These are not file marks, but rather the surface finish left by a fine grinder or belt sander. The inside of the lockplate shows machine-tool marks as well. The highest-grade Smiths had much better internal finishing. Some had bridles with fleur-de-lis piercing and the swirls of engine turning on the insides of the plates.

But what may be lacking in fit and finish is certainly made up for in the function and longevity. L.C. Smith made thousands of guns, many of which are in service today.

Elsies are well known for their stocks' cracking behind the lockplates. The head of the stock where it meets the action does not have a lot of contact area and can set back from shooting. This setback puts pressure on the rear of the tightly fitting lockplates and the mainspring mounting post, which, under recoil, can crack the stock. Slightly relieving the wood at the rear of the lock inlet goes a long way toward preventing this cracking.

MODERN SIDELOCKS

Armas Garbi Sidelocks

Show up at any shotgunning event, hunting

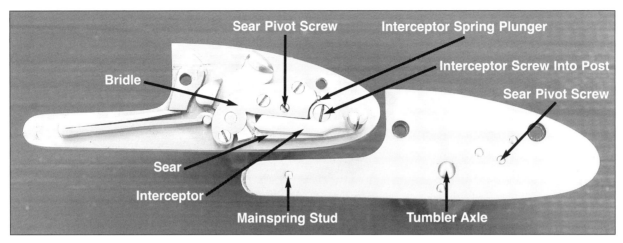

This Armas Garbi version of the H&H-type sidelock is typical of the contemporary Spanish form in that it uses coil springs for the sear and interceptor.

preserve, or Sunday gathering of bird hunters, and if there are sidelock guns present, I'm willing to bet the majority are Spanish guns made for the American market. These days the Garbi/AyA/Arrieta/Ugartechea Eibar-made sidelock has become almost as ubiquitous in the U.S. as the Elsie was in the 1930s.

Shown here are modern Armas Garbi 20-gauge in-the-white sidelocks from another of my workshop projects. Made in Eibar in 2000, these locks are typical of what one can expect to find in many currently imported better-grade Spanish guns. The locks are well made, with nicely fitted and highly polished internal parts. The internals display a robustness that instills confidence in their longevity. They are of the Holland & Holland type.

On the outside of the plate, there are just five pins showing rearward. The mainspring stud identifies it as a true bar action, and the large tumbler axle is easy to see. But where are the other pins associated with a H&H-type sidelock?

On the inside, we see a mostly conventional H&H-type lock, with three bridle screws but no bridle piercing. The sear/interceptor mounting is very different from the conventional H&H type. Notice that the bridle does not overlap the sears and that there is an extra-small screw in it. This screw provides the sear pivot and replaces the nor-

mally integral sear axle. The large-headed screw on top of the interceptor attaches it to the plate.

You might imagine this screw-mounted interceptor pivot to be a weakness, because it is not supported by the bridle. What you can't see is a post integral with the lockplate that protrudes upward through the center of the interceptor. The large-headed screw is recessed into the interceptor, firmly mounting it to the post. The sear and interceptor springs are coil types, eliminating the mounting screws and the other two pins one would see externally. A five-pin lock often indicates the use of coil springs for the sear and interceptor. If you look closely, you can see a tiny plunger on the upper part of the interceptor between it and the rear of the bridle; this is the interceptor spring.

The major difference between many Spanish sidelocks and the true H&H type is this use of coil sear and interceptor springs. I would conjecture that this is to facilitate quantity manufacture and repair; the original V-shaped and flat springs are more difficult to make, easier to break, and require two more screws to mount them. In my opinion, these Garbi locks are very high quality, and they work well with the coil springs. Aesthetically, however, I prefer the older style springs and personally wouldn't own a shotgun with coil mainsprings; it just wouldn't seem right.

In researching this material, I found photos of the insides of three other Spanish sidelocks: an AyA that was virtually identical to an H&H without a pierced bridle, a Pedro Arrizabalaga H&H knockoff with a pierced bridle, and a very interesting Ugartechea. The latter maker thinks enough of the traditional H&H type to try to fool you. Although the Ugartechea lock has a coil mainspring in the rear, a dummy screw is mounted in the front to simulate a bar-action mainspring stud. So much for what you can or can't tell without removing the lockplate.

* * *

I've had the opportunity to inspect quite a number of different Italian sidelocks—many are examples of innovation and evolution. It seems the Italians have taken up the developmental continuum of the sidelock where it stopped in England around 1900. It is obvious that ease of manufacture, lowering costs, or quantity of production did not inspire the changes we see.

The three pairs of sidelocks shown here are singular to their makers. The first, a Fabbri, is from a side-by-side pigeon gun. Fabbri is well known for over-and-under shotguns and, to the best of my knowledge, the company has not made side-by-sides for a number of years. The second set is from a Luciano Bosis 16-gauge over-and-under made a couple of years ago. The third is from F.lli Rizzini, the company I visited in Italy and described in Chapter 5. Each maker has improved or advanced the locks in a different manner for a different reason.

Why have several Italian gunmakers continued developing the sidelock? These locks answer that question with very different messages. English guns often have been criticized for being fragile, or at least for needing to go back to the maker periodically for maintenance. For decades several Italian makers have become known for the durability and longevity of their guns in the face of stiff competitive shooting.

These Fabbri locks are from a beefed-up, won't-shoot-loose-with-ten-thousand-rounds competition gun. The refinements are a product of the maker's goal of ensuring that its guns will not fail when the going gets tough. These particular locks are from a gun that has been shot a lot—maybe forty thousand rounds—by the current owner on trips to South America, in international box-bird matches, as well as at trap and Helice competitions. It shows no sign of looseness and, as near as I can tell, the locks are as sound and tight as the day they left the factory. The owner has had the gun for fifteen years, and he bought it used.

The Bosis development is a product of family pride. As with several small-shop Italian makers, generations of gunmaking tradition have led to the desire to improve upon the archaic and develop a singular legacy for one's own family or firm. Pinless lockplates, integral bridles, and removable trigger groups have been pioneered and perfected by Italian makers and have started a legacy now being adopted by other makers in other parts of the world.

The Rizzini locks are the product of many years, and a couple of generations of family development. They are strong, simple, and advanced in design.

The best part of the Italian innovations is the sanctity in which the makers hold the traditional form of the double shotgun. The improvements are internal; while the guns retain, for the most part, the traditional external aesthetics—as well as handling qualities—formulated at the peak of double-gun development in earlier times. Unlike some recent, and to my mind distasteful, "revelations" in American double-gun design, certain Italian firms are making some of the most beautiful and internally innovative shotguns of all time.

Ivo Fabbri Sidelocks

The outward appearance of Fabbri side-

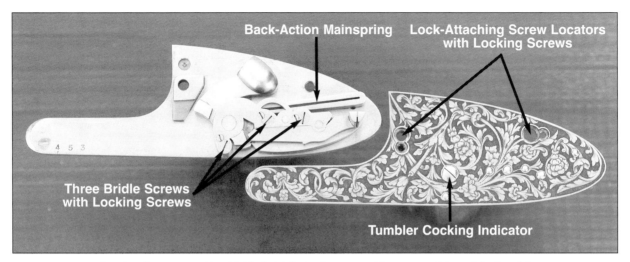

A pair of 12-gauge Ivo Fabbri sidelocks from an older competition side-by-side.

locks would suggest that they are bar-action H&H type. As I mentioned, the beautifully made locks shown here (with engraving by F. Iora) are from a side-by-side pigeon gun. There are seven pins rearward. Note that the lock-attaching screw holes also have locking-screw counter-bores. The large tumbler axle is easy to see and has a thin-line cocking indicator.

This example illustrates why it can be difficult to tell what is on the inside of a lock from looking at the outside. This appears to be a bar-action lock, but there is no mainspring mounting stud on the outside front of the plate.

Looking inside, we find something very different. It is a back-action lock, with the mainspring to the rear of the tumbler. On the outside of the plate, where the sear-spring hole might be, is the mainspring stud. The back-action mainspring location leaves more meat in the action body, making a stronger gun.

Otherwise, the Fabbri is very similar to a conventional H&H-type lock, with a similar pierced bridle, sear and interceptor arrangement, and bridle-screw configuration. But where are the sear and interceptor springs? They are coil springs hidden beneath the bridle. Although nontraditional, the coil springs work very well and are more durable and easier to make and attach than V-shaped or flat springs. Modern

Italian makers have centuries of their own tradition to call on and have no qualms about developing innovations that will improve function and ease manufacture without cheapening the guns.

Also note the three tiny locking screws securing the bridle screws. There's not much chance of these working loose through thousands of rounds of 1¼-ounce loads.

Luciano Bosis Michelangelo Sidelocks

The Bosis sidelocks pictured (with engraving by Pasotti) come from a 16-gauge, over-and-under and illustrate another form of modern Italian sidelock evolution. Four pins show on the outside of the plate. The front is the tumbler axle, the rear is the mainspring stud, and the two central pins are the interceptor and sear pivots.

Note the absence of screws on the interior. The Bosis lock has an integral bridle, which makes for a much stronger and simpler lock. Imagine a bar of steel the combined thickness of the lockplate and the bridle, then imagine a milling machine cutting away all of the extraneous external steel and removing the steel between the bridle and the plate. A web of steel is left between the bridle and the plate at the round boss below the tumbler pivot and just below the sear pivot hole. Two-diameter pins are used for the three axles. The smaller diameter goes

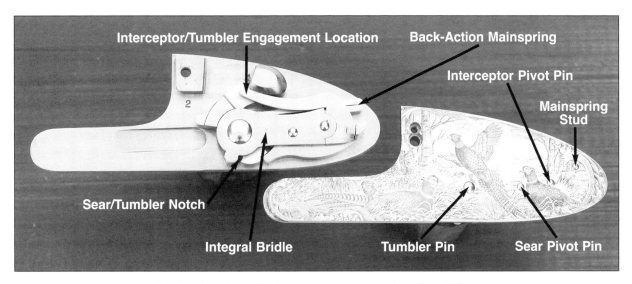

A pair of Luciano Bosis 12-gauge over-and-under sidelocks.

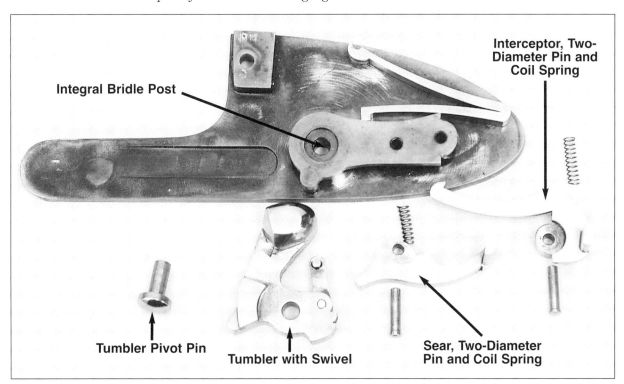

A Bosis 12-gauge sidelock, disassembled.

through the plate so that the pins can be removed by pushing from the outside. These pins replace the more difficult to manufacture and fragile integral pivot pins on the traditional tumbler, sear, and interceptor. Also note the absence of a through-screw between the two locks.

The sear and interceptor springs (coil) are tucked underneath the bridle. This lock also sports an overhead interceptor on top of the mainspring with a hook just in front of the hammer. These are wonderfully simple locks with advanced engineering, and they are beautifully made and finished inside and out.

F.lli Rizzini Sidelocks

First impressions being what they are, these

F.lli Rizzini locks could be described in numerous ways: crisp, clean, simple, uncomplicated, or, perhaps more accurately, evolved. And that is exactly what they are: evolved. Although they look simple, their simplicity is the result of complex geometry and sophisticated manufacturing techniques. By comparison, the Purdey locks shown earlier in this chapter look like Rube Goldberg affairs, but I like to think of each as being engineered according to the manufacturing bent of their particular period. The Rizzini locks are so straightforward that they remind me of the percussion lock I mentioned previously, but they are not at all alike.

The percussion locks—as well as all others made before about 1985—relied on the concepts of forge technology. Parts were manufactured starting with forgings. Metal was preformed in its heated plastic state with dies and hammers. Today's technology involves CNC machining, which removes metal from a bar or block of steel (called "stock removal"). I'll get back to this process in a moment.

The Rizzini locks have just two screws, which act as pivots for the sear and interceptor. When comparing these locks to the percussion locks, one may think that the screws also attach the bridle to the lockplate. The most amazing part of this modern engineering is that the bridle is integral with the lockplate. That's right, the bridle and lockplate were machined from one piece of steel, similar to the Bosis locks above.

When I first saw one of these locks in the hands of Stefano Rizzini, I'm embarrassed to say I didn't get it. I couldn't comprehend how a sidelock could have an integral bridle. It simply didn't register. I was stuck in the notion of forge-manufactured sears and interceptors with integral axles and couldn't understand how they could be slipped under an integral bridle.

One of the differences between these locks and the working parts of other sidelocks is the use of removable axles for the tumbler, sear, and interceptor. Most conventional sidelock sears and tumblers have integral pivot axles. In these Rizzini locks, however, screws are used as axles for the sears and a two-diameter pin for the tumbler. The removable axles allow the parts to slip into place under the integral bridle.

If you look closely at the exploded view, you can see a couple of integral supporting blocks between the bridle and the lockplate. One block is at the bottom of the tumbler circle, perhaps an eighth of the diameter. The second block is rectangular and hidden just below the "Brev. Rizzini" (Rizzini Patent) engraving. It is about $5/8$ inches long and $3/16$ inches tall. It is through-drilled front to back, and the sear/interceptor coil spring, plunger, and strut fit inside of it. The front of the plunger spring powers the sear, pushing it forward to contact the tumbler. A pointed strut on the rear of the spring pushes back on the flat vertical face of the interceptor. The parts are positioned accordingly in the exploded view.

Comparing forging to stock removal for manufacturing, it would appear to be extremely difficult—I hate to say impossible—to make a lockplate with an integral bridle by forging. A handle hole can be pierced through a hammer head by forging, but it is difficult to imagine removing the metal between the bridle and the plate by this method. But it was relatively easy to forge a bridle and a lockplate as two parts and screw them together. That technology was accomplished almost entirely with hand tools until the nineteenth century. I've seen Wallace Gusler, the original Williamsburg gunmaker, hand-forge all of the parts for a flintlock.

Four-axis CNC machining allows both the cutting tool and the stock to be moved to various positions, making it possible to mill out the lockplate and remove the metal underneath the bridle, leaving it integral with the plate. Once this is programmed into the machine, it could be looked at as simplification by eliminating the several steps and parts involved in manufacturing and mounting the bridle to the plate.

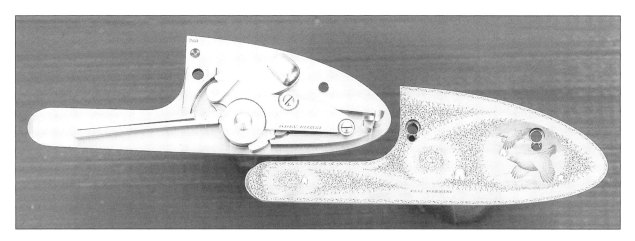

For the author, these R1-E locks by F.lli Rizzini represent the peak of sidelock perfection.

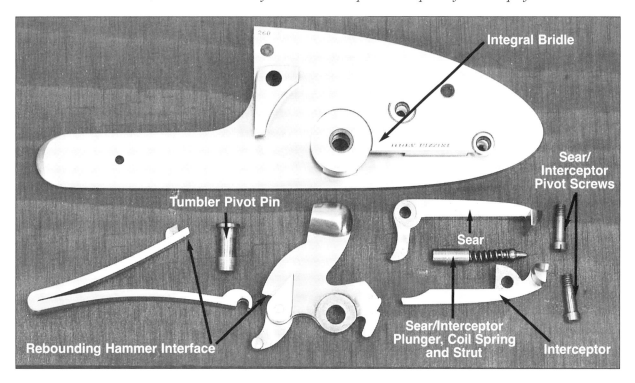

The R1-E sidelock—a study in sophisticated simplicity.

Although, in reality, this may be unnecessary, the integral bridle certainly strengthens the lock. More functionally, the resulting strength of the bridle-bridge eliminates any chance of the lockplate's flexing as it is drawn into the stock with the rear attaching screw. There is no possibility of the sear-to-tumbler geometry changing with the solid bridle and plate arrangement.

The interceptor is a clever arrangement as well. Note that, contrary to the previous locks, the interceptor on this Rizzini lock is below the sear. Looking at the tails of the two, the interceptor leg is also slightly below the sear leg. As the trigger pushes up on the interceptor leg, the front is disengaged from the tumbler before the sear can be disengaged from its notch. Also note that the interceptor engages a notch in the tumbler, rather than a lug or external boss as the previous locks did, and that the interceptor is nearly engaging the notch when the lock is cocked.

As with any well-designed sidelock, the sear itself has a long bar, and the trigger contact location is well behind its pivot point. This offers great leverage, and the length between the pivot and the sear face offers even more mechanical advantage for a good trigger pull with adequate sear engagement.

The tumbler pivot is a through-pin with a smaller diameter at the plate and a larger diameter at the bridle. It is tightly fit and pushed in from the bridle side. Each side of the tumbler has a circular boss, so that is the only area that contacts the lockplate or bridle. The sear has a similar boss. (Note that this antifriction engineering goes back to the flintlock era.)

Another neat trick is the rebounding tumbler/hammer, which uses the flex of both legs of the mainspring. It is very similar to that used long ago with external-hammer guns. When the lock is fired, the bottom front of the tumbler contacts the tip of the upper leg of the main-spring, pushing the tumbler back slightly off the firing pin.

Although it takes some special machining to make the bridle integral with the plate, doing so reduces the total number of parts. Also, once everything is set up, it is no more difficult to manufacture a F.lli Rizzini lock than an H&H-type lock; it may even be easier.

I have studied lock geometry for three decades and have long been a fan of exquisite gun mechanisms. As a stick-in-the-mud traditionalist, I have been surprised by how much I have enjoyed seeing the evolutionary process and the continuing refinement of the sidelock, always mindful of the goals of an earlier time in small-shop gunmaking for simpler, safer, and stronger designs and better manufacturing quality. This ongoing refinement demonstrates a blend of modern machinery and skilled handwork that does not sacrifice beauty or kowtow to the engineers of mass manufacture.

SECTION 4
Custom Gunsmithing

CHAPTER 8

Refinishing Gunstocks

Refinishing a gunstock is very different from finishing new wood. When refinishing, the craftsman can't shape the wood to correspond with the metalwork and must avoid damage to existing checkering. Repairing dents or blemishes is always part of any refinishing job. The stock needs to be stripped of old finish, dents have to be raised, and the refinisher must be careful about the height of the wood where it meets the metal. Some of the process—at least the wet- and dry-sanding—must be done with the stock attached to the action and forearm iron; thus, it is easy to scratch the metal. For that reason, I hate to refinish a stock without also redoing the metalwork. Of course if one is extra careful, refinishing jobs don't always require that the metal be redone.

I believe that a prerequisite to refinishing a gunstock should be the ability to completely disassemble and reassemble the mechanical parts of the firearm. I know that many amateurs have refinished a stock without completely stripping the gun, but not only is this the perfect opportunity to strip clean the mechanism, it is also imperative to remove *any* sanding dust, excess finish, or accumulated crud before final reassembly.

Most of us have seen the Fox, Parker, Elsie, or other gun that was "refinished" years ago with coarse 120-grit sandpaper and hardware store lacquer. Let me emphasize that professional quality restoration is very different from refinishing. It has been only in the past fifteen years or so that this distinction has been accepted. The goal for a competent restoration is to return the firearm to its original, as-new condition. In the case of American guns, original finishes are well known and understood by those who restore them professionally. Duplicating an original Fox finish or the glossy look of a Winchester Model 21 is not a great challenge for these craftsmen. However, it can be challenging for an amateur.

In the case of English shotguns, the parameters are somewhat broader. English guns are commonly "redone," and few people can tell if the original finishes were different from those applied later. Thankfully, most British gunstocks, regardless of vintage or refinishing, wore the same linseed oil "slackum" look. Nevertheless, problems may arise if one chooses a more durable or water-resistant finish rather than the straight linseed oil that was commonly employed. (It is possible to refinish an English gunstock with a more durable finish that looks like straight linseed oil. Later in this chapter, I will cover the authentic methods used to finish and refinish English stocks.)

For the amateur and professional alike, it is how a stock finish performs that is most critical. In restoration, the most important criterion is how the finish looks. In the case of a hunting or clays gun, use in inclement weather dictates performance requirements as well. I've come to the conclusion that the ultimate stock finish should be waterproof, quick-drying, easy to apply, non-messy, applicable without removing the metal, natural oil, synthetic, dust-resistant, easy to repair, scratch-resistant, grain-filling, capable of lasting a lifetime, built up, flawless, gloss, semigloss, low gloss. and of course hand-rubbed. All without requiring much work.

Of course, it just ain't so! No finish is everything, and every good finish takes a lot of careful work. When asked how to refinish a gunstock, one custom maker I know says, "Buy a bottle of Tru-Oil and read the directions." Although he is being facetious, there's some truth in his advice. Years ago, I finished my first two stocks with Tru-Oil. I don't like it and I don't use it, but it is possible to achieve a reasonably good finish with it. My only other advice is to be careful mixing or using Tru-Oil in conjunction with any other finish—and watch out for the shiny, chrome-like look!

At this point I should admit that in the thirty years I've been in the gun trade, I've refinished fewer than a dozen stocks. I simply hate doing it! I will refinish only the custom guns I build.

For the hobbyist, refinishing can be fun and rewarding, and the results can be delightful. Refinishers range from the meek and unpracticed to the self-assured and experienced. The methods range from steel wool and three coats of finish to weeks of lavish care. The refinishing products range from straight wax (which I can't even imagine) to raw oil to polyurethane.

• • •

I'll begin by relating my own methods of refinishing using an oil-modified urethane, then I'll discuss the techniques of some master-class associates who have refinished hundreds of gunstocks. My hope is that, using this information, you'll be inspired to attempt the project yourself, or at least you'll be able to discuss refinishing intelligently with a professional. What follows is not a step-by-step, how-to description, but it will give you an idea of how to approach refinishing like the pros.

First, I'll take a look at what's involved in a competent stock refinishing. For starters, it is going to take a fair amount of time and care. The last two-piece gunstock I finished—new wood, that is—took approximately seventeen bench hours, including the final dry-sanding with 320-grit. The wood pores were completely filled, the stock was wet-sanded four times with 320- to 600-grit, and I applied three hand-rubbed top coats of my favorite GB Lin-Speed Oil. Those hours did not include disassembly or any of the stripping or dent removal associated with refinishing. It was a pistol-grip, single-shot-rifle stock with a cheekpiece, which complicated the job.

The result was a pore-filled, red-toned, low-gloss sheen that is very moisture- and scratch-resistant. It shows the color and figure of the wood nicely, and the client was pleased. I know it won't water-spot, and with reasonable care it will provide years of handsome durability. I can refinish it to new, if it doesn't outlast me.

Some people relish the opportunity to invest the minimum of ten to twelve hours that it takes to do a straight-grip shotgun stock. In my shop, very little setup is needed. I hold the stock in a checkering cradle while applying the final top coats, so handling is kept to a minimum. I also have reams of each grit paper, mixing bowls, and preformed sanding blocks ready to go.

I do the least amount of prep work I can get away with. This isn't because I'm lazy; rather, it's because the less you do, the less likely you are to screw up the original surfaces. I start with a commercial stripper available at hardware stores. If the wood is oil-soaked, I use the stripper on the inletting as well as the external surfaces. Drastically oil-soaked wood requires more drastic measures. I go over the checkering lightly with stripper and an old, soft toothbrush.

The goal is to remove as much of the surface finish as possible without removing all of the finish from the pores. If the stock is badly dented or will need staining or toning color, it is best to remove as much finish as possible to facilitate these processes.

The Hughes/Britte Custom Shotgun

Throughout these pages, a singular custom shotgun has been presented in several chapters, with photos, as examples of gunsmithing processes. As the most sophisticated and complicated custom shotgun from my workshop, its creation has provided some of the greatest challenges of my gun-making career.

In 2001, after delivering a custom boxlock 16-gauge upland gun, I was asked by the client, Pete Treboldi, about the possibility of crafting a 12-gauge sidelock gun for duck shooting. I explained the problem of locating and securing an appropriate barreled action to begin the project. The following year, at the Safari Club International Show in Reno, Nevada, I found exactly what we were looking for.

A Belgian exhibitor displayed the in-the-white barreled action. He had just the one, which he had brought into this country for display only. Fortunately, I ran into friends James Tucker and Jerry Fisher, two American custom gunmakers whose work I most admire. The three of us looked over the metalwork and came to the conclusion that the quality was as good as I could hope to find for beginning a custom project.

The metalwork had been made in Belgium by Britte Armes En Blanc, which translates to Britte Guns In The White, and had been supplied to a variety of smaller gunshops in Belgium for finishing. In 1936 Britte secured a contract with the Belgian government and ceased making sporting-gun parts. This barreled action had been sitting in the basement of the former company for close to seventy years.

Over the course of the next nine months, I managed to purchase and import six of these barreled actions. Griffin & Howe purchased the remainder of the inventory. The shotgun shown in the accompanying photos, and described in many of this book's chapters, was the first completed in my workshop.

The Holland & Holland-type sidelocks detailed in Chapter 7, "Understanding Sidelocks," are from this gun. It appears again in Chapter 11, "Balancing a Double Gun," with photos of the recoil pad, cut-off butt section, and hollowed buttstock. In Chapter 12, "Arcaded Fences," the action chiseling is explained and illustrated. Before-and- after photos of the gun's fences appear in Chapter 13, "Double Gun Metalwork," as does the shaping of the safety button and top lever. Fitting the tang screw is shown in Chapter 16, "Machine Screws and Gun Screws," and the installation of my hallmark is detailed in Chapter 18, "Hallmark: Signed in Gold."

Presented here are multiple color views of the finished shotgun. This project totaled somewhat more than three hundred hours at my workbench, with many more hours by other craftsmen. Gunsmith Dennis Potter choked the barrels .012 in the right barrel and .020 in the left. He also chambered the barrels at $2^3/4$ inches, completed fitting them to the action, finished the forend iron fitting, and machined several screws for the gun. He removed the action bolsters below the barrel flats and shaped the top lever.

I accomplished all of the tasks presented in this book, made the forend escutcheon, shaped the trigger guard for the pistol grip and hand-filed its finial, altered and fitted the grip cap, stocked the gun, finished the stock, and did the barrel rust bluing and nitre bluing of the screws and small parts. The $29^1/2$-inch barrels were fitted with an elephant ivory front bead. All of the metal parts were hand-polished to 600-grit at my bench.

E.L. "Larry" Peters accomplished the wonderful layout and execution of the engraving, the color case-hardening was by Doug Turnbull Restorations, and J. Peter Mazur charcoal-blacked the furniture and gold-plated the lock parts.

As with the guns presented in Section 2, "Custom Shotguns," this one was created in a specific style—Woodward guns, London, England, circa 1900—with an intended purpose: duck shooting over decoys. I am pleased and proud to report that four days after taking delivery, Pete was shooting pintails and canvasbacks from a blind on the shores of Lake Erie with the Hughes/Britte.

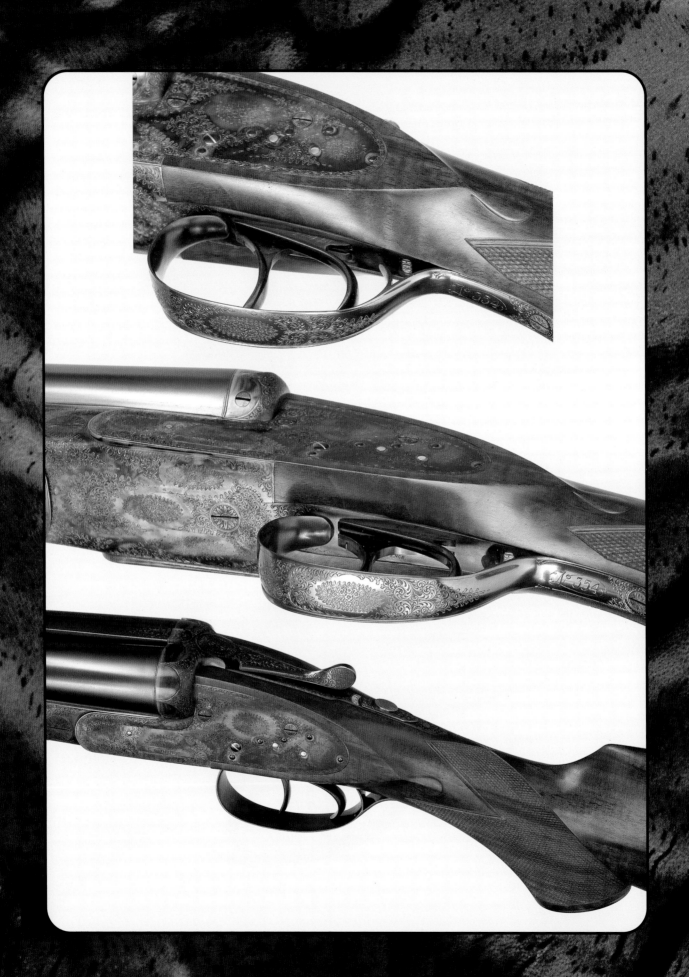

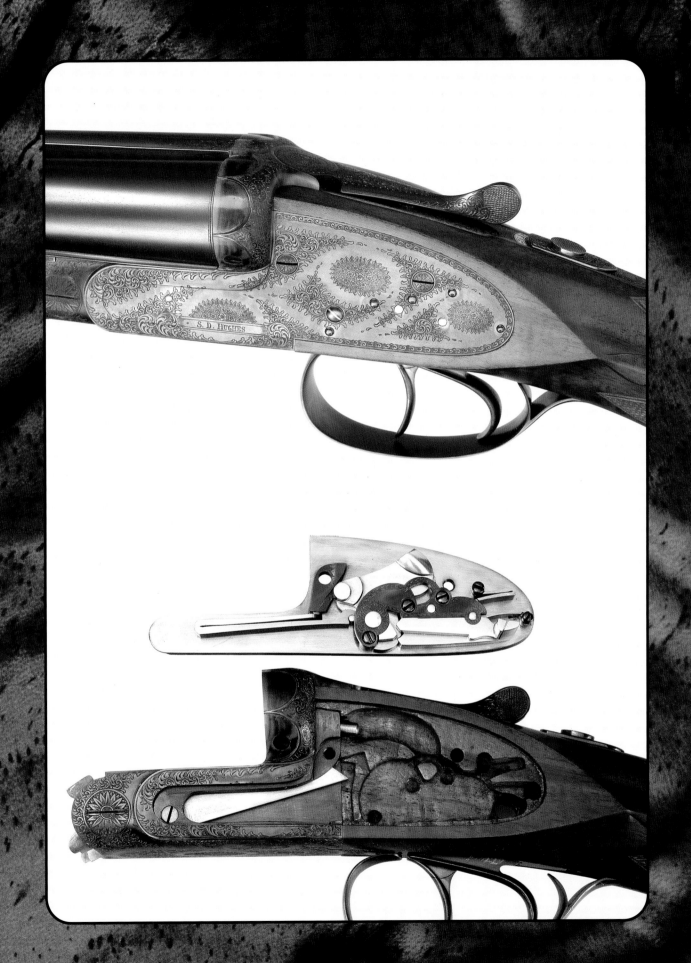

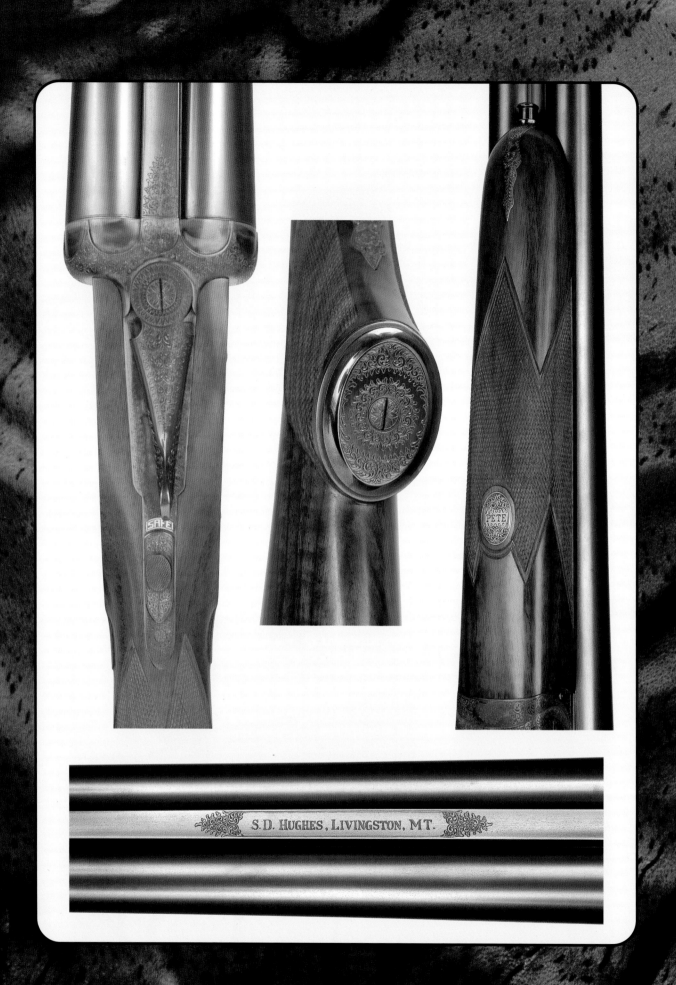

S.D. HUGHES, LIVINGSTON, MT.

Metal Finishes for Fine Guns

This 1890s-era J. Purdey & Sons gun (left) has been "redone" with all of the original metal finishes: color case-hardening, bright polishing, rust, charcoal, and nitre bluing.

The author's custom Fox (right) as new in 1993.

The author's custom Fox (above) as it is today. Note how the metal finishes have worn, especially at the typical points of hand contact.

After a decade of use, the Fox's bow is shiny on the edges, and the triggers are bald on the shoes but blue on the sides.

Evaluating Shotgun Stock Blanks

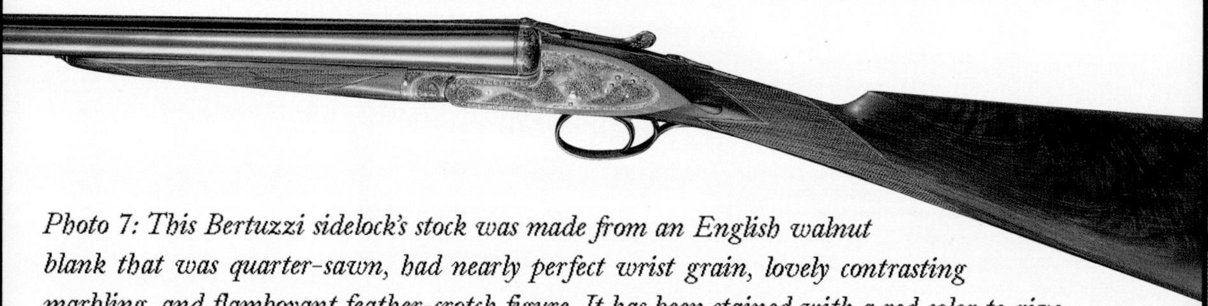

Photo 7: This Bertuzzi sidelock's stock was made from an English walnut blank that was quarter-sawn, had nearly perfect wrist grain, lovely contrasting marbling, and flamboyant feather-crotch figure. It has been stained with a red color to give it the look of an early English gun and to tone down the feather-crotch figure.

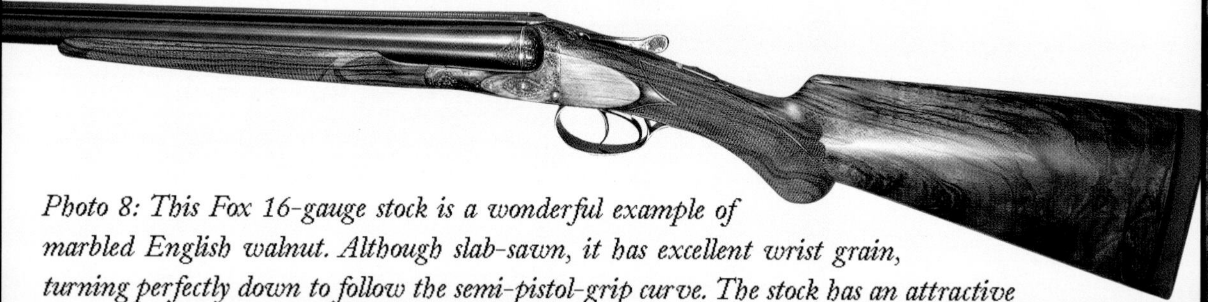

Photo 8: This Fox 16-gauge stock is a wonderful example of marbled English walnut. Although slab-sawn, it has excellent wrist grain, turning perfectly down to follow the semi-pistol-grip curve. The stock has an attractive brown background color, with a bit of red toning.

Photo 9: This English walnut blank is quarter-sawn, is well laid out for a grip stock, and is fairly fancy. It has good color contast and most of its fancy character comes from the feather-crotch grain in the butt. The feather is easy to see on the left side of the blank as it spreads from the comb down toward the toe.

Photo 10: The right side of the blank shown in Photo 9 is a bit light in the feather.

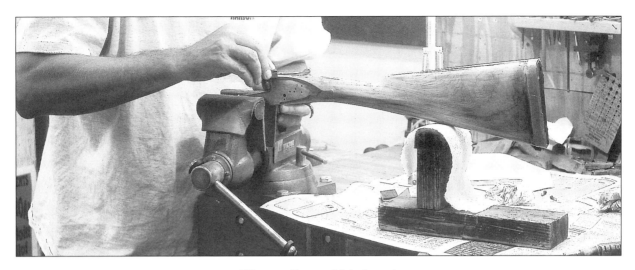

Wet-sanding a sidelock stock.

All of the metalwork is left in place when wet-sanding.

To raise dents, I use a massive, torch-heated copper soldering iron. (Brownells offers an electrically heated dent-raising tool; I'd buy one if I did more refinishing. Several fellows I know use a standard household iron.) I place several layers of folded and water-soaked cotton T-shirt material on top of the dent, then judiciously and carefully apply heat with the iron. The water softens the wood fibers, then the heat and attendant steam restore the crushed grain to its original conformation. Raise as much and as many of the dents as you can;

you'll want to keep the sanding to a minimum.

Now the buttstock is reinstalled on the action and the forend to the forearm iron. I mask the metal, where it joins the wood, with painter's tape. All dry-sanding is done after dent removal. I wet the stock with water, then dry it rapidly with a hot hair dryer to raise and "whisker" the grain. Starting with the finest-grit paper I can get away with, I lightly sand the stock to remove the whiskers and any scratches or blemishes left from dent removal. (If the stock is badly dented or scratched, this probably will be with either

120- or 150-grit and will require concentration on the bad areas.) I prefer to start with 240-grit and finish dry-sanding with 320. The wood is on the metal at all times, and I back the paper with small semihard blocks I've made by grinding old recoil pads to shape. After lightly sanding with 320, I'm ready to seal the stock.

My basic procedure for "best grade" refinishing or new-wood finishing starts with a coat or two of sealer. I prefer Laurel Mountain Forge Permalyn, a polyurethane/linseed oil blend that is available as both a sealer (which is almost thinner than water and penetrates very deeply) and as a higher-viscosity finish, which is useful for filling. The sealer saturates all surfaces of the stock, including the head at the action, all inletting, and the area beneath the buttplate or pad. I use a shoe-polish dauber or fine paintbrush to apply it.

I apply sealer to the end grain at the head and butt until it won't take any more, and I douse all the screw holes as well. I want all surfaces of the stock sealed from gun oil as well as moisture. (I like to think that someday someone will thank me when they open up the stock and don't find the head soaked with gun oil.)

After sealing, I hang the stock, with a wire through the tang-screw hole, in a dust-free drying cabinet for about ten minutes, then wipe off any runover. After another eight hours or so in the drying cabinet, the stock is recoated, if needed—with less sealer this time, as the first coat will prevent deep saturation. Again, the stock is set aside for a few minutes, then the excess is wiped off.

It is important to keep after a stock-finishing job, as modern natural/synthetic oil blends will not bond well from coat to coat if left much more than twenty-four hours between applications.

Once the stock is sealed, I go over it with fine, gray-colored Scotch-Brite (synthetic steel wool) to remove any shiny areas where sealer is standing on the wood surface. I don't mask the checkering during filling, but I am careful to keep the excess goop out of the diamonds. For filling, I mix a paste of rottenstone and Permalyn Finish to about the consistency of toothpaste (wet but not runny) and apply it with cotton T-shirt material, wrapped around my index finger, in a circular motion, packing it into the pores. I wipe off the excess so there is just a film remaining on top.

The proper consistency, application technique, and amount of filler left on the surface are learned through experience. There are no set guidelines. If too much is left on the surface, there will be more work to remove it with wet-sanding. Hang the stock and let it dry for about eight hours. This poly-type finish dries very hard, and if left too long will be that much more difficult to wet-sand.

I wet-sand using water. I learned this technique from gunmakers Monte Mandarino and Mark Silver via the book *Professional Stockmaking*, by David L. Wesbrook. Wet-sanding with water has a distinct advantage over the same process using stock finish. As the wet-sanded areas dry, they turn a very ugly gray, which may make you nervous and does nothing for the look of the wood. Trust me, it will look fine once the finish coats are applied. This hideous gray will show you exactly where all of the surplus stock finish has been removed; any dark or shiny spots will indicate areas where finish remains on the surface and that need to be gone over again.

For wet-sanding, I scissors-cut the sandpaper into two-inch squares and back it at all times with the small sanding blocks mentioned earlier. Paper and block are dipped into a dish of water, then used on the stock.

For most in-the-wood refinishes, one filler application will be enough. Yes, some pores will remain showing, but most English guns show lots of pores. For my own guns and for new wood, I repeat the filling and wet-sanding two or three more times and progressively wet-sand to 600-grit.

When I'm satisfied with the evenness of the surface and the amount of pore filling, I lightly wipe the entire stock with mineral spirits to produce a clean surface. I like to tone my stocks with a bit of red to enhance the background color and give extra warmth to the look. For this I use Behlen Solar-Lux non-grain-raising stain in American Walnut color (product No. B503-6A235). If the stock is naturally dark, I mix the stain in a ratio of 1-to-1 with Behlen Proprietary Solvent (No. B650-2816); no other solvent is compatible. For wood with a lighter background, I use the stain straight from the bottle. I apply it with a shoe dauber quickly and evenly and do not let it run across the stock, which can cause streaking. I hold a cotton rag in my other hand and wipe and blend as I go to get the most even coating possible. The tone should be slightly darker than the finished look desired, as a bit will rub off with top-coating.

Yes, this stain will penetrate through the filler and into the wood. No, it won't come off later, if a few coats of quality final finish are applied as a top coat.

For top-coating, I prefer GB Lin-Speed Oil. On the jar it says, "Contents: boiled linseed oil; petroleum thinner." I also use boiled linseed oil as a top coat, but for reasons I can't explain, prefer the Lin-Speed Oil. I dot a small drop on one area of the stock and hand-rub it out. Then I dot on another small drop next to that area and rub. I continue doing this until the whole stock has the same thin top coat rubbed almost dry. Too much will gum up; too little will not completely coat the surface. With overnight drying between coats, a second or, perhaps, a third coat will do it. If you have thin spots or thicker areas, they can be lightly blended by rubbing with a felt pad and Lin-Speed thinned with mineral spirits.

GB Lin-Speed Oil has a cure time, as do most finishes. The top coats will be soft and fragile for a couple of days and then will harden more than you might imagine. Most natural oils and blends will cure only when exposed to ultraviolet rays—sunlight. I hang the stock out of the way for a few days to "catch rays." This settles the finish, and small inconsistencies fade.

When the finish is completely cured, I recut the checkering by hand, then finish it with a thinned coat of Lin-Speed Oil mixed with artist's burnt umber oil paint (for color) applied with a fine paintbrush.

I'm not a big fan of waxes because they are often too shiny and certainly aren't permanent, but when I do wax I use Renaissance Microcrystalline Wax, the same product museums use. It is not quite so bright as others and is easily removed with a wipe of mineral spirits. A once-a-year waxing will clean the stock surface and provide a temporary barrier to moisture and abrasion.

As I have already admitted, I don't enjoy refinishing stocks, but when I'm forced to do the work, I use this method. The Permalyn filler is highly water resistant and the top coats give that look of an oil finish.

Author's Note: I have more recently used Daly's, of Seattle, Washington, marine finishes with the same process. Benite for the sealer, ProFin for filling, and BenMatte for top coating.

• • •

Having stated that I'm not the last word on refinishing gunstocks, I've solicited the opinions of two other professionals who use different methods and products but achieve excellent results adaptable for home application.

Pete Mazur has been professionally restoring guns for about three decades. His work is legendary, and I have seen much of it in person. The following method was developed by Mazur for achieving a durable, relatively easy to apply, natural oil finish. Although the result isn't the perfect duplicate for every factory finish, it is handsome and easy to repair, and Mazur's clients, including hunters, shooters, and collectors, have been universally delighted.

Mazur begins the process with a commercial wood stripper—available at hardware stores—that is water-soluble and easy to use. However, his method of removing the stripper is on the dicey side for the hobbyist: wearing rubber gloves, he applies the stripper with a paintbrush, and when it starts to bubble he plunges the entire stock into a tank of boiling water laced with liquid dish soap. (For the home hobbyist, I recommend hot tap water in a plastic basin.) No more than five minute later, he pulls the stock out of the water and removes any remaining stripper and finish with a very soft-bristle brush.

This drastic treatment accomplishes three things. First, it ensures that all of the stripper is removed from the wood. Second, the boiling water helps suck all the finish and grime out of the wood. Third, it raises the dents in the wood. Mazur makes sure all surface water is removed, then he puts the stock aside for two weeks to air-dry. He puts it in a safe place where it won't get knocked over and, to avoid warping the stock, doesn't apply any heat in a drying cabinet or with a hair dryer.

After air drying, Mazur removes any gun oil that has seeped back to the surface. He does this with powdered whiting (calcium carbonate) and solvent, which are mixed into a paste, applied to the offending area, and, when dry, brushed off with a soft-bristle brush.

If further dent removal is required, Mazur uses a household iron on top of several layers of water-soaked cotton cloth. Be careful with the iron, as its sharp edges can put more dings and dents in the wood.

Because Mazur works on many antiques and rare guns others won't touch, he is accustomed to replacing wood where it has been broken, chipped, or gouged. His methods are too numerous to describe here, but suffice it to say that if such work is needed, this is the point in the procedure to do it (in other words, wood repair should be done prior to sanding).

For sanding, Mazur prefers to use the finest-grit paper possible. The paper is always backed with a sanding block, and the metalwork is installed on the wood. For large areas, Mazur backs with a thin sheet of cork gasket material glued to a wood block. Smaller areas are done with a pink eraser backing the paper. All sanding is done by hand, starting with 320-grit and progressing through 400- and 600-grits. In the case of a bad dent in a large area, Mazur may use 220-grit, but never any coarser. He does not "whisker" the wood, believing that any whiskers would have emerged previously.

Almost all the old stocks Mazur sees were originally stained, so he reapplies stain to the bare wood. He uses Laurel Mountain Forge Antique Walnut Stain, applied by wiping it in with a paper towel. He cautions to avoid streaking and to blend as you go. The wood is stained a bit darker than desired as it will lighten during oiling. The stain must have several hours to dry—overnight is best—and to allow the solvents to dissipate.

Mazur uses a commercial filler—Herter's French Red—that he works into the pores using a rag and finger pressure. He works over the entire stock for at least twenty minutes. He strives to get the filler down into the pores and leave as little as possible on the surface. After twenty-four hours, he rubs lightly to remove any residue.

Pete Mazur has graciously revealed his secret stock finish. He calls it Pete's Mix 36, because he finally got it right on the 36th batch. It is essentially pure tung oil mixed in a 1-to-1 ratio with boiled linseed oil. He adds a dash of Japan dryer, thins it a bit with gum turpentine, then adds the above-mentioned stain to suit. The linseed is for the look, the tung for its superior moisture-resistance, the dryer to help the finish dry, and the stain for color.

Mazur uses a surprisingly small amount of finish—just six to eight drops per coat to cover

This Holland & Holland 8-bore double rifle was completely restored by Pete Mazur. The wood was refinished using the techniques described in the text.

an entire straight-grip buttstock. A few drops are applied to one side and rubbed in by hand with a circular motion. Then a few more drops are added, followed by more rubbing. Because this is a hand finish, the more he rubs, the better it works. When the butt is done, he sets it aside and use about four drops on the forend. When the forend is done, using a lengthwise motion, he lightly wipes off any surplus from the butt with a paper towel. Then he wipes the forend and sets everything aside to dry for twenty-four hours. A minimum of five coats is applied using the same procedure.

If there are any imperfections—Mazur says that if the procedure was done correctly, they should be minor—they can be rubbed out using Brownells Triple F Rubbing Compound applied with light pressure. The finish tends to be glossy, and the shine can be broken by very lightly wet-sanding with 600-grit paper and mineral spirits. Rub lightly afterward.

Mazur does nothing to protect the checkering during the refinishing process. He says that the stripper/boiling procedure really cleans out the diamonds and, with minimal care, very little finish puddles in the grooves. The pattern is recut by hand one line at a time. It is then colored with

thinned stain—which, if used full strength, would overly darken the bare wood. After the stain evaporates, a couple coats of thinned Pete's Mix 36 are brushed in with a toothbrush. The checkering is left slightly lighter in color than the stock and dull in appearance.

Mazur supplies a bottle of Pete's Mix 36 with the refinished stock, if the client desires. The slightly built-up natural oil finish is lovely to look at, water-resistant, and simple to touch up.

• • •

For a mostly polyurethane finish that is relatively easy to apply, I contacted longtime professional stockmaker James Tucker. Tucker has refinished many stocks and does some of the best work I've seen. He's developed a procedure for a tough, waterproof finish that can be achieved in a comparatively short time.

Preparation is paramount to any good refinishing, and Tucker's method is a bit different. He avoids using commercial stripper unless there is a considerable buildup of finish on the stock. Most English gunstocks have an in-the-wood finish with little surface buildup, and Tucker prefers to leave as much of the original oil in the wood as possible to lessen the need for filling during refinishing.

His first step is to steam the dents. Tucker uses a twelve-inch flat file that was surface-ground perfectly smooth and had all its corners rounded. Water-soaked, pure-cotton bedsheet or T-shirt material is laid on a section of the stock. About half the length of the file is heated with a propane torch, then placed on the wet rags to steam and lift the dents. Tucker goes over the entire stock in this manner. A lot of the dents won't raise well, so he'll lightly sand around them with 220-grit paper. He's careful to use a block backing and not sand down into the bottom of the dent; the idea is to bring the surrounding surface down, not deepen the dent. For really bad dents, he repeatedly steams and lightly sands until the dents have disappeared.

Tucker ignores the existing checkering unless it is worn nearly off or dinged along the borders. If the checkering is badly worn, he'll reestablish the individual lines before they get worse. Edge blemishes will be filed and/or sanded out, then reestablished before sanding.

The stock is then given one complete sanding with 220-grit paper unless it has a lot of deep scratches, in which case he will start with 150 or 180 grit. Tucker backs the grit paper with cork blocks. The idea is to get the flaws out and produce a flat, even, blemish-free surface with a minimum of sanding. He notes that he wears magnification at all times so he can see exactly what he's doing. He avoids whiskering and thus minimizes pulling any finish out of the pores.

Tucker has been using Daly's wood-finishing products for many years. Although he doesn't stain when using this finish, the result is one of the toughest and most water-resistant surfaces possible.

After preparing the stock, Tucker soaks all surfaces, inside and out, with Daly's Benite Clear Wood Sealer—which, according to Daly's literature, is an exterior "deeply penetrating wood seal-

er [that] will harden wood from 15 to 30 percent." After letting the sealer dry overnight, Tucker switches to Daly's ProFin gloss, described as "a hard, fast-drying finish designed primarily for professional use [with] an oil-modified urethane base." The pore filling begins with this product but, because Tucker leaves as much of the original finish in the pores as possible, filling should be minimal. The stock is then wet-sanded with 320-grit and ProFin as the wetting agent —one small area at a time—blending until the entire surface has been gone over. The stock is wiped off as it is wet-sanded, but a small amount of finish/sawdust slurry is left on the surface to dry overnight.

The next day the stock is wet-sanded with 400-grit using the same method. This time the finish is sanded and 70 to 80 percent of the slurry is wiped off, with a bit more left in any areas where pores are showing. By now the pores should be nearly or completely filled.

The next day the finish is wet-sanded and wiped again with 400-grit, with particular attention paid to areas that aren't quite filled. This gives the surfaces a very even look. The stock pores should be filled by this 400-grit wet-sanding with just a trace of finish left on the surface. One more wet-sanding with 600-grit paper is done, leaving almost no finish on the surface. Using light pressure on the sanding block, the 400- and 600-grit wet-sanding should go very quickly.

The stock is then wet-sanded using gray Scotchbrite and wiped off. One more coat is wet-sanded with white Scotch-Brite and wiped, leaving little finish on the surface. In effect, these Scotch-Brite sandings and the previous 400- and 600-grit sandings are more a polishing of the wood than sanding it.

The final coat is applied and wiped off without sanding. Tucker applies the finish with acid brushes and wipes with cheap paper towels because of their lack of absorbency. This is simply a wet-and-wipe application.

The look of the finish is very low gloss. Tucker recommends not trying to build up this finish, because, in his experience, using more than a coat or two on top has led to bonding problems. If you want a brighter finish, top with coats of Daly's BenMatte Danish Tung Oil Finish until the desired gloss is achieved. It is applied by dotting and hand-rubbing everywhere until the surface has a smooth, even finish. Tucker says this is the most forgiving top coat he has used, and it requires no final rubbing with rottenstone to even it out.

After completing the refinishing, Tucker recuts the entire checkering pattern. He brushes in a light coat of Benite to seal the checkering.

With a drying cabinet or dry atmospheric conditions, the elapsed time can be shortened substantially by doing two coats a day. Daly's products are very fast-drying.

As mentioned, both of the refinishing methods described are used by professionals. They require a healthy dose of time and attention. Experience is a bonus as well. Although the methods are very different in procedure and products, both results are good-looking and durable. The oil finish is a bit more delicate, but it is easy to touch up. The harder urethane finish is tougher, but tougher to repair.

• • •

So far I have presented three different methods of stock refinishing that share some commonalities. Even the most basic approach presented isn't easy or quick, but these are professional methods that produce professional results. I've heard many "shop tips" and claims about how "easy" it is to refinish a stock, and I blanch at such suggestions. A fellow once told me how he leaves an old stock in a bathtub full of hot water overnight to soak out the dents. I've heard about using steel wool, which most stockers abhor

because it can rip the filler out of wood pores or stick shiny steel particles in them. And the real corker for me was learning of a method of stock finishing using egg whites. The notion of quality varies so widely that one man's "super finish" may look awful to another.

Obviously a one-hundred-year-old, oil-soaked, bar-in-wood, drop-pointed London sidelock will require much more careful work than a new, mass-produced over-and-under. But no matter which stock the refinisher begins with, which finishing products he uses, or what look he's going for, careful preparation and conscientious application are necessary to achieve professional results.

I have two more techniques from two more professionals: they involve a sophisticated sidelock refinished in British fashion, and what the hobbyist might expect who wants a duller, oil-type finish for his new over-and-under.

Starting with the latter, I contacted Doug Raebel, of Berlin, Wisconsin, who bills himself as the "Stock Doc." Raebel has been repairing, rebuilding, altering, refinishing, and making new gunstocks for more than fifty years. He has redone many "shiny" over-and-unders and knew exactly what I meant by the amateur desiring an "oil finish" for his new shotgun.

Raebel says that most Berettas and nearly all Brownings are stained and that this can present a problem if one is not careful. The secret is to enhance the original finish without completely stripping or removing it. Beretta finishes are not very thick or particularly durable, and it is easy to break through them and into the stain. If a stock is dinged or dented or scratched, it is best to remove the finish entirely and start with bare wood. For complete refinishing, Raebel uses a polyurethane-tung oil blend and the same Behlen's non-grain-raising stain I mentioned earlier.

For retaining and enhancing the original finish, Raebel masks the action and buttplate or pad with masking tape and lightly wet-sands the stock with 400-grit wet-and-dry paper. He prefers using Pro-Custom Oil stock finish as a lubricant for wet-sanding. About 95 percent of the resulting slurry is wiped off using paper napkins. The idea is to polish and refine the finish that is already on the wood, removing any ripples or inconsistencies without breaking through to the stain.

With the wood installed on the metal and the paper backed with appropriate sanding blocks, the stock is wet-sanded using 600- then 800-grit paper. The oil is allowed to dry overnight between sandings. All of the slurry is removed with the final 800-grit wet-sanding. This will give a matte finish with just a bit of sheen. For a top coat, Raebel prefers a very light application of Dem-Bart stock finish, using just a couple of drops to hand-rub the entire surface.

If you break through the finish into the stain, the resulting light spot will need to be enlarged, the entire area restained, and the finish built back up and feathered in to match. Raebel has had good luck matching the color of Beretta wood with Chestnut Ridge Military Stock Stain.

New Browning Citori finishes are heavier and thicker than those on Beretta guns, making them a bit more durable and more difficult to break through. They also are more likely to have ripples and inconsistencies, according to Raebel.

Doug Raebel says he has seen many over-and-under stocks with the finish checking cracking along the edges of the buttplates. He surmises that a lack of sealer at the butt end causes the stock to swell in a moist environment, then, as it dries, the stock shrinks back and the inflexible poly finish cracks. For this reason Raebel is a believer in sealing all of the end grain and inletted surfaces when refinishing.

. . .

To learn about refinishing using the hallowed "London oil finish," I contacted Holland & Holland-trained stocker Paul Hodgins. Hodgins uses commercially prepared finishes, preferring Purdey's Slackum, by Wart Hog, or another English finish called Trade Secret. These are linseed-oil-based finishes with dryers.

In preparation for refinishing, if the head of the stock is oil-soaked, Hodgins will remove the metal and submerge the head in acetone for a few days to draw out the oil. He cautions that acetone is very volatile and that anyone using it should be extremely careful and keep it away from any source of ignition.

He then puts the stripped action and lockplates back into the wood and starts sanding the stock from the checkering back using 120- to 180-grit paper, depending upon how badly the stock is dinged. He raises the grain, or feathers the wood, once to make sure all the fibers are lying down. If he's had to make some alterations to the stock by filing, which tears the wood fibers, he will raise the grain several times.

Hodgins hasn't had much luck steaming dents from old stocks, and he prefers to remove as many of the bad ones as possible using a file or sandpaper. He doesn't mind leaving a few dings, though. "I try not to make the thing look brand new," he said. He also likes to brush a light coat of oil into the inlets to seal the wood and prevent oil-soaking.

In the case of an old sidelock that has metal standing proud of the lockplates, he will let in the locks one-half turn to a full turn on the sidenail. In other words, he inlets the lockplates and all their innards deeper into the stock. Bringing the lock screw around one-half turn or a full turn will realign the slot. This process will leave some wood standing proud to redefine the panels around the lockplates and the drop points. He considers this part of a sidelock refinishing job, if it is needed. This doesn't work for a single-trigger gun, though, because the sear locations are so critical. If the metal at the plates, action, and top strap is too proud, he suggests a restock.

The front end of the stock is then sanded, starting with a light pass with 120-grit paper. He tries to avoid the checkering but concedes losing the border lines. The entire stock is sanded to 320-grit.

To begin filling the pores, a single coat of oil finish is applied; then he wet-sands with the oil finish and 400-grit paper. He leaves the resulting slurry on the wood and lets it dry for a couple of days. This step is repeated using 400-grit paper, then 600-grit. Each time, some of the slurry is left on the surface. The stock is wet-sanded again with 600-grit, but this time Hodgins wipes off all the slurry. Now he can inspect the surface to see whether any pores are unfilled. If they are, he wet-sands a third time with 600-grit.

When the pores are filled to his satisfaction, Hodgins removes the metalwork and carefully clamps the stock grip in a padded vise. He then finishes off the ends of the four horns at the front of the stock between the lockplates and the top and bottom straps. This area cannot be reached with the metal in place.

Although Hodgins rarely uses stain, if the wood needs color he applies a non-grain-raising, alcohol-based stain after the wood is filled but before the final finishing coats of oil are applied.

Hodgins applies the final finish with the metal off the wood, using his fingers to dab on just a bit of the same finish he filled with, then rubbing it in by hand. After the finish has set up for an hour to an hour and a half, it will get sticky—"about like what we call toffee in England," Hodgins said. The stock is then dotted with linseed oil—Hodgins prefers raw linseed but says boiled will work—and wiped off with a rag, using the linseed as a vehicle to remove what was left of the sticky finish from the first coat. This process leaves a very thin film of oil on the surface, and in this manner, successive coats of the prepared finish are built up and wiped off using linseed oil and a rag. Hodgins

Holland & Holland–trained Paul Hodgins refinishes using the hallowed "London oil finish."

says he likes to do a coat in the morning and one in the evening.

How many coats? "Never less than a half dozen," Hodgins said. "Sometimes ten to fifteen very thin coats." (This is still a very thin finish.) "If it needs it, about every third to fifth coat I will rottenstone it to buff it down a bit." For this procedure, linseed oil is dabbed on the stock and a small quantity of rottenstone is sprinkled on. Then it is lightly rubbed out with a cotton rag on his index finger and wiped off with a clean rag.

Hodgins warns that if you forget to rub off the finish with the linseed oil after an hour and let the finish harden, you'll have to rottenstone it, which is a lot more work. He also cautions that if you've stained the stock, you must build up several coats before rottenstoning to prevent rubbing through the finish and blotching the stain.

After ten to fifteen coats have been applied, he recuts the checkering. When all the checkering lines are restored, the checkering is finished with a coat or two of linseed oil. If the stock has been stained, Hodgins will put a bit of stain into the checkering while it is still wet with linseed to keep it from darkening too much. He uses a toothbrush to lightly blend the stain and oil to match the stock color.

The final steps are to very carefully scrape out any finish that has inadvertently found its way into the inletting, then clean up the metal-work and reassemble and mate it to the refur-bished wood.

"I'm sure this will all look very straightfor-ward when it's written down, but it takes a lot of experimentation and experience," Hodgins said. "And every stock is different."

Although there are obvious similarities in these methods, I'd like to point out a few specifics. None of these craftsmen uses straight linseed oil, nor do they mix up special concoc-tions (except Pete Mazur); none use alkinet root or chemicals to stain or tone the wood, and with each the method and expenditure of labor is quite intensive. They each use commercially available finishes and stains (even Mazur's is a

mix of commercial products) because they each believe that the current products lead to a better finish. And one more tip: leather dyes are terribly light-fugitive and will fade over time.

Having related five different professional techniques for stock refinishing, I can assure you that if I were to interview five more gunsmiths, I'd come up with five more variations on the same themes. If you're thinking about refinishing your own wood or having a professional do it, you should now at least be armed with a reason-able notion of the products, procedures, and techniques involved.

Author's Note: Most finishing/refinishing products are extremely volatile! Any rags, paper, brushes, and other materials that have been soaked in stock finishes or solvents must be carefully cleaned or properly disposed of because they may combust spontaneously. Personal health care and common sense dictate the use of gloves, glasses, and proper ventilation for many of these procedures.

CHAPTER 9
Stock Bending

The first time I heard about stock bending was in gunsmithing school in the mid-1970s, and I was skeptical. I couldn't imagine how—or even why—someone would bend a gunstock. But these days, at least among the double-gun crowd, the practice of stock bending is common knowledge, and competition shooters have understood its benefits for years. The first fellow I heard of who bent stocks was a man from Oregon who followed skeet and trap tournaments on the West Coast during the summer and in Arizona during the winter. He bent stocks on site, and, although I have no idea how he did it, he was well known in those circles.

The first time I saw a stock bent was on a video produced by the American Custom Gunmakers Guild. California gunsmith Bill Nittler (now deceased, formerly of the Purdey American repair station) was shown doing it. Nittler used a somewhat sophisticated jig to hold the shotgun in a fixed position and hot linseed oil to heat the wood. The jig was set up to hold the stock firmly in its new conformation until it cooled. The video showed the process in detail and gave a complete explanation of how and why stocks are bent. I was astounded. Indeed, I could see the stock being bent, and it was obvious that this was a common job for Nittler, with relatively predictable and consistent results.

Since then, I've learned a great deal about stock bending, most importantly that it can be fraught with problems. As Birmingham-trained gunmaker John F. "Jack" Rowe says, "It may be a bit more of black magic than science." Any pro-fessional stock bender will make it clear that there are risks that are the client's rather than the gunsmith's.

Breakage is risk number one, and, although they seldom like to admit it, many stock benders have broken—or at least cracked—a stock or two. Which makes the possibility of cracking or splitting risk number two. All the stock benders I've talked with are careful to make a thorough inspection of a gun before attempting to bend its stock. Some even disassemble the gun to see if repairs have been made that aren't visible from the outside. Cross-grain wood and earlier repairs may prompt the bender to say no to a project. But some individuals, if they simply can't shoot the gun the way it is, will still ask the smith to try, but if the stock breaks, they're pretty much left with having a new stock made.

These days there are a lot of new guns coming out of Europe with cross-grain wood, pin knots, or burls in the wrists of the stocks. New or old, these stocks are not good subjects for bending. In Chapter 19, I offer a detailed look at stock-blank layout, which should help you recognize a cross-grain stock. If not, a competent stock bender should let you know; he won't want to break your gunstock.

Previous repairs may have been done with an adhesive that will let go if heat is applied. Even if the glue remains good, if the stock cracked through the wrist once, it might do it again. The benders I've talked with are very reluctant to bend a stock that has a wrist repair.

A third risk is what's known as spring-back.

Because it's abnormal to heat and bend a stock, it's not hard to imagine the wood wanting to return to its former position. Spring-back usually occurs after bending, when the stock has cooled and after it has been removed from the jig. If this happens, the bender typically will heat it and try again. Some stocks may take a third try, or not retain much bend at all. Allegedly, it is possible for a stock to spring back over time—weeks, months, or even years. I recently measured a stock that I'd bent two years earlier, and it measured exactly what it had been bent to. Stock benders will tell you that they believe in delayed spring-back, but most say they've rarely had to deal with it.

Damaging a stock's finish is another concern. The amount of heat applied and the way it is applied can seriously mar both the old varnish finishes and some of the newer synthetic ones. More often than not, the stock might be slightly darkened or a bit of the finish lifted or "crazed" in the grip area. Spot refinishing—in the checkering, where it is easier to camouflage—is usually all that is necessary, but in some extreme cases a complete refinish may be necessary.

With these caveats, why would anyone want to bend a gunstock in the first place? Why would they risk cracking or breaking a perfectly good gunstock with unnatural heat and contortion? The answer is gun fit. If your gun doesn't fit, spending a couple of hundred dollars to have it bent becomes an attractive alternative to the time and expense of making a new stock.

I can find no early reference to stock bending in my library, but knowing of the ability of British gunmakers to alter shotguns and the secrecy in which they held these methods, I have no doubt that stock bending has been done for a long time—maybe two centuries or more. The standard straight-grip (wrist or hand) configuration of a typical British gunstock lends itself well to bending. In fact, benders will tell you that these are the easiest stocks to work on.

With the sheer number of used British guns on the market today, there has been a lot of stock bending done lately, which can be a good thing. Let's say your newly acquired Birmingham boxlock suits you just fine except that it is consistently shooting a few inches to the left. Or perhaps the early Holland & Holland you coveted has a bit less drop than you desire. Taking into account the various risks, bending can put you on target with a minimum of expense and hassle.

And that is the purpose of stock bending: to get your gun as close as possible to your dimensions and, thus, shooting to your point of aim. Some stock benders will recommend a few shooting lessons to be sure your gun mount is credible as well as a fitting with a try gun to ensure that your measurements are accurate.

Older American guns are another story. Many were stocked with excessive drop compared to today's standards. Also many were stocked in American walnut, which I've heard is harder to bend than the English variety. Many had thicker pistol-grip stocks as well, which adds to the difficulty of bending. If your gun has all three of these traits—as is the case with most 12-gauge Fox Sterlingworths, Parker Trojans, and Field Grade Elsies—you may be out of luck.

That's not to say your stock won't be bendable, but there is a limit to how much and where a stock can be bent. Many years ago, I purchased a near-mint Fox Sterlingworth 20-bore with 30-inch barrels. I really liked the gun, but the trouble was the more-than-three-inches of drop at the heel. There was no way I could shoot the Fox effectively. That was when I started researching bending for my own application. No stock bender I talked with could imagine getting the 3/4-inch upward bend I wanted. Furthermore, because bending takes place in the middle of the grip, the comb nose would rise far less than the heel. To cap it off, the pitch also would change dramatically, so this would need alteration as well.

To visualize this problem, picture the profile of the butt with a pivot point in the middle of the grip. As the stock is bent upward at the pivot point, the comb nose rises less than the heel, as it is closer to the bend. Because the toe of the stock is farthest from the bend, the pitch is significantly altered.

Let's say the stock is bent upward 1/2 inch at the heel. The comb will come up appreciably less, and it still might not be high enough. Likewise, if the comb nose is proportionally higher than the heel, the comb might be too high when the drop at the heel is correct. Either way, the pitch will be altered, which must be considered beforehand.

Another gun of mine was bent upward nearly 1/2 inch at the heel, bringing the comb to shootable dimensions. To finish the job, I recut the butt for my pitch angle and installed a recoil pad for the length I needed, all of which, in this case, worked out fine. It may seem like putting the horse before the cart, but I'd recommend that you have an accurate idea of your stock dimensions before shopping for a used gun. Of course, I realize that this isn't the way it usually works.

Illinois gunsmith Steve Downes has a slightly different approach. He is most interested in the stock measurement known as "drop at face"—the area where the shooter locates his face on the stock. This is usually about three to four inches behind the comb nose. When making a new stock, the drop at face is determined by the drop at comb and heel, as there is (usually) a straight line between them. It may be possible to bend a stock to the correct drop-at-face measurement leaving the comb and heel slightly off, but still locating your eye where it needs to be to shoot straight. Make sure your fitter gives you the drop-at-face measurement along with the others.

Bending for cast isn't so much of a problem, because it doesn't substantially alter the other stock dimensions. Bending for drop does, and this factor must be taken into consideration before embarking on that adventure. What I hear

Gunsmith Steve Downes's sturdy stock–bending jig holds a stock during the bending process.

Hot oil drips on a stock protected with aluminum foil during the bending process.

around the trade is that roughly 1/2 inch at the heel is about the most that can be reliably bent in any direction. If the stock needs to be bent for both drop and cast, most benders do it as two different operations and charge accordingly.

Can you imagine bending a stock that has a through-bolt holding it to the action? If it is a pumpgun or an autoloader, it's best to adjust the dimensions by altering the inletting where the stock meets the action. (Forget bending recoil-operated autoloaders with a spring housing in the midst of the butt.) Other through-bolt guns, such as Browning Superposeds, are good candidates for bending. If you have trouble believing this, remove the buttplate, through-bolt, and butt from such a gun and note that the size of the hole in the wood exceeds the size of the bolt body enough to allow some movement. You'll see how it could be bent without bending the bolt. If the hole is too small, sometimes it can be enlarged before bending. When bending for cast with these guns, the bender must be careful not to spring one side of the stock's head out the side of the action.

Thick, heavy through-bolt target guns with palm swells and American walnut stocks simply may not bend. In such cases you might consider "shaving the face," as Jack Rowe calls the procedure of removing wood from the side or top of the comb to obtain more suitable dimensions.

Stock bending, in many cases, is a viable alternative to restocking a shotgun. It is not a cure-all for every shooting problem, and I want to stress that you're probably not going to achieve all of your dimensions perfectly by bending. But within the variables of shotgunning, bending could get you a lot closer.

• • •

Having related the reasons for bending a gunstock and the potential problems with doing so, let's take a look at some of the methods and procedures used by experienced stock benders around the U.S.

Oklahoma gunmaker Jack Rowe was taught to bend stocks in Birmingham, England, so long ago that he doesn't remember exactly when. Rowe started his apprenticeship about the time World War II was ending. More recently, he's been teaching stock bending and other double-gun work at National Rifle Association summer gunsmithing classes at Murray State College in Tishamingo, Oklahoma, and Pine Technical College in Pine City, Minnesota. Rowe says that,

"there's usually a bit of smoke and fire involved" with his method. He stresses that it is a small-shop procedure requiring a minimum of tools and no bending jig.

With the barrels removed, Rowe clamps the gun's action in a lead-jaw vise on a workbench solidly mounted to the floor and wall. (The vise jaws are parallel to the length of the bench.) If the stock is to be bent for cast, the action is held bottom up, with the butt on the right side of the vise. If it is to be bent upward for less drop, the gun is held with the right side of the action up and the toe toward the wall.

His other tools are two-by-four-inch blocks of wood cut to lengths matching the distance between the wall and the stock, plus a bit more than the amount of bend desired. In other words, if the distance from the wall to the stock is twenty-four inches and $1/2$ inch of bend is desired, the block will be about 24$3/4$ inches to create a bit of over-bend. Rowe has many different-length blocks, and each is padded with leather on the end that contacts the stock.

Rowe wraps the stock wrist with multiple layers of old cotton T-shirts and ties them on with string. These rags tightly cover the grip area. A pan is placed under the wrapped stock, and the cotton rags are saturated in linseed oil.

Now comes the fun—and dangerous—part. (Don't try this at home!) Linseed oil has a relatively low flash point, yet it must be brought to a temperature that will make it boil. Using a propane torch with about a $3/4$-inch tip, Rowe, holding the stock in his hands, heats the oil-soaked rags right where he wants the bend to be. The stock is rotated over the flame, preventing the cloth from catching fire. If it flames, Rowe blows out the fire and backs away with the heat. Over the course of fifteen to twenty minutes, he heats the oil-soaked rags, taking the torch away at times to let the heat soak into the wood.

According to Rowe, "There are two things you need to know: when the wood is ready to bend, and when it has bent as far as it will go. I tell the customer that about a half inch in any direction is the maximum, but that guideline doesn't always apply. Sometimes you can't even get that; sometimes you can get almost double that."

Rowe says that "feel" is more important than keeping track of the heating time or temperature. "You can tell when it's hot enough by pulling on the stock," he said. "You can feel it."

To do the actual bending after heating, Rowe clamps the action in the bench vise and by hand pulls the butt away from the bench. Appropriate-length wood blocks then are inserted between the back wall of the bench and the stock.

"Some stocks are so stubborn—resistant to bending," Rowe says, "that you let them cool in place for a half-hour, then take them out to check them, and they just spring back again. You pull them over to their limits—to where you feel that if they went any more, they would crack or break—and when you check them, they spring back and you have only half the amount you need. You have to take them past the point you need, because you have to allow for spring-back. There is always going to be some amount of spring-back when you take a stock out of the vise. But with some, you have an eighth or a sixteenth and that's all you're going to get."

Glenn Baker, of Woodcock Hill in Pennsylvania, blends new and old methods of stock bending. He learned the craft from Peter Stevens, a retired Purdey craftsman who gave him all of his equipment, including a bending jig. Baker uses hot linseed oil, infrared lamps, or a combination of both to heat the stock. His jig is based on a twelve-inch-square, oak beam that holds the entire gun, barrels and all. A screw mechanism, hand tightened, pushes the stock over for cast once the wood is heated. By turning the gun in the fixture, drop can be increased or reduced using the same heating and bending routine.

Baker wraps the wrist of the stock with cotton rags, old T-shirts, or sheets, from the end of

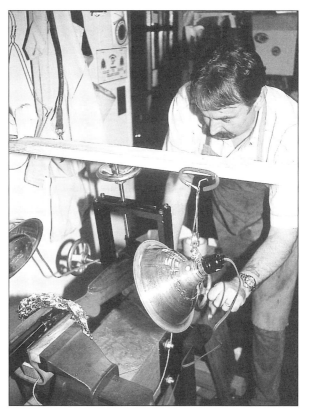

Woodcock Hill's Glenn Baker uses a combination of hot linseed oil and infrared lamps to bend stocks in his specially made jig.

the top strap to the comb nose. He soaks the rags with linseed oil and mainly uses infrared lamps for heat. A lamp is situated on each side of the grip, with the locations of the lamps and their distances from the stock regulating the amount of heat. Baker heats the grip for about twenty to thirty minutes and says he can tell by experience when it is ready to bend.

His jig is calibrated to show the amount of bend in the stock. Like Jack Rowe, Baker notes that one must always over-bend, as the wood will spring back to a greater or lesser degree. He said, "Three things can happen when you bend a stock; two of them are not good. One: It will bend just fine and you'll live happily ever after. Two: It will break and you'll end up with a pile of splinters. Or three: It will have a memory and come back. You pay your money and you take your chances. In most cases it will bend and everything will be fine."

Baker bends quite a few stocks and often will do it while the customer is visiting his shop. His usual turnaround time for bending is one day. Baker bends mostly for cast, avoiding the problems associated with changing pitch when changing a stock's drop. He also says that many would-be clients simply don't know how to properly mount their guns, and that often, with a few lessons, they are able to shoot well without modifications.

Gunsmith Steve Downes definitely believes in a gunfitting—if not shooting lessons—prior to bending a stock. Fitting gives the client more confidence in his mount and his gun's dimensions as well as gives Downes a complete set of numbers to work from. As I mentioned earlier, Downes thinks the drop at face dimension is the most important drop figure and that the client should specifically ask his gunfitter for it. He also feels it is important to be fitted with a try gun similar to the gun you will be shooting; for example, use a side-by-side for fitting if that is the type of gun whose stock is to be bent.

Downes bends quite a few through-bolt guns, such as Berettas and Brownings, and always makes sure there is sufficient clearance around the bolt to allow for a bit of bend.

He also has no qualms about telling someone he won't bend a stock. "If it doesn't look good, I'm not going to bend it," Downes said. "I'd much rather do that than have to call the customer and tell him he's got two pieces of stock." So Downes thoroughly examines every gun prior to bending. When I asked him what he would turn away, he listed cross-grain, pin knots, burl through the wrist, or any gun with a touchy single trigger like a Fox—the latter because the trigger is not going to function properly after bending. He takes guns apart and examines them inside and out. "Sometimes you'll open up a gun and find numerous repairs that couldn't be seen from the outside," Downes said, "or it will have some ancient repair with some unknown type of glue that probably won't withstand the heat used in bending. I then tell the customer up front that it's at his own risk, but I just dread having to call them and say, 'I broke your stock.'"

Traditional oil-finished guns are least likely to suffer cosmetic anomalies from the heat of bending. American guns with old varnish finishes, such as L.C. Smiths and Parkers, will sometimes "craze." When this happens, Downes carefully scrapes away the crystallized varnish and spot-refinishes the area. Sometimes newer Brownings will turn yellow, but Downes keeps the heat in such a small area that it is usually a minor job to touch up the color.

Downes's bending jig is a modified version of the one in the video *Special Gunsmithing Techniques of William J. Nittler*, the American Custom Gunmakers Guild production I mentioned at the first of this chapter. It is based on a large, rectangular box made of two-by-six-inch boards with a stainless-steel sink below to catch the oil. The oil is heated in two deep-fryers—one above and one below—with a recirculating pump that feeds the oil back up to the top. A simple nozzle with a valve drops the hot oil onto the stock.

Downes wraps the stock in aluminum foil from the action to the comb to protect the wood from the oil. In fact, the oil never touches the stock; soaked rags are wrapped around the outside of the foil. Downes no longer uses linseed oil, because of its vulnerability to flash fire and because it stinks so badly he can't stay in his shop afterward. He substitutes vegetable oil and says, "The place just smells like a burger joint for a while."

The first step is to remove the trigger guard, then the whole gun is put in the jig and locked down with clamps at the action and muzzles. The oil is heated to between 375 and 400 degrees. If bending for cast-off, the left side is faced upward and a steel bar with a padded foot for holding the stock in place is located over the butt. If the bending is to lessen drop, web straps secure the stock while cooling after bending. The jig is fairly simple, but it is sophisticated enough to accomplish any bend reasonably desired. Downes can measure directly from the sides or bottom of the jig at any time to determine the stock dimensions and the amount of change.

The oil is dripped onto the stock for forty-five minutes or more. "I don't need to rush it," Downes said. "I'll keep heating it until it's ready to bend. I'm not going to force it over." He accomplishes the bend with hand pressure, believing, as Rowe does, in feeling the wood move and feeling just how far it will go. If the stock needs to be bent in two directions, occasionally both can be done simultaneously. "Sometimes you heat these guns up and they bend like a wet noodle," Downes said. "Then I can get both bends at once, though sometimes I have to heat and bend them twice." He also keeps the heat on the stock for a while after the bend is accomplished, believing this reduces the chance of spring-back.

Downes says there is no accounting for the amount of spring-back there will be after the gun is removed from the jig. A stock must always be over-bent, then measured after it is cool. "That's

why you wind up bending it twice on occasion," Downes said. "You take an educated guess, bend it as far as you think necessary and see what you get. The heavier the grip section, the more likely it will spring back and need a second go."

He leaves the stock in the jig until it is completely cool. Then after removing the stock from the jig, he removes the buttstock from the action to clean up the inside. The heat from bending will cause all sorts of stuff to ooze out of the wood into the inletting, and this may interfere with the function of the safety or other mechanisms. Downes stresses the need for this post-bend cleanup. After reassembling the gun, he bends the long tang of the trigger guard to fit the new conformation. A final check is made to ensure that the gun functions correctly.

Owners considering having this work done should examine their guns for suitability and make sure that they have the appropriate dimensions. A client also must understand the associated risks and realize that no matter how careful a gunsmith is, there are no guarantees that the proper dimensions will result or that the stock won't break in bending.

CHAPTER 10
Stock Machining

Custom stockmaking brings to mind an image of a lone craftsman standing at a bench littered with hand tools. Chisels and gouges, powered by a mallet, inlet the action. Drawknife and spokeshave, razor sharp, peel away long curls of walnut to shape the contours. Although these techniques are still employed by many gunstockers, the number of custom stocks that are inletted and/or shaped by a duplicating machine might be surprising.

Machined stocks are nothing new. Eli Whitney invented the stock-carving machine in the first half of the nineteenth century, and all of the great American arms manufacturers have used them since. While gunmakers in this country were refining machining processes, British and European makers were clinging to traditional handwork methods. It's hard to believe that large-scale gunmaking firms such as BSA and J.P. Sauer didn't use stock machines, building as many guns as they did. (When it comes to gunstocks, the terms "machined," "semi-inletted," "duplicated," "carved," and "turned" are largely interchangeable. The duplicating machine is also called a pantograph, though this is not technically correct.)

Semi-inletted stocks became a big business when surplus military bolt-action rifles flooded the market after World War II, and machine-duplicated stocks have made the custom rifle market what it is today. Similarly, today's few professional muzzleloading gunmakers have developed stock patterns to cut down the hundreds of hours required to create sophisticated Pennsylvania long rifles.

Although production-machined replacement stocks for factory shotguns have been around for years, I feel they often leave much to be desired. The shooter who thinks about buying one for that "good-deal," broken-stock Parker may be in for a big surprise.

When restocking or creating a new stock for a double gun, there are many factors to consider. The curve, flex, and distance between the tangs, as well as the fact that just two tang screws hold the works together, are major considerations. Vagaries of wood such as seasonal stability, stress relief, and pore density are others, as are shootable dimensions and strong grain through the wrist. Equally important are the quality of the pattern stock and the precision capabilities of the duplicating machine.

Any stock that isn't bedded solidly to the action and tangs is subject to splitting under recoil. If the tangs aren't in the proper relationship to one another, the sears, triggers, and safety will malfunction. Single-trigger guns require extra careful stocking if they are to work reliably. If the wood is machined before it is completely cured—and even after it is—it may later move around slightly or even radically.

Production-machined or factory-styled replacement stocks usually have the same dimensions as the original gun, which limits custom alterations. Sometimes the blank layout may not be good. If a pattern stock is worn or the cutters are dull or a machine rattles as it carves four stocks, how good can the replacement be?

Now consider a professional using a precision stock-duplicating machine. With this device, a custom maker can machine a stock and avoid the problems mentioned above. George Hoenig, of Boise, Idaho, built the duplicators preferred by today's professionals. Although Hoenig/Rodman machines (as they are known in the trade) are not currently available new, they are a very desirable item on the used market and may sell for as much as the low five figures. In addition to being found in shops of American stockmakers, I believe they are employed by Holland & Holland, Purdey, and Hartmann & Weiss. Gene Simillion of Gunnison, Colorado, has used a Hoenig/Rodman machine for many years and has duplicated quite a number of stocks for me.

Using a Hoenig/Rodman machine sounds simple, but it is a delicate and sophisticated operation. The pattern stock is set up with fixtures on both ends to center it. A stock blank is positioned on the centers of another spindle. When the pattern is rotated (by hand), the other spindle rotates exactly the same way. One chuck holds a stylus above the pattern stock and another holds a precisely ground and sharpened cutter, driven by a high-speed motor, above the blank. As the stylus is moved side to side or up and down, the cutter exactly mimics this movement. Different styluses are used to adjust the amount of wood left on the stock. The principle is that each movement of the stylus along the pattern stock is mirrored on the stock blank by the cutter, thus duplicating the pattern exactly.

There are several advantages to precision-machined stocks, not the least of which is saving time for the craftsman. Although George Hoenig was trained in the traditional German school, he says "Making a stock from a blank is about the worst way to do it."

That is a strong statement, but any experienced stocker will tell you it is not unusual for a stock to move as stresses in the blank are relieved during shaping. Inletting can open or close up;

quarter-sawn wood can bend up or down; slab-sawn wood can cup or twist. The fancier the blank, the more likely it is to move around as the bulk is removed to take it down to the final shape. Stockmakers will tell you that when major movement occurs, it is often the result of trying to remove a lot of wood in a hurry.

The procedure of machine-duplicating a stock can help the wood normalize. First, the outside of the stock is rough cut to remove the bulk of the wood and most of the stress. (This process may turn up voids, bark inclusions, nails, or even bullets or musket balls in the wood—flaws that otherwise wouldn't have been discovered until hours of hand inletting and shaping had been invested.) Then the inletting is roughed in, after which the stock can be set aside for a couple of days or weeks to stabilize.

The stock and the pattern are then returned to their exact centers on the duplicating machine and the outside and inletting is recut to within $1/32$ of an inch. A final pass is made on the inletting to bring it down to close tolerances.

The stockmaker is left with a fully machined stock cut within $1/32$ of an inch on the outside and within a few thousandths of an inch on the inside. The inletting is still slightly undersize, while the outside is left a bit more oversize, so that if the cutter takes out a small chip or tears the grain, there's still some wood to work with. The metal can be inlet by removing the last bit of wood with hand tools, compressing the grain a bit, just as if the stocker were working from a blank.

This may sound like reducing stockmaking to assembling a drugstore blackpowder kit, but it's far from that. The machined stock is only as good as the pattern stock, and therein lies the rub: the stocker must first have—or produce—a quality pattern.

For example, I recently stocked a fine Italian sidelock that was imported in-the-white. The original stock was unfinished, dull and drab, with a huge beavertail forend and a severely hooked pistol grip. I converted it to a pattern stock. After shortening the forend iron, I reinlet the forend tip and carefully glass-bedded the iron and forend. I shaped the oversize wood to a pleasing splinter, and I made and fitted an oval escutcheon.

The metalwork was glass-bedded, which involved coating both the stock head and inletting with a fiberglass bedding compound. (Glassing the head and locks is not for the foolhardy or light-minded. Bedding compound can permanently bond the metal to the wood if release agents and metal recesses are not respected. Believe me, you don't want to chisel the stock off of glued-in metalwork.) This gives a perfect impression of the metal components and a hard surface for the machine's stylus to follow.

The client's stock dimensions were compared to those of the sidelock's original wood and appropriate adjustments made. In this case, the comb was quite high and needed to be quite low. After roughing off the pistol grip, I drew and shaped a straight grip and made a new trigger guard. The stock needed more cast and toe-out, so I bent it.

To achieve a diamond grip and remove all traces of the pistol grip, I built up several areas around the wrist with body putty. Just as I would shape any stock, I pared this one down to final form, except that I left small flats on the comb and toe lines to establish centers. (Possibly, the most difficult part of using a machined stock is establishing center lines on the curved surfaces, as opposed to those on a square blank.) I then then spray-painted the pattern stock a uniform brown so its lines were clearly visible, and sealed the wood.

At this point, several advantages of machining came into play. With the exact dimensions established, I hollowed the pattern stock's butt to balance the gun. I shipped it to the client (an active and discriminating shooter),

who shot, patterned, and tested the gun's feel and function for a month. Then, after minor alterations to perfect the stock pattern, I traced its layout onto the new blank and took the bandsaw to this very expensive stick of sumptuous walnut. For machining, it went to Gene Simillion, who cut me an exact duplicate with .030 inches of extra wood on the outside, .003 inches of wood on most of the inletting, and .006 inches at the head. He left the tang-screw holes uncut so I could locate them exactly. The stock was then headed up with a draw clamp and hand chisels, just as I would have done working from the blank. Because duplicating-machine cutters are circular, I also needed to square up the corners of the inletting. The forend was left with quite a bit of external wood (in such a way that it could be held in a bench vise for inletting) because of the jig required for the machine.

Working with tiny allowances is delicate; there is not a lot of extra wood to support the inletting during the stocking process. With careful work, however, the results are the same—perfect inletting with compressed end grain, no wood-to-metal gaps, and nothing binding the mechanism.

Does this process save money? From my perspective, that's not the point. Perfect pattern work takes care and time, and the cost of precisely running the duplicating machine will set you back a few hundred dollars. If a stocker quotes prices, how he does the work is determined by what he has to work with. Simply put, some stocks aren't good candidates for duplication, and their replacements should be made from the blank.

On this subject, I spoke with Paul Hodgins, a Holland & Holland-trained stocker who actually ran the carving machine there. He now works in Utah, making most stocks from the blank but also using machined stocks when it's practical. What determines which process Hodgins uses are the quality of the original stock, the amount of alteration needed, and the overall difficulty of the project.

Sometimes Hodgins will have just the head and inletting of a sidelock machined. This saves him from hand-inletting the difficult mechanism but gives him unlimited latitude for custom dimensions. Other times the stock head is oil-soaked, badly broken, or nonexistent, necessitating that a new stock be made from a blank.

Having an accomplished stocker like Gene Simillion running the machine is an advantage. He understands when I need extra wood and when I don't. I often have special requests (leave more wood at the lock panels, don't locate holes, leave the butt extralong), which he accommodates. Simillion marks the amount of extra wood he leaves on the stock, so I know what has to be removed. What I end up with is a custom-machined stock, and my clients get the finest work available by any method.

When to machine and when to work from the blank is a decision best left to the professional. A few years back, I built a semi-pistol-grip Fox, making the pattern stock from a commercial, preinlet blank, then having it machined very closely. In this case, the metalwork (tangs, triggers, and guard) had been substantially altered, the stock design and dimensions were quite unusual, and the client wanted an extraordinary shotgun. I made the pattern stock quite rapidly, without having to worry about botching an expensive blank. The client shot the gun extensively, and we made modifications before machining a gorgeous stick. It probably cost him a few hundred dollars more, but he knows he's gotten exactly what he wants. How much is that worth?

In no way will the duplicating machine replace competent stockmaking. There are too many times when it is best to work from the

Gunmaker Gene Simillion operating a Hoenig/ Rodman stock duplicating machine. The H/R stock duplicator is used in small-shop gunmaking world-wide and is well known for its precision.

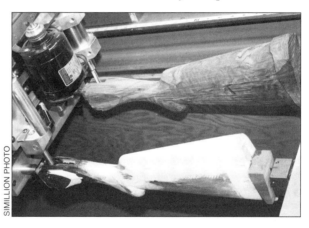

The pattern (left) was made by building up a stock with body putty and as the stylus traces its surfaces the machined stock of fine walnut is precisely duplicated with a rotary cutter.

blank, and I have the utmost respect for crafts-men who do so. But I also respect those who understand and use technology for labor savings and improving their work. Stock machining does not create instant stockmakers; it is more like having an apprentice to do some of the heavy work, in a world where stockmaking apprentices are a rare commodity.

CHAPTER 11

Balancing a Double Gun

As a shooter, I was intrigued by shotgun balance long before I knew why one gun felt like I could hit with it and another handled like an oak post. Whether the firearm is a rifle or a shotgun or even a handgun, appropriate balance is an important part of why some guns can be shot better than others.

As a custom gunmaker, I consider proper balance and handling as necessary requirements of a high-quality firearm. (A gun must also be fully functional and place shot accurately, be correctly proportioned and pleasing to the eye, and have a high degree of detailing from butt to muzzle.) No matter how fine a gun looks, how great it shoots, or how well detailed it is, it can't be "high quality" if it doesn't balance and handle wonderfully. And these inherent features can be determined with the eyes closed and without firing the gun.

In this chapter I'll discuss shotgun balance and explain its how's and why's, then I'll describe the actual procedures I use in my workshop to achieve proper balance. First, let's review some parameters of gun balance.

How much should a shotgun weigh? (I'm talking side-by-side field guns; I have little experience with over-and-unders and target guns.) In my opinion, the 96 to 1 rule is still the best estimate for appropriate weight. This rule states that a field gun should weigh 96 times the weight of the shot charge. For example, when using a one-ounce shot charge, the shotgun should weigh one ounce times 96, or 96 ounces (six pounds). This figure equates to the light side of comfortable recoil.

For me, six pounds is the minimum weight for a gun of any barrel length or gauge. Any less than that is too light for me to control. I own a 30-inch 16-gauge Austrian boxlock, with a recoil pad, that is well balanced and weighs a couple ounces over six pounds. It is a great-shooting gun and, with one-ounce loads, a joy to carry in the field. If I had a 28-gauge, I would want it to balance and handle just about like the 16; the smaller gauge does not equate to lighter weight.

I have little experience with guns on the top end of weight scale. However, I can say that a well-balanced eight-pound 12-gauge gun, such as the Krieghoff I once borrowed while shooting doves in Argentina, will handle remarkably well in certain circumstances. In Argentina, there was always plenty of time to mount the gun, and at the end of the day—some nine hundred shells later—I was quite pleased with the the gun's lack of recoil as well as its ability to follow through without my having to think about it.

The heaviest custom shotgun I've built was a Britte 12-gauge sidelock double. It was created specifically for duck shooting—from a blind—with $1^{1}/8$-ounce loads in the open-choked barrel and $1^{1}/4$-ounce loads in the tight barrel. The double wound up at 7 pounds 2 ounces and has a thick red-rubber recoil pad.

The moderately dense one-inch piece of wood that I cut from the butt weighed 3 ounces. The ground-to-fit, one-inch Galazan recoil pad (with screws and plugs) that replaced the wood weighed 4.64 ounces. So 1.64 ounces had to be removed from the butt to achieve the original

A custom Hughes/Britte 12-gauge sidelock weighing 7 pounds 2 ounces and balancing at the hinge pin.

balance. A smaller pad would have had less effect, but all pads weigh more than an equal amount of wood. That sidelock double might have benefited from the added weight, but the extreme end is always the worst place to add it, and it made the gun feel sluggish and butt heavy. The drilled buttstock, along with the cutoff wood and pad, are shown in the photos.

In my opinion, a 12-gauge field gun should weigh about 6¾ pounds. At that weight, the gun is not a burden to carry and isn't brutal in recoil with 1⅛- or 1¼-ounce field loads.

I am not embarrassed to admit being recoil sensitive, and the same sub-seven-pound gun without a pad would give me a headache after a box of 1⅛-ounce, AA trap loads. I prefer one-ounce light loads or a heavier gun with a recoil pad for even informal target shooting.

I'm not a believer in heroics to lighten a gun—most of us simply want to improve the gun that we have in any way that will help our shooting. I shudder when I hear of things like striking the barrels for weight loss or better balance. It is difficult for me to believe that it was ever done, but I've measured barrels whose wall thicknesses varied tremendously between the outboard side (where a file can work) and around to the ribs (where a file can't work), so I can't deny that it may have been done.

Although an extreme measure for weight reduction, back-boring (given safe wall thickness) is a better option. At least it removes metal symmetrically, resulting in more uniform wall thickness. Some smiths say it improves patterns.

So how should a gun of a given weight correctly balance? This is simpler than it might seem. As near as I can tell, there are only two ways for a double gun to balance properly, and they are determined by the type of shooting one wants to do. One way is for snap shooting, as at grouse or woodcock in heavy cover, when the gun has to come up quickly and is fired once it touches the shoulder. The other way is for more deliberate shooting, when leading the target in some manner is involved. I find no practical use for the extremes, for having a gun butt or muzzle heavy.

For snap shooting, I want a dynamic-handling shotgun to balance on the hinge pin. For more deliberate shooting and to increase natural follow-through, a slightly weight-forward gun is in order. I know all the reasons not to use the hinge pin as a point of reference; in any case, the pin is a good place to start. If I were balancing a Winchester Model 21, I would take the extra length of the receiver into account.

Moving the balance point as little as ⅜ of an inch forward or back of the hinge pin will drastically change the "feel" of the gun. Some people have suggested experimenting with balance by adding weight to the muzzle or butt, but I believe this to be largely ineffectual if the method of balancing is going to be by reducing the weight.

The best way to learn how a well-balanced gun "feels" is by handling as many well-balanced guns as possible and noting what your hands tell your mind about how the weight is distributed. How do you know when a gun is well balanced? Having a variety of guns to handle, and someone who understands balance discuss it with you as you handle them, is the ideal situation. Otherwise, you may have to locate the balance point of several guns, then compare their feel as you contemplate what you have read about proper balancing. To determine a gun's balance point, set up a balancing block (a small triangular piece of wood) on a table and place the gun upside down on top of it, or place the gun through a loop of rope suspended from above. I can get a pretty good idea by simply resting the gun on the edge my hand, but I wouldn't recommend doing this at a gun show.

Most quality British guns and a lot of pre-World War II continental guns were built with balance in mind. Few American factory guns are well balanced except by accident—certain frame-size and barrel-length configurations, such as the Parker "O" frame and Fox 16-gauges with 28-inch barrels, are good examples. I was fortunate that the first quality side-by-side I owned was a very well-balanced French boxlock. There is simply no substitute for handling the genuine article.

Many years ago, I read Gough Thomas's *Shotguns & Cartridges for Game & Clays* and developed my notions of correct balance from his writing and by holding that French boxlock in my hands. To condense Thomas's thoughts, a well-balanced gun should have half of its weight between the hands, one fourth toward the muzzles, and one fourth toward the butt. These are referred to as the "half weights."

Thomas developed the notion of "moment of inertia," or MOI, as applied to shotguns and to my knowledge was the first to use the term "dynamic handling." He credits Americans with the expression "a fast-handling gun," which is probably the best description of what every gunner desires.

Thomas built a gauge for measuring balance and MOI. A brief definition of MOI is the amount of energy needed to get a shotgun into action (mounting, but mostly swinging) as measured from the balance point.

He states that for optimum MOI, the distance from the trigger to the balance point "should preferably not exceed $4^{1/4}$ inches." My own Hughes/Fox 12-gauge balances at $4^{3/8}$ inches ahead of the trigger, as does the heavier Britte sidelock that I mentioned earlier. My 30-inch Austrian 16-gauge balances at $4^{1/4}$ inches with its added one-inch recoil pad and hollowed butt. Few repeaters are even in the ballpark, but the only one I own—a 16-gauge, 28-inch Winchester Model 12—balances at $4^{1/2}$ inches in front of the trigger. After I added a $^{1/2}$-inch recoil pad, it weighs 6 pounds 3 ounces. Maybe that's why I enjoy shooting the full-choked gun at long-range targets.

More recently, mechanical engineer Don Amos developed his own version of an MOI machine and established a data base of the guns he has measured with it. Several years ago, I met Amos at a Las Vegas gun show, and he had his new—at that time—MOI machine and was beginning to build his data base of recorded MOI measurements. I had my Hughes/Fox 12-gauge, and we got together to measure the gun. When I told him it was a 28-inch, 12 gauge Fox, he commented that it would probably come out being "slow." I left the gun for him to measure; when I came back, he seemed amazed at how fast handling it turned out to be.

Frankly, I was surprised he couldn't feel the handling qualities. This is no knock on Don Amos; in the mass of gun-show humanity and with the line of folks wanting to have their guns measured, he was focused on the task at hand. I had been pretty certain how the MOI would come out because I had balanced the gun with dynamic handling in mind. I had built it at 6 pounds 10 ounces and had skeletonized the forearm iron and severely hollowed the buttstock to get it down to that weight and to balance near the pin.

From a workshop perspective, balancing a

A one-inch recoil pad (above) with screws and plugs and the one-inch section of walnut cut from the stock. The pad weighs 1.64 ounces more than the cut-off walnut.

Two holes were bored in the buttstock of the Hughes/Britte 12 gauge to counter the weight of the pad and balance the sidelock. Note the end grain and holes are well sealed with stock finish.

gun is a matter of procedures and consciousness; that is, it is knowing what the gun is supposed to feel like. Achieving the desired result means carrying out the appropriate procedures with the least amount of trial and error. In other words, I don't believe that gunmakers strike barrels as an afterthought to achieve the proper balance: I like to think they are smarter than that. I imagine they determine the probable finished weight and balance for a given gauge and barrel/stock length, have barrels made to an appropriate wall thickness and taper for their length, pick out a corresponding piece of walnut (light or heavy), and know if the gun was going to have a particularly long or short stock. With these parameters in mind, I believe they attempt to get the gun as close as possible to the proper balance in the course of creating it.

Then, if it isn't quite right, they will tune the balance and weight after building the gun. Gunmakers know that most guns will come out butt heavy, and they know as well that the butt will have to be drilled out to lighten it. By drilling one hole rather deeply, the weight will be reduced; but as the hole gets deeper, the balance will be less effected. By drilling two shallower

holes at the butt end, the same weight reduction can be achieved with a more significant change in the half weights. As with any fulcrum, the further away from the balance point that the weight is reduced, the more effect it has on the balance. By taking the weight out of the butt end of the stock, dynamic handling could most often be achieved with the minimum of hassle. Look at the butt end of a finely balanced gun and you will typically see two bore holes.

Early gunmakers didn't have a method of measuring or quantifying MOI, so how did they achieve it? Common workers didn't get to shoot the guns on which they worked, so how could they reproduce these "felt" concepts in the shop? I wish I knew exactly what they did, other than hollowing the stock, but I do know that balancing a gun was a required procedure, similar to ejector timing and stock finishing, and it was accomplished as accurately and quickly as possible by the person responsible for that phase of the work.

As part of my procedure, and to confirm stock dimensions, clients often get to shoot their guns before final finishing. This gives them a notion of how the guns will balance. Fortunately, I have enough workshop intuition to achieve my clients' requests for a dynamic-handling shotgun.

And I do it without measuring MOI or shooting the gun. I surmise that balancing was originally done using procedures similar to those I use: identifying the balance point, "feeling" the balance, then altering the stock until a given balance point and feel were achieved.

Fortunately, most shotguns are butt-heavy. I say "fortunately" because it is far easier to remove wood, thus weight, by drilling holes in the butt than by any other form of weight reduction or balancing alteration. Adding a recoil pad is one of the most common alterations to shotguns, but in almost every case a pad will add weight and change the balance point.

When I started hollowing buttstocks, I used the tools at hand—flat wood-bits, which are accurately named. These are *not* the best tool for the job, but I have become so adept with them, I hesitate to change.

Forstner bits (with a centering teat and radial cutters) used with an electric drill are better tools for boring deep holes in wood stocks. They are available in the one-inch and 1 1/8-inch sizes I most often use. Auger bits in a hand-powered drill would probably work well. I have no personal experience with either Forstner or auger bits. I also use brad point bits, the kind with the teat for starting the drill, for smaller holes.

The problem with flat bits is the difficulty controlling them. A 1 1/8-inch flat bit on a 1/4-inch shank mounted in a handheld electric drill can wander as it bores into the wood, which presents the possibility of drilling out the side of the stock. If you are going to try this, you should invest in quality Forstner or auger bits, and practice with them before attempting to drill a gunstock.

Before drilling, I determine the balance point by resting the gun on a balancing block held in the bench vise. (Note that the actual weight of the gun is of little importance to its balance.) I start around the hinge pin area, then with a grease pencil I mark the true balance point on the barrels.

For boring the holes, the stock must be held very tightly in a bench vise. So tightly, in fact, that I have all but given up balancing finished guns for fear of damaging the stock finish. The vise jaws must be well padded, but the padding must not interfere with firmly holding the stock, which cannot be allowed to move during the boring process. I bore my custom shotguns when they are completed, but before the final stock finish is applied.

I mark a centerline on the back of the butt and pencil on the layout for the size of holes to be drilled. Correct layout includes missing the butt-pad screw holes and allowing plenty of thickness between the hole and the outside of the stock. It is also wise to check the thickness of the tapered comb to gain an idea of how deep it is safe to drill with a given bit size. A 12-gauge stock might be 1 5/8 inches at its thickest; a 20-gauge somewhat less.

I prefer to drill the top hole first, so when I clamp the stock in the vise, I position it with the comb-line level. If I keep the drill and bit level, the hole will be level as well. When drilling the lower hole, position the stock with the toe-line level. Typically, I bore the upper hole with a 1 1/8-inch bit about 1 inch to 1 1/2 inches deep. Then I drill the lower hole as I continually check the balance. Eventually the two holes will meet, but there is usually sufficient weight removed before this happens.

What should a hole's diameter be, and how much weight will be removed? The truth is, I've never owned a scale that was accurate enough to record precisely how much weight was removed from the stocks I've drilled. I was concerned solely with handling, which, as I have said, I determine mainly by feel and by knowing the actual balance point of the gun. So my new workshop sidekick Michael Harney brought in a laboratory balance scale calibrated in hundredths of a gram. We took a sample of moderately dense English walnut, weighed it, then drilled some one-inch

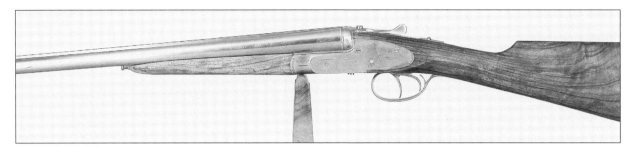

This custom Hughes/Garbi 20-gauge was balanced after completing the gun but before applying the final stock finish.

diameter holes, an inch deep, weighing the walnut before and after each hole was drilled. As accurately as we could measure, a one-inch hole drilled an inch deep removes 9.5 grams (.334 ounces), or a third of an ounce.

I often step down a drill size (1¹/₈ inches to one inch) when I need to deepen the hole to remove more weight. I frequently check the wall thickness of the stock by measuring the depth of the hole and determining the total thickness at that point with calipers. Because this is an inexact measurement, if I err, I do so on the extra-thickness side.

The 20-gauge Garbi stock shown in the photo has two large holes bored in the butt. The upper hole 1¹/₈ inches by 1³/₄ inches deep, then steps down to 1 by ³/₄ inches deep to a total

depth of 2¹/₂ inches deep. The lower hole is 1¹/₈ inches by 1¹/₂ inches deep and 1 inch by ⁵/₈ inches deep for a total depth of 1³/₄ inches. If you look closely at the photo, you can see where the holes step down from 1¹/₈ inches to 1 inch. There are also three ³/₈-inch holes about 1 inch deep between the major bore holes.

By calculation based on the one-inch hole an inch deep equaling .334 ounces, we determined that just a shade under 2¹/₄ ounces were removed from the Garbi with the two major holes. But I wasn't boring holes for weight reduction, and the gun now balances about 4¹/₄ inches ahead of the front trigger. It has a very lively feel in the hands. The client and I hashed this over and determined that he wanted a tad bit of weight-forward balance, and that is exactly the

Before boring the holes to balance the gun it must be solidly held in a well-padded vise. It is best done prior to final finishing. This custom Garbi (right) had two large holes and three smaller ones to shift the balance point forward.

way it feels to me. He shot the gun to confirm dimensions when the stock was ready to finish but before the pad was installed or the gun balanced. He had a very good idea how much he wanted to change the balance.

There are many variables to consider when balancing a gun. For example, the Garbi 20-gauge shown has very dense and heavy feather-crotch wood at the extreme butt end, although the rest of the stock is less dense. The slab I cut and weighed from the 12-gauge gun's butt had dense wood throughout, though not as dense as feather-crotch. The height, length, and width of the butt as well as the thickness and type of pad will vary from gun to gun, so the amount of wood needing to be removed will rarely if ever be the same.

It is interesting to note that a 1896 vintage Purdey 12-gauge 30-inch sidelock I have weighs 6 pounds 12 ounces and balances at $4^1/4$ inches ahead of the trigger. Even more interesting is that under the leather-covered Pachmyr recoil pad (a much later addition), three $^3/4$-inch holes were bored into the stock. As these figures correspond exactly with Gough Thomas's recommendations, it seems safe to assume that the Purdey was built (more than one hundred years ago) with dynamic handling in mind. And whoever added added the pad had proper balance in mind. I'll bet there wasn't an MOI measuring gauge in sight!

CHAPTER 12
Arcaded Fences

The first "quality" double shotgun I have owned had arcaded fences—the kind that look as if an umbrella is opened on them. It was a Belgian-proofed, lightweight, French side-by-side 12-gauge boxlock marked "LaCouture A Lyon." At the time I bought the gun, my major determinant of its quality was the arcaded fences, which were similar to those I'd seen in photos of shotguns made by James Woodward. Before that, I had never actually held a shotgun with arcaded fences.

I clearly remember looking at my side-by-side and marveling at the arches on each fence. This gun also had sideclips, which added to the look. The relieved areas were shallow but crisp of edge, with rounded arches that were finely pointed on the ends.

The arch theme harks back to the Egyptians, Babylonians, and Greeks who built with them, mostly below ground. The origin of the words "arch" and "arcade" comes from the Latin *arcus*, or something curved, and relates to the curve of a bow or the flight of an arrow. It is also the root word for architecture. I recall the arches that supported aqueducts and other structures built by the Romans, who apparently were the first to use them structurally above ground. Centuries later, Europeans revived these themes in art, design, and architecture, and I have to believe that's how arches wound up on guns.

So how were the arcaded fences on my shotgun accomplished? They had to have been hand chiseled. It's obvious that the arcades were formed by removing the metal below and leaving the metal above. But why would a gun with so little ornamentation incorporate such time-consuming chiseling? The only clues I could find on my French gun were the pre-World War I proof marks and the overall quality of the construction, fit, and finish of the boxlock. The gun had been made at a time when labor had been cheaper than materials, and it displayed the French penchant for the esoteric.

I was no stranger to hand chiseling, although I had done relatively little of that kind of work. In the 1980s, I had built a late-seventeenth-century-style English flintlock fowler. All of the metalwork, except the barrel and a few cast lock parts, had been handmade. As part of the project, I designed and made a serpent sideplate using only chisels and files. Although it may be difficult to imagine, hardened steel will cut soft steel quite cleanly and predictably. Chiseling steel to give architectural shape to a shotgun action is no different than hand-engraving, except that the chisels I use are $1/8$ inch to $1/4$ inch wide rather than the tiny ones used for embellishment.

I did more steel-cutting when I built my first Hughes/Fox gun. In that case, I chiseled beaded fences from the barrel bar around each ball to the top rib. Once the case-hardened action had been annealed, the metal was quite malleable. The hardest part was taking the first swat of the hammer to the cape chisel. After that it was challenging and enjoyable to sculpt the action.

With subsequent Fox projects, I did more chisel work and kept thinking about arcaded fences, but my clients wanted to preserve the Fox flavor, which didn't include umbrellas. Then along came a sidelock Bertuzzi project in-the-white and in need of fence-shaping. The client and I talked about creating arcaded fences, but the bottom line was that I didn't have the nerve. We decided to trim the action with traditional Holland & Holland-style fences, and I gained more experience with the chisel. About that time, I bought a long-barreled, 16-gauge Austrian boxlock that was nicely ornamented with, you guessed it, arcaded fences. After studying the fences for several weeks, I decided that one day I would sculpt the arches on a shotgun action.

A few years ago, I acquired a half dozen 12-gauge sidelock-barreled actions that had been built in Belgium in the 1930s. Although completely assembled, they were like blank canvases, offering unlimited opportunities for stylistic improvement. One of my clients, Pete Treboldi, was the reason I had been looking for such a project, and he was instrumental in the purchase of the actions. We talked about arcaded fences; he liked their form and, particularly, their uniqueness. I warned him that the work would require many bench hours, but Pete enjoys the notion of handwork in his projects and encouraged me to accept the challenge.

On my own time I studied photos and my guns, and I contacted engravers about appropriate tools. I didn't know anyone living who had actually done similar work. I knew that the cape chisel used for the Fox fences wouldn't allow cutting the hard, ninety-degree edge in a tight half-circle. I ordered a 1/8-inch-wide diesinker's chisel from Brownells, then I looked for advice on how to sharpen it properly.

After talking with engravers Eric Gold and Terry Wallace, I ground away the upper face of the tool so there would be less metal to sharpen, then I ground the face to about a thirty-five-degree angle to give me a good, flat cutting edge.

I used consecutive medium and fine stones to carefully perfect the cutting surface, sides, and bottom of the tool. It was brought to a mirror polish with a superfine ceramic stone, and then stropped with Simichrome Polish. The final step was to clamp the chisel bottom-up in the vise and carefully stone the relief, or clearance angle, at the point where the chisel meets steel. This slight, five-degree bevel right at the cutting edge is required to remove metal.

The chisel has to cut into steel to do its work, but without the relief angle it will bury itself deeper the more it's hammered. With the tiny relief angle and the angle at which the chisel is held in relation to the work, the craftsman can control the depth of the cut and raise a curl of metal similar to a curl of wood that comes off with a wood plane.

With a final stropping, the chisel was ready to cut.

But I wasn't.

I like to prepare for challenging new aspects of gunmaking, so this preparation took place months before the actual work began. Then one day when the decks were cleared, it struck me that I would need to practice on something before gouging the multithousand-dollar Belgian metalwork. Glancing over to the corner of my shop, I spied a rusted relic of a hammer gun that five minutes later was broken down and the action firmly clamped in my bench vise.

I'm happy to report that the chisel did cut the steel very cleanly and crisply. I used a brass hammer I'd made in gunsmithing school to power the cutting, and in just a few minutes I was raising curls of bright, clean metal from the rust. But how was I going to precisely lay out the three petals on each fence?

I thought for a moment, then got out my French boxlock that I hadn't looked at in months. Taking a tool made from a thin-bladed tape measure, I measured the distance from the barrel bar around the curve to the top rib. Then I took calipers and checked the distance between each of the petals, which turned out to be uniform.

I was into it now, so I retrieved a new Belgian barreled action to measure its fence circumference: it was almost identical to that on the French gun. One less difficulty to deal with. Now there were three disassembled double guns on my bench—not unusual when exploring new possibilities.

The rusty hammer gun's fences were a bit larger, but that didn't matter; it was merely a practice plate. I made a paper tracing of the French gun's arcaded fences and carefully cut it out with scissors and a razor knife to make male and female impressions of the total layout and individual petals. Being a nut for patterns and templates, I created another template of one petal from brass, but that didn't work because it wouldn't bend to correctly conform to the curve of the fence. I made a third template from X-ray film, with tabs to stop on the breech face to measure the depth. This one would flex to the curve.

Just looking at the French and Austrian guns told me that the hardest part would be uniformly removing enough metal while preserving the crisp edge. Another challenge would be finding out if the chisel would allow me to cut the tight radius of each petal without the heel of the tool hitting the raised edge. I also knew it would be mandatory to maintain the ball shape of the fences to conform to the curvature of the barrel.

Using the templates, I scribed the first and second petals on the hammer-gun action. I started lightly with the chisel, getting a feel for its angle and how it altered the depth of the cut. There were two basic steps to the work: cutting the outline and removing the metal forward toward the breech. This was one of those times in the life of a craftsman when time stands still. When I next looked at the clock, two hours had disappeared.

Stopping to evaluate my progress, I was

The author's inspiration for carving arcaded fences came from a 16-gauge Austrian boxlock and a French 12-bore boxlock.

faced with a new dilemma. The chisel wasn't going to do all of the work, and somehow the bottom of the recess would need to be leveled and all the chisel cuts removed. The problem was getting right up to the crisp edge without damaging it. Furthermore, eventually the area would need to be refined and bright-polished. But I was working on my own time—not my client's—and I'd cross that bridge later.

A Bertuzzi sidelock the author is chiseling with traditional Holland & Holland-style fences.

To level the recess, I chose a flat needle file—a "fine" onc, in which the teeth on the edges had been ground off. It would cut only on the top or bottom and would help preserve the edge. Using short strokes, I tried to stay away from the edge but kept running into it. The file was cutting very effectively, removing the chisel cuts and establishing the circular contour of the breech. To help preserve the edge, I ground the end of the file to a rounded shape, removed all the burrs from the end, and polished it. This time it was a lot easier on the edges.

It was obvious even after a couple of hours that I wasn't nearly deep enough. I was going to have to get more aggressive. Out came the two arcaded guns, the French and Austrian boxlocks, and with calipers I made depth measurements at different locations on the arcs. They were just .030 inches deep, but I was only halfway there.

I spent twenty minutes sharpening the chisel, and then began the second petal on the action. By now I was familiar with the tools and the metal and was able to smack harder and cut deeper. In the next forty-five minutes I peeled away as much steel as I had in the previous two hours. Now I was getting somewhere.

• • •

The next week I was off to Italy to visit the gunshop of Perugini & Visini, where I hoped to see someone chiseling actions. I lucked out, and the first day there I was introduced to the shop foreman, Agustino, who was fitting the parts to an Anson & Deeley boxlock double-rifle action. The rough-machined receiver would need to have the fences and reinforcing bolster chiseled. I asked when this would be done.

Fortunately, it was only four days before Agustino started to chisel-shape the bolsters on the sides of the action. Simple lumps of steel were left on the action, and Agustino began by rough-chiseling them into an S-curve. As this

was a standard shop procedure, there was a basic template already made. The hammer strokes, angle of the chisel, and quickness of the work indicated a competency that comes only with great experience.

All week I periodically had watched Agustino fitting parts almost mechanically, and he had been stoic and steady about it. Now he was smiling; like a sculptor he was working free-form, shaping the action with hand tools. Clearly, he was happy to be doing the work, and he seemed to appreciate my interest and enthusiasm.

Agustino was working with a 3/8-inch-wide, 1/8-inch-thick chisel that was about 3 inches long and set into a 5/8-inch-square steel handle that was 6 inches long. He was using a 10-ounce hammer, and the chisel handle was severely mushroomed, perhaps an inch across. Vincenzo Perugini, the shop master, came over because he could see how fascinated I was. He showed me his own chisel, pointed to the concrete floor, and then pointed out the rear window of the shop at the mountain behind. I drew a blank. He did it again, making a sawing motion. I shook my head and shrugged. Perugini ran into the parts room and came out with a piece of saw blade that was heavier and had more aggressive teeth than anything that ever came out of the North Woods. Again, he pointed to the mountain behind the shop.

Then I got it. The chisel blanks were made from a saw blade used to cut marble blocks in the hills out back. I'd seen trucks hauling marble on the highways, and there was a quarry on the hillside near town.

Perugini gave me two chisel blanks, and when comparing them to the one Agustino was using, I noticed something odd. The chisel was sharpened like a cold chisel, with a sharp wedge for the cutting end, but on one side, instead of being flat, the edge was ground with a slight curve. I pointed this out, and Perugini gestured at the curved side and motioned as if chiseling a horizontal plane. Pointing to the flat side, he motioned as if the chisel, when struck, just dug deeper and deeper. (Remember the clearance angle I ground on my chisel?) The curved side forces the steel to curl when cut, so the depth of the cut can be adjusted. Without it, the cut chip wouldn't curl and the chisel would dig in.

Perugini snatched the chisel blank from my hand, raced to the grinding wheel and proceeded to grind the cutting bevels—one flat, one slight-

The author at work with a brass hammer and chisel.

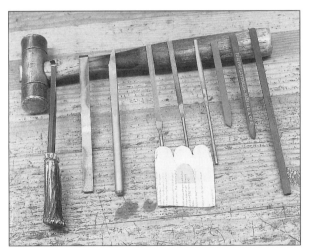

The tools used for shaping a shotgun's fences: brass hammer, and (left to right) scraper, Italian chisel, diesinker's chisel, three needle files, stones, and various templates.

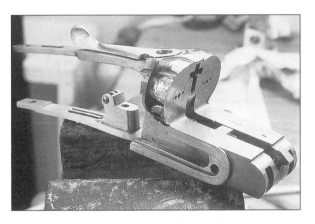

The Britte sidelock action with the left fence stoned and finished, and the right fence after two passes with the chisel.

ly curved. He sharpened it on an oilstone, stropped it, and made a few cuts on a piece of scrap steel to test it. With both of us beaming, he handed it to me and bowed.

"Grazie, grazie." I thanked him.

That day Agustino went on to finish the bolsters and start the fences. Other than his chisel, the only other tools he used were safe-edged files and small scrapers. The files were much like the ones I had used, but he was quicker and surer with them. I tucked away the scraper notion; I had forgotten that method when doing my practice fences.

Agustino had a couple of templates for this operation as well. One side was perfected, then he started the second. Of all the work I observed him doing, this was the only procedure that he noticeably slowed down to do. Agustino spent quite a bit of time carefully matching the templates to the work and visually studying the fences, side to side. When it came to the final touches, he discarded the templates and worked solely by eye. I didn't have to ask why; I do the same thing in my work. With any sort of sculpting, especially when both sides must look identical, the craftsman's eye is the last word. If one doesn't have the experience, then measurements and templates and patterns are useless. If the work looks right, side to side, to the artist, it will look right to the client.

I hadn't been back from Italy a week when I chucked one of the 1930s Belgian actions in my bench vise. My tools were sharpened, and the paper template and X-ray film template had been made. I coated the left fence with blue layout fluid and started arranging the petals on the action. I used calipers to perfect the spacing of each point and the dimensions of each petal. An "order of procedure" had been determined to provide direction and enhance efficiency, and I had visualized the individual operations. I wasn't going to be as efficient as Agustino, but who else would have a gun with arcaded fences that had been chiseled by an American gunmaker?

My plan was to do as perfect a layout as possible, then start by taking down a layer with the chisel, staying away from the finished lines. I would then file down the recess, removing as much material as possible with the file and perfecting the roundness of the fences. This would be done in three layers to achieve the needed depth. After the recess was deep enough and cleaned up, I would go back with the chisel and cut the edge. I would use the scraper to finish the hard edges. The process would be repeated one petal at a time until one side was done.

To remove the bulk of the material, I found it best to cut the complete outline of the arch with the diesinker's chisel, and then chisel forward toward the breech in facets with the Italian chisel. Working around the ball contour was like cutting around a globe, peeling away the tops of the continents. Working forward with facets is a process of cutting a series of small flats, then cutting the tops off of them to create smaller flats. This is an old method of achieving a rounded surface using a flat tool. The more you can remove with the chisel and the smoother the cut, the greater the efficiency.

I modified the procedure to make two passes with the chisel before starting work with the files. As I had seen Agustino do, I used a second, very fine needle file to clean up the coarser file marks.

The first petal took serious time. I finished the second faster, but that part of the fence was more rounded than the top, and I had to pay more attention to the "globe" effect. The middle petal was also more challenging because the action was difficult to position in the vise. But thanks to the learning curve, the work went faster than it had with the top petal.

Mind you, speed was not the issue; it was efficiency. One thing I've heard European-trained gunmakers comment on—and that I observed in the Italian shops—is that they spend less time admiring their work than Americans do.

The lower petal—the one that connected with the barrel bar—offered another challenge. There was a screw in it, as there is in this location in many high-grade sidelocks. It was drilled through with a tiny hole, to vent the firing pin in case of a blown primer. First, I tried chiseling with the screw removed, but the tool wanted to dig in on the edge of the empty hole. The solution was to leave the screw in and cut right over the top of it.

Stylistically, the arcades on my French gun had the deepest cuts next to the top rib; the Austrian 16 had the deepest cuts down at the barrel bar. This Belgian action had plenty of metal in both places, so I decided to go for good depth top and bottom, to maximize the effect. Blending these two areas to mate to the barrels required that I frequently mount the barrels to the action to check the adjoining surfaces. To complete the lower juncture, I did quite a bit of filing to reshape the barrel bar, and then I did some finish chiseling with the barrels in place, working the tool over both surfaces. I noticed that the barrel steel was considerably harder than that of the action.

While performing all of these operations, I had been thinking about how to polish the recesses. I largely use grit paper to polish, but it wasn't going to work in that small an area, and it would be extremely difficult to prevent abrasive erosion to the hard edges. I decided to try mold-makers' stones. They come in grits from 150 to 600 and are used wet by dipping them in stoning oil. The unusual thing about these stones is that they're relatively soft and break down and conform to the surfaces being stoned. For my purposes, the stones would take on the shape of the arc, making polishing easier and less damaging.

With all three petals chiseled, filed, and scraped, the arcades had uniform hard edges and nicely leveled recesses. The finish left by the extrafine needle file and the scraper was very good but not polished. I'd noticed that both of my arcaded guns had engraving at the bottoms of the ledges and wondered if this was to cover up less-than-perfect polishing.

Regardless, I started with the 320-grit mold-makers' stones on the flats of the recesses and worked my way into the edges. They conformed nicely to the surfaces and did an excellent job right out to 600 grit. Even at that fine grit the stones left a dull surface, which I later high-polished with a bit of 600-grit paper and Scotch-Brite pads.

The final step was to take down the barrel steel to match the fences. If you look closely at arcaded fences, you'll see that the points are above the barrel steel and the recesses are flush. This was accomplished by putting layout fluid on the barrel breech, assembling the barrels to the action, and scribing to define the amount of metal to be removed. The barrels then were filed down to match the contours of the fences.

I'm fussy about keeping track of bench hours on all jobs. Because I bill by the hour, this is a must, but it also helps in planning future projects. My records show that it took me exactly $15\frac{3}{4}$ hours to complete one side of the arcaded fences. That included filing the barrel bar, blending to the top rib, and polishing. I was quite pleased with that level of efficiency, though I wondered how long it would have taken Agustino.

For the second side, I made a tracing of the completed fences. When doing any detail shaping that must match from side to side—such as carving drop points—I use a template for the first side but always make a new one, from the existing work, for the other. This is the best way I know of to make both sides alike.

To further increase efficiency, I made a rough layout on the right side and chiseled away the bulk of the metal for each of the three petals. Then I did a more detailed layout using the new template, and I proceeded as I had for the left side. The work progressed much more quickly, and I expected to save at least a couple of hours. In reality, it took quite a bit more time than my initial estimate: nearly forty bench hours were required to complete chiseling and polishing the arcaded fences.

The most difficult part of the entire operation was determining when to call the work finished. Fortunately, the French and Austrian guns were here for comparison, as was my memory of watching Agustino and Vincenzo. I often asked myself, what would they think of my work?

CHAPTER 13

Double Gun Metalwork

How much time does it take to build a double shotgun? You'll hear that it requires hundreds of hours to create a London "best." Then you'll hear about annual production figures and imagine dozens of craftsmen working night and day spending those hundreds of hours building the volume of guns the maker achieves. In my experience, which is probably greater than most gunsmiths', I can tell you that it is difficult to imagine the sheer number of operations required to put all of the bits and pieces together to make a gun.

Presented here, largely via digital images of two shotguns, are some of the individual metalwork operations and a bit about the processes to provide some notion of the techniques and time involved.

The first gun is the Belgian Britte sidelock you've seen in Chapter 12 and that is featured in the Color Section of this book. The second is a 20-gauge Garbi sidelock with a two-barrel set nearing completion. Each gun has had extensive metal shaping that is not commonly done in this country and that is often camouflaged with engraving and finishing.

Let me emphasize again that in an ideal world all metalwork should be completed before stockmaking begins, though it rarely works out that way in my shop. Initially, the action body of the Garbi was shaped, but for a number of reasons—one of which was a much-needed break from the demands of tedious metalwork—I didn't begin chiseling the fence beads until after the gun was stocked and test-fired.

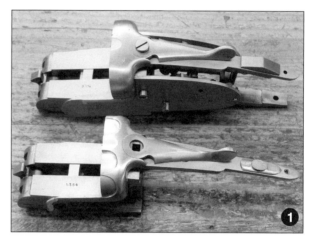

Photo No. 1: Two Britte 12-gauge actions: the one on top just as I received it; the one on the bottom after I completed the arcaded fences, toplever shaping, and contouring the safety button. Chiseling and polishing the arcaded fences took forty bench hours.

Photo No. 2: Before-and-after safety buttons for the 12-gauge Britte. The pyramid-shaped safety blank (right) was leveled in the milling machine and milled down to the final height (thickness) of .125 inches. The oval thumb pad was located and scribed on top, then the rest was milled down to about half the total thickness, leaving a rectangle of steel about $5/16$ by $7/16$ by .065 inches for the oval pad. After scribing with a template, the thirty-five-degree oval was hand filed to shape, the front of the safety was filed with a slight crescent ("SAFE" was later inlaid in gold underneath), and the rear filed with a spear point matching the end of the tang. The button was then contoured, giving it a slight dome that carries down both sides next to the thumb pad.

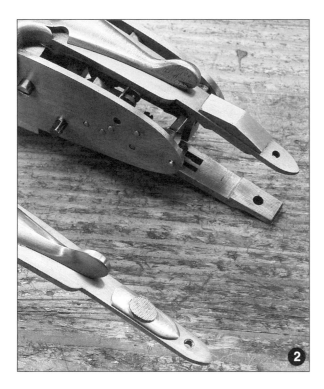

Then all was polished.

The final step was to checker the thumb pad at 50 lines per inch using a No. 2 metal checkering file. After the safety was completed, all of the underlying surfaces, including the spring and the place where it contacts the safety, were hand-polished for smooth operation. These procedures consumed five bench hours.

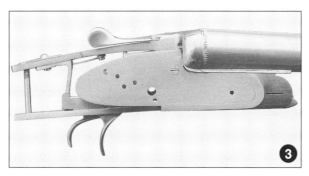

Photo No. 3: A 20-gauge Garbi action as received—imported in-the-white—with only the beginning of the fence bead at the barrel bar. The buggered lock screw was for assembly and was replaced.

Photo No. 4: The same Garbi action after extensive metal shaping. The action body was altered by removing metal to form a concave cove

molding just below the barrel bar. This difference makes the action appear lighter, slimmer, and longer, adding character. The work was begun with a chisel, continued with small round and half-round files, and finished with scrapers, stones, and polishing paper. Nine hours were required for this alteration.

The toplever has been filed to eliminate some of the "lollipop" look of the original and to make it appear a bit longer and more slender. Fence beads have been chiseled, beginning at the barrel bar, continuing up the back of the ball fence, turning at an angle where the top of the wood will be, and then curving around to mate with the top rib. No metal was added nor was welding done; the bead was formed entirely by removing metal from the ball fences with hand tools. Adding the fence beading consumed seventeen hours. The oversized lever screw was later fitted and the screw slot aligned.

Photo No. 5: A close-up of the Garbi action shows the fence bead as an angled trough on the front edge, with a rounded top and a steep, almost perpendicular rear. Most of the shaping was done with a $1/8$-inch diesinker's chisel and a chasing hammer. Finish-shaping and cleanup were accomplished with a series of fine needle files, scrapers, stones, and polishing paper. Note how the bead diminishes and nearly disappears at the junction of the top rib.

Photo No. 6: The finished action with some of the important tools used to shape it. I always have good photo support at hand for inspiration and instruction when taking on a challenging project. Chasing hammer, diesinker's chisel, and No. 6-cut Grobet Swiss needle files were indispensable for this delicate work.

To my knowledge, little of this type of hand metalwork is being done in the United States. These processes may not mimic the exact methods used by English or European gunmakers, as my techniques were chiefly developed by extensively studying existing work, assembling the

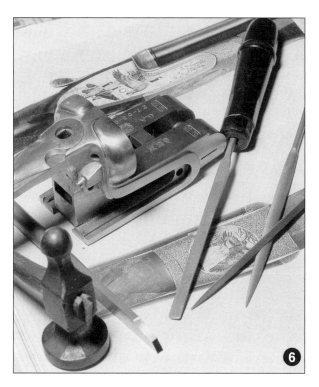

appropriate tools, and having the confidence to take sharp tools to gunmetal.

CHAPTER 14
TIG Welding

During discussions of shotgun repair, you may have heard someone say, "You can have that TIG welded and it'll be good as new." Well, I've been gas-welding gun parts for twenty years and TIG welding for five, and I'll tell you up front, *it just ain't that easy.*

The way TIG (tungsten inert gas) welding is spoken of, it is as if a magic wand can be waved over a worn gun part, instantly bringing it back to life and restoring it to as-new condition. TIG *can* be magic, but only in the hands of a magician who knows the proper "potions and incantations," one who can ward off the evil trickery that can be unleashed in the process.

The fellow at your local welding shop can probably fuse a lump of weld on the sear notch of your Army & Navy sidelock's tumbler. He can probably weld together the two pieces of the broken trigger guard of your DHE Parker. But can he remachine the tumbler to the correct arc, cut a .020-inch-deep notch at the proper angle, and reheat-treat it to the appropriate temper? Will the thin guard be misshapen by heat and have its engraving fouled-up, and will it fit back into the inlet in the stock?

For gun repair, proper welding technique is only the half of TIG process. The other half is gunsmithing. Without a knowledge of—and respect for—archaic manufacturing techniques, metallurgy, lock geometry, hardening, and a host of other skills, many demons *can* be unleashed by a TIG welder.

In this chapter, I'll explain alternative welding, how TIG works, and why it is so adaptable

to gun repair. I'll talk about specific shotgun repairs, how gunsmiths use TIG, and what needs to be done, before and after the welding, for proper repair.

Welding is probably as old as gunmaking. I imagine its origin was near the time of iron smelting. Converting iron ore to a usable product requires intense and prolonged heat to render the metal molten, drive off the impurities, and convert it to bars of iron. Welding is the process of mating two pieces of iron (or steel) together to form a single homogeneous unit. It is accomplished by heating the adjoining surfaces until they are softened to the point at which they can intermingle to become one.

The earliest method of welding was accomplished with heat from a coal-fired forge, thus it is called forge welding. Most gun barrels, from the inception of firearms until the mid-nineteenth century, were made by heating and welding a single "skelp" (a strip of iron) to an elastic state and, with hammer and anvil, wrapping it around a long mandrel. When the edges were nearly joined at high heat, the small gaps between were "fluxed" and the near-molten surfaces hammered together. The flux, usually a borax compound, was used to drive the impurities from the joint.

Twist, or damascus, barrels were manufactured by wrapping a long skelp around a mandrel in a spiral form and forge welding the continuous edges together.

There are two points I want to establish. First, welding and gunmaking have a long history together. Second, a necessity for a strong and successful weld is removing impurities from the joint or preventing them from entering it.

Today, there are two basic types of welding: gas and electric arc. With gas welding, oxygen and acetylene are blended through a lighted torch nozzle for a heat source. The heat is controlled by regulating the gas pressure, the blend of gasses, and the size of the hole in the torch tip. No flux is used with gas welding; heat alone is relied upon to drive out the impurities.

Electric-arc welding is accomplished by running an electric current through the metal, with the heat supplied by the resistance to this current at the point of the weld. The heat is controlled by the amperage output from the welding box and by the size of the welding rod, which is usually coated with a kind of flux.

Most electric welding employs a ground (positive) and an electrode (negative). (This sounds reversed, but hook up a car battery backwards and watch the sparks fly!) The positive current flows through the ground wire into the work piece; the negative lead holds the welding rod; when the rod's tip strikes the metal, it produces an arc of electricity. This arc is actually an intense spark jumping from the work piece to the rod, and it creates enough heat to cause the base metal and rod to flow and fuse.

Arc, or stick, welding is the kind used to join steel plates to make a ship's hull or attach a trailer hitch to a car frame. The welding rod is consumed in the process and provides the metal to fill the joint between the two pieces of steel. With gas welding, the consumable rod is placed near the joint, fed in by hand, and fused into a weld with heat from the torch.

Although most gunsmiths have an oxy-acetylene torch, the problems with using either gas or stick welding for gun-repair applications are numerous. Gas welding require an abundance of heat, and by the time the area to be welded is up to temperature, the whole part is often cherry red. When the part cools, it has likely been covered with heat scale or the metal's temper has been changed or the part has been warped by the intense heat.

Stick welding, even with a small welding rod, is too coarse for most gun work, and the weld will form slag that must be chipped off. The heat can draw the temper or warp the metal.

Both welding techniques suffer from contamination in the form of pits with gas welding and slag in arc welding.

The biggest advantages of gas welding are the ability to apply the rod separately from the heat and to weld small areas using a fine rod and a small tip. The advantages of arc welding are the limited heat applied to the area adjacent to the weld and the fine control of the heat via regulated amperage.

TIG welding blends these two techniques and offers the advantages of both gas and stick welding. The proper term for this process is "gas tungsten arc welding," or GTAW. The popular term is TIG, which, as I said, stands for "tungsten inert gas welding."

TIG welding employs an electric arc to heat the metal to the fusion point. The arc is struck with a *nonconsumable* tungsten electrode, so the stick doesn't burn up or add metal to the joint as the welding takes place. A consumable filler rod is fed into the weld by hand, as with gas welding. During the process the weld is shielded by a bath of inert gas—helium or, more often, argon. The inert shielding gas has no chemical properties and serves only to blanket the weld and exclude the active properties in the surrounding air.

The heat for TIG welding is controlled by the amperage output from the welder and the size of the nonconsumable electrode. Instead of setting the amperage at the welding machine, the welder adjusts the amperage by a foot pedal just like the gas pedal in a car. The harder the welder steps on the pedal, the higher the amperage he produces.

Here's how TIG welding works in the gunshop. The gun part is placed in a bench vise or clamped to a flat piece of steel to which the ground wire is also clamped. A nonconsumable tungsten electrode is held in the welding torch (in this case the torch does not produce flame and only serves as a handle for the electrode). The inert-gas tank valve is opened and the welding machine is turned on. The gunsmith places the electrode near the work surface and steps on the pedal to strike an arc. The arc jumps from the electrode and heats a very small area to the molten stage. The consumable welding rod is fed in with the other hand. All the while inert gas is flowing through the welding torch and surrounding the weld.

The smith simultaneously controls the amperage with the foot pedal, the amount of heat and its location with the electrode in the torch handle, and the amount and location of filler metal with the consumable rod. Both hands and one foot are used.

There are many advantages to TIG welding. The amount and location of the heat and welding rod are almost infinitely variable. Tungsten electrodes as small as .040 inches are commonly used, and the filler rod I use is $1/16$ of an inch. A good welding machine will start at $1/2$ of an amp, as controlled by the pedal. If the operator works quickly, the surrounding heat-affected area will be minimal. It can be seen as color changes in the metal around the weld.

TIG welding is so versatile that it can be used on stainless steel, nickel steel, titanium, aluminum, magnesium, copper, brass, bronze, and even gold. It is possible to weld dissimilar metals such as brass to copper or stainless steel to mild steel. At the counter of a welding shop, I saw an aluminum beer can that had been cut in two and welded back together.

The biggest drawback to TIG welding is the hand-eye coordination needed. It requires a great deal of practice to become proficient. I've

Tools of the trade: a TIG torch, bronze vise jaws, ground clamp, welding hood, tungsten rod, and filler rod.

made use of my TIG welder for several years and am just scratching the surface.

Another drawback is cost; the most basic TIG welder runs about $1,500. (The low-amp versions for finesse welding run $2,500 or more.) A great addition is an "electronic quick-change filter" for the welding hood. This has the protective glass, but the operator can see through it until the moment the arc is struck. The glass turns dark in a millisecond, allowing the gunsmith to have the rod and the electrode in the perfect position without having to flip the hood down.

My advice to gunsmiths who want to get into TIG welding is to spend the money, then weld every scrap gun part in your shop (all gunsmiths save unrepairable parts forever) for a straight week. *Then* talk to someone who has been TIG welding gun parts for several years.

TIG welding can be a magic wand in a gunshop. It is possible to repair tumblers and trigger guards expertly; sear noses can be built-up; cracked or loose hammers repaired; even barrel hooks can be welded to refit guns with nonremovable hinge pins.

Using a tiny electrode and rod, it is possible to weld the tiniest of gun parts. One gunsmith told me of successfully welding a locating pin on a sidelock mainspring. Another TIG welder reattached one of the three teats on a pineapple-finial trigger guard without damaging the original engraving.

• • •

To provide a more complete description of TIG welding in relation to guns, I will present the experiences of four skilled gunsmiths who have used TIG welding as part of their repair work for more than a decade. Achieving a good weld is only a part of the repair process. Knowing what can and cannot be repaired, then exercising good judgment, are the keys to success.

Let me emphasize, again, several essential points. The biggest advantage to TIG welding for gun repair is the ability to weld a small area without heat affecting the metal around it. This is possible because the amperage output is controllable with the foot pedal and by the size of the electrode. The greatest disadvantage is the long practice needed to become proficient. Many welders around the country have achieved proficiency with this process, but they have no background in repairing fine guns.

To paraphrase gunmaker Michael Ehinger, gunwork has to be better than any other kind of repair because of safety factors and the quality of the items being worked on. One part of the process is knowing what you're doing; another part is knowing what you have to have when you're done.

A critical part of the process is gunsmithing. Simply adding metal where it has broken off or corroded away doesn't renew a gun part. According to gunmaker Ed Webber, "After welding, I treat the part as if I were fitting a new, rough forging."

These fellows are magicians mostly because they were performing quality, safety-conscious gun repairs long before they bought a TIG welder. Mike Ehinger is America's Joe Manton, building the finest flintlock double guns of the twentieth century and doing museum-quality restoration of muzzleloaders. Ed Webber has created superb single-shot rifles and has repaired or restored every type of vintage firearm you can imagine. Another is Dan Cullity, whom I like to call "The Wizard" because of his reputation for diverse and sophisticated gunmaking and restoration. And my good friend Dennis Potter has devoted more than thirty years to quality shotgun work.

None of these craftsmen has a high profile, but each regularly accomplishes the really difficult repairs for many of the higher-profile gunshops, gunsmiths, and gunmakers around the country.

Interviewing these four brought to light many repair applications and techniques. It was also interesting to find that other techniques had been developed singularly and that some smiths won't touch jobs that others do regularly. Dan Cullity summed it up by saying, "If a fellow is clever enough, any metal part can be rebuilt by welding."

They all agree that there are three phases required for successful TIG-welding repairs. The first is preparation. The area to be welded must be cleaned to a point near surgical sterility. All oxidization in the form of rust or bluing must be removed. This means using a degreaser, wire brush, mild acid wash, abrasive, and/or sand or bead blaster. Preheating is called for if the part is case-hardened or to warm up a large part prior to subjecting one small area to intense heat. In both cases preheating helps relieve or prevent stresses in the metal.

The second phase is the weld. According to Cullity, "Welding would have a bad name if you could see the weld." And he isn't necessarily referring to cosmetics. A good weld not only restores the original surface to its full-sized, predamaged self, but it requires deep penetration to ensure the part doesn't break again. When welding two broken pieces together or adding a lump of metal where a piece has broken off, penetration is critical. After the pieces to be rejoined are closely fitted together, welders often file a V-notch (chamfer) at the joint, as well as all the way around the broken part. This allows the base metal to be fused deeply and the groove to be built up with the filler rod.

As I mentioned, the heat-affected area is also critical to a good weld. In nearly all cases, minimizing the total heat applied to the part prevents drawing the temper or warping or heat-scaling the metal. If a large or prolonged weld is in order, the craftsman must weld, let the metal cool, and repeat the process several times until deep penetration and thorough filling are achieved.

The third phase of successful TIG welding is gunsmithing; every part must be returned to its original, unaltered state. This means filing, fitting, and postheat-treating as well. If the part was case-hardened before, it must be case-hardened again. If it was hardened and tempered tool steel, it must be hardened and tempered anew. In the case of a part that was dead soft, it may require annealing, as the welding can draw carbon to it, spot-hardening that area.

The vast majority of older double-gun parts were made of mild steel that was often case-hardened. Many of the lock parts and all of the springs were made of carbon steel, also called spring steel. It's the same with the welding rod used for gun repair: mild steel or carbon steel. When speaking of welding for other gunsmiths, Dan Cullity says, "They either want something stuck back together or they want it to harden like O-1 steel."

O-1 is the carbon steel most of us use for making chisels, springs, and gun parts to be hardened and tempered. The "O" in O-1 stands for oil hardening. To harden the part after it is made, we heat it cherry red and quench it in oil.

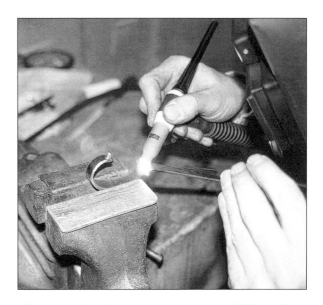

The author fabricates a trigger guard by TIG welding.

The part is then degreased, polished, and the temper drawn to give a spring its proper flexibility or a chisel its proper edge or a gun part its proper wear resistance. In this case, Dennis Potter uses spring-steel "music" wire for a welding rod. This is the thin, round wire used to wind coil springs.

There are many varieties of mild steel welding rods, and each of us has found a favorite—contrary to what you might have heard, none of us uses coat hangers. Sometimes both mild- and tool-steel rods can be used on the same part. An example is an extractor where the stem can be repaired with mild steel and the tip, which is struck by the ejector hammer, repaired with tougher tool steel.

As for technique, there is one major difference in the initial approach. Many smiths choose the proper rod and successively build up layers of weld, cooling everything in between (and sometimes filing out imperfections) until the proper mass is achieved. Others prefer to weld a separate lump of steel to the base metal prior to shaping it. Cullity will build up as much as 3/8 of an inch of metal. Mike Ehinger prefers to weld on a new piece even if he is going to file off 90 percent of it. Either approach is perfectly acceptable, provided that the weld is acceptable.

Let's look at some actual gun parts and case histories of repairs. For example, all the craftsmen featured here have welded a new lump of steel to replace a broken hammer spur. The lump was then filed to match the other hammer, checkered or possibly engraved, and finally case-hardened. Each also spoke of chamfering and welding cracked hammers. Ed Webber and Mike Ehinger have rebuilt corroded percussion-hammer noses, remachined the cups, and built up the flash shields of the breech fences where the worn hammers had dented them.

Trigger guards are commonly repaired or modified. They can break at the weak area of the wood-screw hole when someone is trying to pull the tang out of the stock. The screw stud that threads into the triggerplate is sometimes twisted off. Properly welding them is easy, but it's critical to prevent heat-warping the tang in order to fit it back into the stock inlet. When converting a pistol-grip guard to a straight grip, a section of new metal is welded in place to lengthen the tang. Guard tangs are often engraved, so reengraving is necessary for perfect results.

Sear tips and their arms or legs can break, or they can become worn or shortened by multiple trigger-pull stonings. A short sear can cause failure to detonate a shell because of a short hammer fall, or it can foul up ejector timing. Potter and Cullity choose to build up weld in this case, whereas Webber and Ehinger often choose to make new parts.

Tumbler notches, or bents, often disappear with improper stoning, and sometimes they shear or break off. After determining the appropriate filler rod, gunsmiths generally build these up with weld. Remachining the tumbler arc and recutting the notch is the gunsmithing part of the repair. In the case of both sears and tumblers, the safety factor is an enormous responsibility, and you want a professional smith doing all of the work.

Tumblers also crack on occasion. Cullity speaks of a new London gun—about 5,000 rounds had been run through it—with its tumbler cracked right through the mass of metal in its middle. He successfully repaired the tumbler by welding and refitting. Another 5,000 rounds later the other tumbler cracked in nearly the same place. The shotgun is now going strong after each tumbler was repaired.

Surface pitting is another story. I can't count the number of times I've heard someone say, "You can get those pits welded up." Cullity has done his share, but he says it's often a losing proposition because it's so difficult to clean the rust pits; he may be chasing welding pits caused by impurities. Webber frequently welds pitting, but only after grinding a larger void to expose a bare metal surface. Ehinger's museum restoration of historically important muzzleloaders has led him to weld areas that were horribly pitted and corroded. But if it's the barrel he's welding, he also makes sure the gun will never be fired again. The reason for this is that barrels are usually made of a single piece of an unknown steel. Adding different steel or subjecting one area to intense heat may dangerously affect the barrels' structural integrity. Although some of these smiths have welded barrels in unusual circumstances, none of them promote the practice. To a man, they say it just isn't a good idea.

The sole exception is worn hooks on guns with solid or nonremovable hinge pins. Cullity has built up many hooks by welding. Potter welded the hook on my own Fox after seven years and several thousand rounds loosened it. The hook on a Fox is small and nearly hollow, with cuts for the cocking shoe, spring, and screw. This repair was a delicate process, but the weld is undetectable. Of course, the real work was properly refitting the hook to the pin and breech face. Welding both hooks and barrels is unwise—in my opinion and according to British proof law—but I've heard that "spray" welding (I'm not familiar with this technique) is acceptable.

Cullity has also welded V- and flat springs, including mainsprings. He has even replaced mainspring locating pins, the tiny legs that project through the lockplates. He uses spring-steel rods, and he files, polishes, and retempers the springs. To satisfy his own curiosity, Potter welded a broken mainspring and has repeatedly compressed it in a vise without it's breaking or taking a set, although he never installed it in a gun. After hearing of Cullity's experience, Potter may try this in the future rather than making a several-hundred-dollar part.

Another questionable practice is welding the action body—for the same reasons barrels are off-limits. In certain circumstances corrosion or forging pits can be filled in, but filing, polishing, and heat treating are needed.

Other parts that can be repaired conveniently with TIG welding are toplevers, extractor studs at the knuckle, and, in specific cases, locking bolts. The hidden arm that actuates a Greener-type crossbolt, if broken, is a good candidate. Many expensive or unobtainable parts can be repaired with proper TIG welding.

In fifteen years of TIG welding, Cullity says he has never seen one of his welds break or fail. Ehinger saved a rare gun's trigger guard by welding the tiny teat of its pineapple finial back together. The pineapple was ornately engraved and, with a fine touch and sharp eye, he was able to weld the backside without harming the engraving.

"Fortunately," said Ed Webber, "you can cure a lot of the idiot factor of amateur gunsmithing with welded repairs." Dan Cullity summed it up succinctly: "There is no substitute for experience, judgment, and restraint." He was talking about TIG welding, but his words are equally important for all gun repairs.

CHAPTER 15

Gunsmithing Screwdrivers

I was torn between desire and hesitation when contemplating this chapter's subject—screwdrivers. Desire, because I'm always interested in spreading knowledge about gunmaking, and screwdrivers have not gotten a lot of ink in the past. Hesitation, because of educating—or encouraging—friends like Ian, who freely admits "a screwdriver becomes a dangerous weapon in my hands."

Three of my friends have different skill levels with screwdrivers. Ian owns a set and is justifiably afraid of using them on his guns. Tim has a passable set, with blades I ground for him, and can mount a scope, remove a sidelock, or tighten a loose screw—though when I'm in his gun room he's apt to say, "Here, you do it."

Ross, on the other hand, takes great pleasure in "raccooning" his shotguns. Thankfully, he doesn't bugger his screws, and he'll bring a problem gun to my shop before messing it up. A few years back, he even organized an evening seminar where I demonstrated how to completely disassemble and reassemble sidelock and boxlock guns. The other four fellows just wanted to see how it was done and what the guns looked like inside. Ross wanted to see my tools in action and learn about the assembly process.

In all of the chapters of this book, the following is the most ardent warning I'll issue: The surest way to screw up a perfectly good gun is to forcefully apply chisel-like instruments to its external surfaces. At the very least, those thin, crisp screw slots can get buggered. Much more frightening are the possibilities of gouged lockplates, furrowed stocks, or screw heads so badly damaged they must be drilled out to be replaced. I've seen all these things result from good-intentioned but incautious disassembly.

My desire to provide information about screwdrivers comes also from the number of loose screws I see in pride-and-joy shotguns and the limited access to competent gunsmiths to tighten them. In Chapter 16, "Machine Screws and Gun Screws," I write that the reason for aligned action-screw slots is that it allows for immediate recognition of tightness (or looseness). I've also seen a few cracked stocks because the tang screws had shot loose. Wouldn't it be great if you could feel confident about tightening loose screws?

Most side-by-side shotguns have a similar number of screws in similar locations that fasten metal parts to each other and to the stock. Most screws have fine slots and should be installed tightly to prevent them from shooting loose.

We use screwdrivers, or turnscrews, as some smiths refer to them, to install and remove screws. (A gunsmith's joke: What's the difference between a screwdriver and a turnscrew? About forty-five bucks!) The screwdriver rack above my bench holds nearly two dozen mismatched tools, some of which I use every day. Besides those, I have a set of precision jeweler's screwdrivers with tiny blades, a travel kit with one handle and interchangeable bits, a bench block with another assortment of bits, several long-shank (ten inches to twelve inches) drivers for stock through-bolts, Phillips blades for removing recoil pads, and a drawer full of specially ground blades for specific applications.

Each screwdriver has a handle, a shank, and a blade. The handles are wood, metal, or plastic and should be proportional to the blade size to allow the application of proper torque to the screw head. I prefer wooden handles because I occasionally use them to tap gun parts into or out of place. (I also use wood handles as snap-caps when dropping the hammers on a disassembled gun by holding them flat against the breech face.)

Most shanks vary in length from ³/₄ inches to five inches and are round, rectangular, or octagonal in cross section. Round shanks are best for removing deeply recessed screws as they are less likely to mar the edges of the holes. Round shanks are also proper for removing recoil pads that are slit—as opposed to having removable plugs—for access to the screw heads. A wrench can be used with a rectangular or octagonal shank to increase torque, but this can be dangerous. I have no idea why shanks come in different lengths, but I like the shorter type—no more than three inches—because I prefer to stay close to the work.

Each blade is ground to fit a different screw head, slot depth, and width. Most blades are hollow-ground on both sides. Hollow-grinding makes the best blades for gun screws because the slots are cut with parallel sides; a properly hollow-ground bit also has parallel sides and will fill up the slot. It is equally important that the driver blade match the width of the screw head. It is less likely to slip out of the slot while transferring maximum force because it contacts both sides of the slot for its full width and depth.

For example, a screw with a ³/₁₆-inch head and a .020-inch slot ¹/₈ inch deep should be matched with a .020-inch blade just shy of ³/₁₆ inches wide that will fit snugly to the bottom of the slot. If the blade is too thin, or if it doesn't contact the full width of the head or reach to the

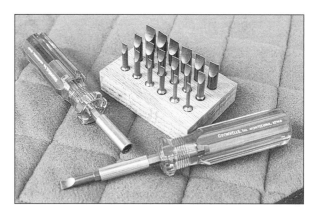

Brownells's Magna-Tip Thin Bit set is a good start for gunsmithing screwdrivers.

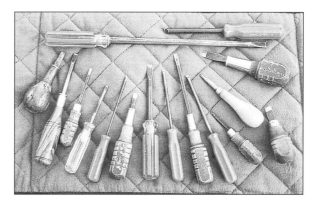

Screwdrivers come in all shapes and sizes as shown in this portion of the author's collection.

bottom of the slot, it is more likely to slip out and bugger the head or damage the gun. If the blade is even a tiny bit too wide, it can mar the surrounding metal when it's placed into the slot.

I looked at several assortments of professional-quality gunsmithing screwdrivers for this chapter. The Browning set is an economical starter set, made by Grace, and so named because the drivers were made to fit the Browning Auto-5, which, for a factory gun, has relatively fine-slotted screws. The five wooden-handled screwdrivers range in blade width from .200 inches to .275 inches and are ground from .022 inches to .030 inches thick. Unfortunately, they are not thin enough for most British and European screw slots. Through the years I've reground several of these sets for friends to match the slots of their favorite guns. If you know a sympathetic gunsmith or are handy, the low price plus regrinding will get you into the ball game.

These Browning drivers have square shanks, are forged of quality steel, and are appropriately hardened. I've used them for nearly two decades and have reground them many times. I suggest adding one smaller and one larger width and grinding them to fit the trigger guard and main tang screw (breech pin) of your favorite double. The screwdrivers are available individually or in sets from Brownells, Inc.

Brownells offers a mind-boggling assortment of screwdrivers for the gunsmith. The "house brand," Magna-Tip, employs separate handles and possibly one hundred bits that can be purchased individually or in sets. The bits are well made, precisely ground, and properly hardened. Each has a short, six-sided section that slips into a magnetic socket on the handle shank.

I enjoy having a wide variety of bits available, and with three separate handles, I'm not changing them all the time. I do prefer fixed-blade drivers for stubborn screws, as there is some wobble with the bits and standard handles. Brownells offers a locking collet-type handle that holds the bits more positively, although they don't interchange as quickly because the collet must be hand-tightened.

The most useful screwdrivers for double-gunners come in the Magna-Tip Thin Bit set. With eighteen bits in nine widths and .020-inch- or .025-inch-thick blades, these are the closest to correct size of any I've found. For the most part, this set will work well for the screws of many American-made doubles.

Brownells also offers the Forester-Bonanza set, with round shanks and blades from .023 inches to .035 inches. This set has been a useful part of my screwdriver collection for many years and offers the only through-bolt, extra-long-shank screwdriver I know of.

Pachmayr sells a Professional set of interchangeable-bit drivers. The plastic-boxed kit includes twelve straight-slot, seven Allen-head, six Phillips-head, and three Torx-head bits. The slotted bits are .125 inches to .400 inches wide and the blades from .017 inches to .055 inches thick, with the wide ones having the thicker blades. This makes a good travel set for factory guns. The slotted heads could be custom-ground to fit your guns.

Unfortunately, none of these screwdrivers has fine enough blades for many of the screws on imported doubles.

I've seen various screwdrivers made in England and offered in this country as "gunmaker's" or "best grade" or as rosewood- or ebony-handled masterpieces to grace felt-lined gun cases. I've heard that the drivers sold in the U.S. as the gunmaker's variety are considered cabinetmakers' tools in England; the published blade thicknesses I've seen were too coarse for British guns. In my experience, the fancy-handled, cased-set variety are of fine quality but aren't ground for use, although they could be. Galazan offers a London Best working set I haven't seen or used, and the catalog honestly states, "All are hollow ground on one side to facilitate custom grinding."

The process of measuring screw-slot width is difficult and even dangerous. Using the pointed prongs of dial calipers (which are very sharp and will readily scratch gunmetal), I have carefully measured slots as thin as .012 inches. If you are going to attempt this, first practice on screw slots that aren't in a gun. Then, after you've mastered the technique, secure your gun in a cradle so you have both hands to guide the calipers. I wouldn't think of trying this without my magnifying visor on.

I prefer to determine slot width first by eyeballing, then by carefully trying different blades until I find the one that fits perfectly. You're less likely to scratch the gun by tipping one edge of the blade into the slot. Once the thickness is determined, find a blade that is nearly as wide as the screw head. Never use a 1/8-inch bit in a 1/4-inch screw even if the slot-to-blade thickness is a perfect match. Maximum force is generated at the outer edges of the screwdriver, and buggering is achieved by using a narrow blade in a wide head.

Of course there are no standard slot sizes except in screws on machine-made American guns. To establish trends in slot sizes, I called gunsmith Pete Mazur, who has experience with doubles from all over the world. Mazur suggests that American screw slots are usually .020 inches to .040 inches; most English, Spanish, and German slots are from .015 inches to .030 inches, with some thinner; and Italian slots are the thinnest, at .010 inches to .015 inches. Keep in mind that these are only guidelines and that you can't readily buy drivers for most of these screws.

Chances are, if you've purchased some screwdrivers, or bits, the blades don't fit the screws of your double gun. They must be ground to fit. If you're not handy enough to regrind blades, you should think twice about using them on a fine gun. You can always ask a gunsmith to tighten the screws or to grind the blades.

I regrind blades and Magna-Tip bits with a rotary stone chucked in a drill press. Brownells sells a large stone (1^1/$_2$ inches in diameter) for Magna-Tip bits and a smaller stone (5/8 inch) for fixed or ultrathin blades. I've found Brownells grinding stones to be aggressive and true, and they don't load up with metal chips. These stones work well for hollow-grinding any screwdriver blades.

Brownells's suggestion of holding bits in a drill press vise often works well. Some bits, however, have their hexagonal section askew to the flat of the blade and are difficult to hold in a vise. These bits I carefully handhold against the grinding wheel, as I do with screwdrivers with attached handles.

For those without a drill press, the grinding wheel can be chucked in an electric drill, which then can be securely held in a bench vise. If the grinding wheel isn't firmly planted, it isn't possible to correctly and efficiently grind screwdriver blades.

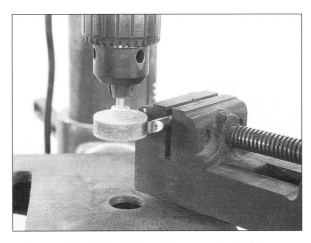

One method of grinding bits to perfectly fit screw slots is chucking a rotary stone in a drill press and clamping the driver bit in a small vise.

Here's how I do it: The larger grinding wheel is installed in the drill press chuck and the key tightened. At the workbench, I clamp the driver bit in a small drill press vise, aligning the ground part of the bit perfectly vertical by holding a square to the bench top. I place the vise on the drill press table, then raise the table until the ground section of the bit is level with the middle of the grinding wheel. I then lock the table at this height.

It is important to note which direction the drill chuck is rotating and to make sure the bit only touches the wheel as it turns away from the tip. In other words, the wheel should sweep away the metal from the shank toward the tip of the bit. This means holding the bit on the right front side of the wheel in a drill press. If the tip is facing into the rotation, the bit could dig into the wheel and cause major problems. This works the same on any grinder; the wheel should rotate away from the tip of the bit. I adjust the speed to a relatively slow setting.

With dial calipers, I measure and note the thickness of the tip before grinding. I determine the desired finished thickness and divide it by two, as half of the metal must come off each side of the bit. (For example, to take a .025-inch-thick bit to .015 inches, I remove .005 inches from each side.) Always wearing safety glasses, I move the bit into the wheel, lightly starting the contact toward the rear of the ground area. I adjust the attitude until the ground section is fully contacting the wheel. Then I back it off and take a look at what's happening.

The ground area should show an even, shiny surface where the bit was ground by the wheel. If not, I adjust the bit in the vise so there is even contact between the wheel and the bit. With gentle pressure, I'll grind the desired amount from one side of the bit. (I verify this by measuring the tip with the calipers.) Then I'll turn the bit over in the vise and grind the other side equally.

As a final step, I take a small sharpening stone—one I'd use for a pocketknife—and lightly dress each newly ground edge to remove any burrs that might scratch gunmetal.

Some points to remember: It's a good idea to do a dry run without the wheel in motion. Always approach the wheel carefully and use gentle pressure when grinding. Grind lightly on the first pass to make sure the bit is truly aligned with the wheel. Check both the top and bottom of the tip with calipers to ensure even thickness. It takes less than a minute per side to remove .005 inches of metal from a wide blade. A narrow blade will grind much quicker and is more difficult to position. If you stop to check the evenness of the grinding and the thickness as you go, the bit won't get very hot. Heat will draw the temper if it's enough to change the color of the steel. I find grinding a hand-held bit much easier. Then again, my hand-eye coordination is fine-tuned daily, and I wear 4X magnifiers.

As I mentioned earlier, if you don't have screwdrivers, I would recommend the Brownells Magna-Tip Thin Bit set for starters. Again, the eighteen bits come in .020-inch and .025-inch thicknesses, and I suggest grinding six or seven of the .025-inch bits down to .015 inches. Better yet, custom-grind them to fit your shotgun's

screws. Adding more bits for special applications is easy, and you can get them all in one place.

The following measurements will give you a reasonable idea of screwdriver blade sizes for typical English, Spanish, and other Continental (German, Austrian, French, Belgian) side-by-sides. Toplever screws (retain the toplever) .015 to .020 inches thick by .340 or .360 inches wide; primary tang screw (or breech pin, under toplever) .015 to .020 inches by .300 inches; triggerplate and inspection plate (on action bottom of a boxlock) .015 to .020 inches by .340 inches; trigger guard wood screw: .015 to .020 inches by .180 or .240 inches; forend iron screws (usually under forend) .015 to .020 inches by .210 or .240 inches; plunger forend tip screw (tiny, sometimes installed from underneath) .015 to .020 inches by .120 or .180 inches. The extractor retaining screw (found on or between barrel lumps) will be from .015 to .020 inches thick and vary in width.

The rear tang screw (hand pin), which comes up from under the trigger guard, is usually thicker (.020 to .025 inches). This screw occasionally comes loose; you can tell by checking whether the threaded end is flush with the rear of the top tang. The trigger guard must be removed to tighten the rear tang screw, which must be tight or recoil can crack the stock at the wrist.

Sidelocks have one less screw on the bottom and typically three more at the locks. There are screws (about .015 inches by .180 or .210 inches) just behind each fence that secure the locks to the action body and one (about .015 inches by .270 inches) that goes from side to side that hold the tails of the lockplate in place. (Hand-detachable locks don't have these.)

In sum, with English, Spanish, and most other Continental guns, you will need different width blades, most ground to a thickness of about .015 inches. This is thin, but the slots on many Italian guns are even thinner. For most American guns, a variety of widths with blades .020 to .025 inches thick will work fine.

• • •

How does one know if screws are loose? On most fine guns, the slots of tight screws should align with the bore. What if the slot is turned past alignment when the screw is fully tightened? In restoring quality guns, I have several tricks to realign slots, but those methods go beyond the scope of this chapter. In most cases, however, it is better to have a screw tight than aligned, which is mostly a cosmetic thing. The exception is the rear tang screw, which I frequently find loose on older guns due to wood shrinkage. Sometimes if this screw is fully tightened it will protrude above the top tang and interfere with the safety's function—obviously, a bad situation. The solution is to remove the screw and carefully dress the threaded end down until it is flush with the top tang when tightened.

To this point, I've discussed tightening loose screws as opposed to actually disassembling or working on a gun. I'll present the following procedures simply for information sake because they are better left to professionals—done incorrectly, they can screw up a gun in a hurry.

The breech pin, or main tang screw, is usually very tight because if it comes loose, the stock is almost sure to crack. To prevent this, gunmakers use a brace and bit—and considerable torque—to install the screw. Most often it will require a similar technique to loosen it.

When I'm trying to install or remove a very tight screw, I keep a close eye on the tip of the bit and will often see it flex a tiny amount. This flex happens just before the tip breaks, which will surely mar or damage the gun. (Magna-Tip bits are hard and brittle and will break before they flex, so I don't use them on supertight or stuck screws.)

There are several techniques I use on screws that are so tight I can see the bit flex without the screw loosening. First, I always try to remove the stock to make the working unit smaller and because the wood is easy to damage. Penetrating oil is a good start for loosening screws, but it seldom reaches the threads and some types will discolor bluing or case colors. Heat applied directly to the screw can help, but a torch can ruin a gun. I sometimes apply heat with a large, copper-tip soldering iron that has never had any solder on it. Solder doesn't look good on screwheads.

Freezing sometimes works, but it means putting the gun—minus the wood—in the deep freeze. This can draw oil from the metal and promote rusting. Some gunsmiths employ a bit in a drill press, using the downward pressure and turning the chuck by hand. This has worked well for me but requires clamping the gun in the drill vise.

For really stuck screws, I have used an impact wrench, definitely an extreme measure. When struck with a hammer, this tool applies up to two hundred foot-pounds of "shock torque" and downward pressure directly to the screwhead. The driver bit must be perfectly ground, the action held solidly in a bench vise, and the hammer judiciously applied. I would never suggest that anyone other than a professional gunsmith try this technique.

The bottom line is to use your screwdrivers to tighten screws and leave the loosening to the professionals.

CHAPTER 16

Machine Screws and Gun Screws

I recently finished polishing a complete set of screws—thirty-six in total—for a custom side-lock shotgun. While polishing the set, I was thinking about the contents of this book and it occurred to me that I'd never read anything about screws, those small parts that are essential to the makeup of a shotgun. There is much to learn about them: you've probably noticed that the screws of high-quality double guns are finely slotted and that they all align with the gun's bore. As noted in the previous chapter, the alignment reveals instantly if the screws are loose.

Before I discuss screws and their importance to fine guns, I need to clarify a few terms. In British gunmaking nomenclature a "pin" means a screw. So the top tang screw under the lever is the "breech pin," and the screw at the rear of the tang is the "hand pin" because it lies under the shooter's hand. Also to Brits, a "peg" is what we call a pin. I prefer the American usage, in which a screw has threads, a pin does not, and a peg secures a tent or is a nickname for Margaret.

There are two types of screws on guns: machine screws and gun screws. Machine screws fasten metal to metal and have fine machine-cut male threads that mate to female-threaded holes. They usually have a square-shoulder head that fits into a counterbored recess in a metal part. Screw threads are commonly cut with a "die" held in a "die stock," and holes are threaded, or tapped, with a tap that looks like a tapered and fluted screw.

Gun screws mate metal, such as buttplates and trigger guards, to the gunstock. They usually

have an untapered shank deeply cut with very coarse threading. (Gun screws are unlike the tapered wood screws found in hardware stores.) The heads are tapered and have either a slight dome or are flush-fit. They are mated to an angular countersink in the respective metal part.

There is no standardization of any screws by double-gun makers around the world. A Fox trigger-plate screw, for example, will fit another Fox but no other gun—each maker came up with his own idea of what he wanted.

I don't know how, when, or where metric threads were developed or standardized. I do know that modern Italian gunmakers have as consistent a system as any. Italian gun repair authorities tell me that metric threads are so standardized that threaded screw blanks in various sizes and with oversize heads can be purchased to fit many different guns. Making a screw for an Italian gun shouldn't be a problem if one has metric dies. However, the ultrafine slots of Italian screws are somewhat of an aesthetic tradition and can make them a problem to remove.

No two American doubles even use the same threads; Fox, Parker, Ithaca, Lefever are all different. Even the later-manufactured Winchester Model 21 had oddball threads. To the best of my knowledge, none of these guns uses what we would call standard threads.

When Jack Rowe (the Enid, Oklahoma, smith quoted in earlier chapters) started his apprenticeship in Birmingham, England, in the 1940s, British Association (BA) threading had been the standard for many years. When I asked

Jack how long, he said, "It's always been that way; it might go back to the turn of the century." He also told me that in the small shops—as well as in some of the larger ones—each craftsman had his own "screw plate" to make screws for his own use. Whereas most were to the BA standard, these plates varied tremendously depending on the quality of the taps used to make them and the wear on the plates themselves. A so-called BA standard made with a thirty-year-old screw plate that was originally made from a worn tap is a far cry from a new thread cut with a sharp die.

Rowe's shop is the American warranty station for Spanish AyA guns, and he says all modern Spanish threads are metric and remarkably consistent throughout the industry. His AyA factory-made screws often fit other Spanish guns with little modification. I have used stock replacement Spanish screws for some other Continental guns.

To my surprise, German guns show little standardization of screw threading, according to Suhl-trained gunsmith Dietrich Apel, of New Hampshire. They commonly have metric threads, but many are in uncommon sizes. Before World War II, there was no standard except in large factories like those of Merkel and Sauer. All small-shop handmade guns had individual screw sizes.

From all this, it's obvious that it's not a simple matter of running down to the hardware store to obtain a screw for a gun. Problems arise when a gunsmith encounters the type of screw that's all too familiar—the buggered variety.

Whenever possible I try to repair a screw before replacing it. Besides the time-saving aspect, I like to keep the gun's parts as original as possible. Sometimes a buggered screw head can be peened back into reasonable shape, lightly dressed with a fine file, have its slot recut, and its engraving touched up. More drastic buggering requires a TIG welder to build up the head.

It is possible to buy oversize head, threaded

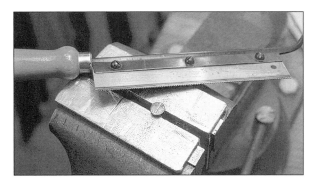

Making new screws involves cutting a slot—often by hand with a saw.

The threads can be cut with a die or a lathe.

screws for some guns, and that is my second choice. Galazan, in New Britain, Connecticut, supplies replacement screw sets for Parkers (eleven action screws), Foxes (three action screws), and Winchester Model 12 pumps (eight action screws). The company also sells Model 21 screws individually. I've fitted a couple of screw sets for clients, and they do require work. For example, the head diameter must be reduced slightly to fit the recess, the bottom of the head must be removed until the slot aligns properly, and the top of the head must be dressed down to fit flush. Screw sets save time and money, and I consider them a blessing.

My last choice is to make a new screw from bar stock. This process takes from one to two hours per screw, at an average cost of at least $100 each. Understandably, I (and my clients) prefer rescuing the originals, but sometimes there's no choice.

To make my own screws, I first determine

Fitting a tang screw to a sidelock shotgun using masking tape to protect the tang.

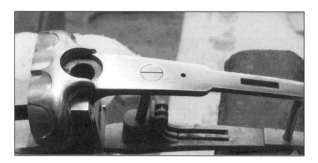

The finished tang screw with the screw slot aligned.

proper size by measuring the external diameter of the original screw with a micrometer and the number of threads per inch with a thread pitch gauge. A gun's era and origin give clues to its screws' threading. I draw a blueprint of all the dimensions so I know where I'm going. When a screw is missing, I must derive all possible dimensions by measuring the recess it fit into. If the female threaded hole is large enough, a thread pitch gauge is inserted to determine threads per inch. If not, I use trial and error with an assortment of screws as well as workshop intuition. The last resort is drilling and tapping the hole to a larger size.

Picking the appropriate steel is a concern. Most screws are made from leaded bar stock, which is "free-machining," or easy to cut with machine tools. This steel has a low carbon content and must be case hardened, so gunsmiths often use drill rod, which is carbon steel that can be hardened by conventional methods.

Oversize round-screw stock is chucked in my engine lathe and one end is faced off to get it square and true. It is then center-drilled to a sixty-degree angle for the lathe's tailstock, so the material can be supported at both ends during the turning process. The head diameter is turned (machined) slightly oversize, then the shank is turned to the right diameter for threading. The base of the head is turned square or to the appropriate angle for the counterbore of the screw's hole.

If a die is available for the right thread, the screw shank now can be die-cut in about ten minutes. Lathe-cutting the thread with a tool bit, called single-point threading, will take much longer, in addition to the set-up time.

For single-point threading, a sixty-degree (fifty-five for Whitworth, forty-seven for British Association) threading bit is set up in the lathe cross-feed and the machine is adjusted to its slowest speed, put in back-gear, and set for the desired number of threads per inch. By advancing the bit a few thousandths of an inch per pass and engaging the lathe carriage at the correct interval, the thread will be cut over and over until proper depth is achieved.

Once threaded, the screw is cut off at the head, which is then turned down until its diameter perfectly fits the counterbore in the gunmetal. The head is then reduced in thickness until it sticks up slightly when it's threaded into place.

The screw slot can be fashioned with sophisticated slotting cutters and a milling machine, but most gunmakers use files or a saw. To accomplish this by hand, I cover the head with layout fluid, and locate the center with a center square and the slot scribed across the top. To start the groove, I use a three-corner file with one edge ground smooth. Once the file is centered, I cut the slot with a slitting saw to a width of about .020 inches. It can then be opened with screw-slotting files to the correct width and depth. Most custom screws are simply cleaned up and left with .020-inch slots.

The slot is then aligned in the gun and the head dressed down flush with the gunmetal. This final fitting can take some time to ensure the screw is bearing well in the bottom of the counterbore when the slot comes to alignment. The head can't be filed while in the gun for fear of marring the surrounding metal. In other words, the screw goes in and out many times before it is perfectly fitted. Many gunmakers can reproduce simple engraving, but if the job requires something at all complex, I send the screw to a professional engraver with another engraved screw from the gun for a sample.

Of course, the heads first must be polished to 600 grit. Then it's time to fire up the nitre tank and blue all those small but critical fasteners. The sapphire sparkle of a nitre-blued screw is the final touch for a fine gun.

CHAPTER 17
Metal Finishes for Fine Guns

Given the subject of this book, it may surprise you to learn that the last custom gun I completed was a Marlin Model 1894 lever-action rifle. The project was commissioned to replicate "best-quality" American riflemaking of the 1900s, the same period that witnessed the birth of best-quality gunmaking worldwide.

During the finishing process, I was struck by the fact that the techniques and processes of the Marlin's metal finishes mirrored those used on quality double shotguns. Then I began thinking about how and why contemporary gunmakers use the polishing techniques and metal finishes we employ and what my decades in the trade have taught me about the utility, durability, and longevity of metal finishes for fine guns.

I will relate some of the history of the processes, preparation, and application techniques, and I will compare advantages and longevity in usage. The best example of durability that I have is my own custom Fox shotgun. It was completed in 1994, and I have shot and hunted with it extensively since that time. Examining, evaluating, and illustrating the various parts and finishes will serve as graphic examples of the aging and wear processes of gunmetal finishes.

The appropriate metal finishes for fine guns were determined long ago and are startlingly similar, regardless of a gun's type or manufacturing origin. In other words, the 1890s Deluxe Marlin or Winchester lever-action gun, Sharps single-shot rifle, best Purdey sidelock, Colt or Smith & Wesson revolver, Austrian boxlock, or German drilling, all would have had some of the

same bluing, case-hardening, and bright polishing to complete the metal finishing. The processes evolved from earlier guns and gunmaking, with all but rust bluing having been in common use during the flintlock era. Although the advent of mass-manufacturing techniques has altered this scenario, most of the contemporary high-quality, small-shop gunmaking done worldwide today employs many of these techniques and processes.

As an example of best London gun finishes, there is an 1890s-vintage J. Purdey & Sons hammerless sidelock in my shop showing five different metal finishes that are true to the original type but have obviously been redone. (See Color Section, page 7A.) The finishes are: 1) color case-hardening—action body, triggerplate, lockplates, lock screws, forend tip, and triggers; 2) rust bluing—barrels; 3) charcoal blacking—trigger guard, toplever, safety button, some screws, forend iron, and plunger; 4) nitre bluing—some screws, hinge-pin caps, and striker disks; 5) bright polishing—bores, muzzle, lock screws, barrel flats, lumps, extractors, breech faces, knuckle of action, and iron. (The terms "bluing" and "blacking" are used interchangeably in this case, although they can be very different processes, which I will explain later.)

The barrels show a high-polished rust bluing that was typically done in England and makes the color appear very similar to highly polished charcoal bluing. I assume the small parts have been charcoal blued, but they nearly match the barrel color and finish. The bright-polished metal surfaces of the barrel flats and so on are noted because this is a distinct metal-finishing technique that takes place after the rust-bluing process. It's more than pure instinct that tells me the Purdey's refinishing was done in England.

In the earliest times, all gunmetal was bright finished, as evidenced by the patina shown on surviving examples. Just as armor and edged weapons were polished or possibly burnished, so were guns. Finding out what finish was used for what old gun part is largely accomplished by looking at the protected surfaces that haven't been subjected to external wear: the barrel and iron under the forend, the backside of the buttplate, the underside of the forend tip, and so on.

Early metal-polishing techniques are a bit trickier to research. It is known that various grades of pumice and shark skin (shagreen) were used to polish metal in ancient times. Why the metal was polished is easier to decipher. The finer the steel or iron is polished, the less friction there is between moving parts, the less likely the metal is to corrode, and the more refined is the metal's appearance.

Although it is conjecture on my part, it is easy to surmise that the rust browning of gun barrels was a natural progression from tarnishing. Just as a shovel or garden tool will resist severe corrosion once it has built up a patina of fine rust, so will gun barrels. Controlling the process was certainly one of the earliest applied firearms metal finishes. Progressive coats of a mild acid solution that are allowed to bloom into red rust and then brushed, or "carded," off between coats will build up a minute surface oxidation that will resist corrosion much better than bare metal. At some point someone likely spilled boiling water on rusting metal to discover rust bluing—which is exactly how red rust is converted to blacking. Interestingly, rust bluing seems to have been discovered around the turn of the nineteenth century, at least one hundred years after rust browning was a common practice.

W.W. Greener's classic book, *The Gun and Its Development* (1881), is one of the first texts to differentiate between browning and blacking, although in some circles rust bluing is still referred to as browning, which differentiates it from charcoal blacking. The rust-bluing process was in general use in the firearms industry by the 1850s.

Case-hardening is another matter, and it is easily traceable to the earliest development of steel. Whoever discovered that melding carbon with iron produces a harder substance is lost to time, but I'd be willing to bet that the discovery came hand in glove with arms development.

Steelmaking—the amalgamation of carbon and iron to create steel alloys—was a rare and guarded process possibly developed by alchemists. This development certainly took place in regions with available iron ore and a history of smelting and refining it. It would be logical to assume that the coal or charcoal used to smelt the iron ore was, by accident or experiment, found to harden it. Many of the arms-making centers of Europe were developed around iron-mining locales.

For a couple of centuries at least, wrought iron was used to make all gun parts except springs. There was no need to purchase the vastly more expensive alloy steel, because the process of case-hardening iron was perfect for most gun parts. So in the flintlock era, all of the lock parts (the plate, tumbler, sear, cock or hammer, bridle, and screws) were forged and filed from iron, then case-hardened for sturdiness and wear resistance.

The process involved finely polishing the metal surfaces; packing parts in a vessel with charred bone, leather, or animal body parts; then heating the "pack" (it is still called pack-hardening) to the critical temperature and quenching the red-hot metal in water. During the heating process, the organic carbon in the charred animal-matter would bond with the surface of the iron and would be fixed with it during the shock of the water quench.

The depth of the carbon penetration—and therefore the depth of the hardness—would depend upon the temperature, the length of heating time, and the concentration of carbon at the surface of the metal. The surface hardness might vary from a few thousandths of an inch to as deep as .025 inches.

This process provided four distinct improvements to a flintlock, and none of them was cosmetic. The engaging sear face and tumbler notch were hardened, making them less likely to break. The contacting surfaces of the lockplate, tumbler, and sear pivot areas became resistant to friction wear and considerably "slicker" than unhardened surfaces. All of the hardened metal surfaces became much more resistant to corrosion or rusting. And the frizzen, or steel, that the flint struck was hardened to provide a shower of sparks to ignite the priming powder.

Case-hardening was (and is) also known as "carburizing"; that is, the imparting of carbon to the surface of the steel. Shallow carbon penetration left the center of the lock part the original soft, malleable iron. This provided another advantage; the metal parts were subject to warpage when quenched, but with a malleable core, the part could be straightened after cooling without fear of breakage.

Nowhere was the process used to impart fanciful colors to the metal for the visual enhancement we enjoy today. This came along much later. In fact, I've owned original flintlock and percussion guns with bright-finished, case-hardened lockplates that showed no trace of external case colors, even in protected areas, but had traces of case colors on the backs or undersides of the plates.

Fire bluing (also called heat, temper, or nitre bluing) is another archaic process often used as a contemporary firearms finish. Although I haven't personally seen one, there are eighteenth-century fowlers and rifle barrels that show the brilliant hues of fire bluing underneath their full stocks. It is obviously seen as the temper color of lock springs. I remember an original flintlock fowler I owned that had brilliantly blue-tempered main and sear springs exposed when the lock was removed. I shot more than a thousand rounds through that gun before looking at that gorgeous sapphire-blue mainspring and thinking what a crime it would be if it broke. I immediately retired the gun and sold it to a collector.

These days we most often see fire bluing as a coloring for screws and small parts. Most fine-gun fanciers have seen the ends of fire-blued screws showing on the lockplates of many guns pictured in books and magazines. I tend to think of fire bluing more as a byproduct of the tempering process, but I also use it as a colorfully decorative metal finish for my own gunmaking.

The third type of bluing, or blacking (the least practiced and understood today), is charcoal bluing. This is a heat-bluing process. I know very little about small-shop techniques except what I've gleaned from the few fellows I know who still use them. As for mass-manufactured firearms, prior to World War II charcoal bluing was almost universally used. All of the prewar Winchesters had rust-blued barrels and charcoal—or "Carbona"—blued actions and small parts. The luscious blue seen on early Colt and Smith & Wesson revolvers was charcoal bluing. Most of the small parts of double shotguns made anywhere in the world, if blued, were charcoal blued. The barrels were always rust blued, because the soft-solder rib joints couldn't stand the heat. And to further confuse the terminology, this bluing was given a very bright polish but remained a dark blue-black color, quite unlike the pitch-black of modern caustic blue and much shinier than all but the finest rust bluing.

* * *

Whether refinishing older guns or preparing metal for new custom guns, all of the craftsmen I know hand polish gunmetal instead of using wheel polishing. At one time, wheel polishing was a job title in the trade, and there were professional polishers who, with a number of different wheels and compounds, could competently polish the many contours of firearms metalwork. These days wheel polishing is mostly buffing and more likely to ruin a fine gun than improve it. Likewise, hand-held rotary tools are the bane of quality gunwork. Both buffing wheels and rotary tools run at high speeds by inexperienced hands can easily distort or disfigure metal surfaces.

Prior to polishing new work, I like to go over all of the metal surfaces—the complete action, iron, triggers, guard, and so on—with a fine-cut file to perfect all of the flats and curved surfaces. The polishing itself is done almost entirely with grit paper. I prefer cloth-backed roll abrasives called Metalite made by the Norton company. I buy it in 1¹/₂-inch-by-50-yard rolls in grits from 100 to 400. I also stock, for special applications, 600-, 800-, and 1,000-grit wet and dry paper along with crocus cloth, which has almost no grit at all.

Different metal finishes require different degrees of polishing, but everything gets a minimum of 320-grit. Unless one has personal experience—and preferably someone to illustrate the technique—he or she is not likely to appreciate what thorough hand-polishing entails.

Beginning with 100- or 150-grit, I like to back the paper with a hard surface, most often the same file used to complete the metal shaping. These coarser grits are aggressive enough to alter the shape of the metal, and care must be taken to preserve the corners and hard edges. Finer grits of 180, 220, and 320 can be backed with slightly softer materials. I have numerous blocks and backers made from specially ground pieces of wood, recoil pads, hard rubber, erasers, and gasline tubing with wood dowels down the middle. These match the various sizes and contours of

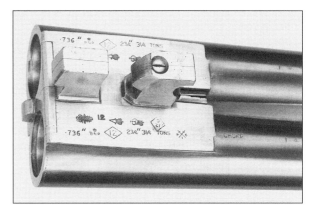

Bright-polished metal is also a planned finish, as shown by these flats and lumps.

the individual parts being polished.

Probably the best advice for complete scratch removal in polishing is to "cross polish" with each grit at a forty-five-degree angle to the previous polishing. If all of the polishing is done in the same direction, it is virtually impossible to know when all the scratches are removed. Sometimes it isn't possible to cross polish because of the surface, and one must be especially careful to look for scratches when advancing to a finer grit.

For refinishing—preparing the metal and replacing the original finishes—some craftsmen prefer to use stones of different grits. There are basically two types of stones used for gun polishing, with multitudes of sizes, shapes, and grits. Soft stones wear away as they are used and are great for conforming to unusual contours, such as the corners where ball fences meet raised fence beads. Hard stones are preferred for refinishing other areas, such as large uninterrupted flats. Both types must be used with lubricant—generally light oil or water—so in effect the polishing is being done somewhat blind behind a smear of wetness.

Hard stones are excellent for refinishing because they won't break down, and they can be used for polishing around and over engraving without fear of degrading the cuts below the surface. With even the hardest backing, grit paper or soft stones can dig into and degrade engraving cuts. When polishing for refinishing, one must be extremely careful with engraved surfaces and those that meet with the stock inletting. With some refinishing, it may be necessary to take down the metal to match shrunken wood or to remove pitting. In this case it is best to first take a rubbing or "smoke pull" of the engraving so there is a record of its original appearance for the person recutting it.

Professionally hand-polished metalwork is a joy for the stockmaker, engraver, metal finisher, and, ultimately, the owner of the firearm. It may be difficult for the novice to appreciate fine polishing, because perfect surfaces draw little attention. The best word I can use to describe it is crisp, and you know it when you see it. When compared to the guns we've all seen with poor buffing, mismatched side-to-side shaping, dished screw holes, and scratches that show right through the bluing, there is no doubt that fine polishing is worth the extra effort.

It is quite possible to achieve a high-quality rust blue with 320-grit polishing if all of the coarser scratches are removed. Some prefer a higher polish, say 400-grit, for a shinier look, but the shine also can be accomplished with finer rusting and faster carding-wheel speed. (A carding wheel is a wire wheel with extremely fine, soft iron wires that gently brush the surface.) Personally, I don't like rust bluing to be too shiny, as it can be confused with caustic bluing. Conversely, quality double-gun barrels should never have a matte finish. Don't let anyone tell you to sandblast or glass-bead the barrels prior to rust bluing or that a nonreflective surface is preferable. In my mind, this is poor preparation that produces inferior results.

To complete polishing by hand, I go over all of the metal surfaces with Scotch-Brite. It is possible to blend all of the polishing marks in the same longitudinal direction, even the contours that can't be grit polished this way. Scotch-Brite

is graded by color, and I use the finest maroon to blend 320-grit, gray to blend 400, and white to blend 600-plus. Simply scrubbing by hand will show grit-paper scratches that haven't been completely removed and will brighten the steel surface without removing any metal.

Color case-hardening requires a minimum of complete 320-grit polishing; 400 grit is better, and some craftsmen use 600. The polisher must be sure to remove all of the scratches with that final grit; 320 scratches showing through 600-grit polish are far more unsightly than a uniform 320-grit surface.

Charcoal bluing looks good when polished to at least 400-grit and best at 600 or finer. The same caveat regarding scratch removal applies to charcoal bluing as it does to case coloring. The bluing will appear darker when polished to finer grits. Unmolested charcoal bluing from the nineteenth century will show an almost mirror polish underneath a true blue-black color. I've been told that the metal was burnished with a hardened steel burnisher as a final step prior to charcoal blacking. I've experimented with burnishing but have had little success. The conclusion I've come to is that even our mildest steel—say, 1010 on the steel code—is quite a bit harder than pure wrought iron and doesn't take well to manual burnishing.

I know of only three craftsmen currently experimenting with charcoal bluing, and, of the three, only Doug Turnbull offers it commercially. Turnbull suggested the highest-quality polish possible for the best results. Pete Mazur wheel-cards parts between heatings to burnish the blued finish. Steve Moeller offers wheel-burnished metal, which he achieves with a superfine wire wheel, superfine polishing compound, and decades of experience. This is not wheel buffing, but, rather, soft burnishing using a mild compound.

I employ Doug Turnbull Restoration for charcoal bluing and color case-hardening. I know of no other firm that can offer as much experience, as predictable results, as little chance of warpage, and as beautiful colors. Turnbull also can alter the colors to match particular themes. Parker colors, for example, are different from Fox colors, which are different from most English guns' colors.

I like my custom guns to present a palette of colors, and nitre bluing small parts adds the appearance of sapphire jewels scattered on fine guns. This deep cobalt blue requires a very high polish, and this is the only time I buff metal. (I do spin polish the inside of trigger-guard bows with grit paper on a split dowel.)

After hand-polishing or spinning in the drill press to 600- and 800-grit, I cross polish the screw heads, holding them in the bench vise, to remove the spin marks. The heads and tails (the ends that show on the outside of the lockplates must be polished) are very lightly touched to a high-speed, loose-muslin polishing wheel using Brownells 550 buffing compound. This gets them bright, and once they are degreased they are ready for nitre bluing. Although this heat bluing can be done with a torch, I prefer to soak the screws at about 590 degrees in a bath of melted saltpeter until I see them come to color, then quench them in warm water. (Warning: At this temperature, any water entering the melted salts will cause them to erupt violently. Eye, hand, and body protection is a must.) This soaking at heat makes the light oxidation wear better and last longer. Still, in terms of longevity, nitre blue is the first metal finish to go.

I have sweaty hands, and sweat means salt. The nitre bluing of my guns' trigger-guard screws may start coming off before the first winter's cold arrives and I start wearing gloves. Likewise, even the most durable rust bluing on the guard tang will show some signs of wear after a few seasons in my hands. By way of example, I finished my custom Fox 12-gauge in 1994. I did all of the metal polishing and rust and nitre blu-

ing. Doug Turnbull Restoration did the color case-hardening, and I put a fine coat of lacquer—the same oil/polyurethane blend I used on the stock—over the case colors and the nitre-blued parts. Then I started shooting the gun.

Before the first year ended, I had shot at hundreds of clay targets, soaked the gun in western Oregon rain forests, scorched it on Idaho chukar slopes, and plunged it into mountain snow. At season's end, I completely disassembled and inspected every surface of the gun to see what had happened.

As it sits here next to my desk, the Hughes/Fox is my benchmark for metal-finish survival. The case colors have held up remarkably well, although you might not think so viewing the photos. (See Color Section, page 7A.)

The legendary engraver Lynton McKenzie once told me, in his refined Australian accent, "Case colors are only as good as the lacquer put over top of them." Looking closely at the scroll clusters on the bottom of the Fox action, one can plainly see the lacquer flaking and the progressive graying of the metal. I purposely left the case-colored forend iron without a lacquer topcoat, and the metal where my hand holds the gun while carrying it lost its colors in year three. As the gun balances on the hinge pin, it is easy to correlate the graying to my carrying position. There is no sign of rust or corrosion of the case-colored metal. The trigger guard is a different matter.

Now I'm pretty good to my guns, but when returning to the vehicle after an outing I have noticed some of my friends treating their guns to good wipe-downs before casing them. Sometimes I do, too. Sometimes I don't.

As a result, there are the faintest traces of surface corrosion along the raised bead on my Fox's guard bow and the edges are shiny, whereas the middle still looks great. The rust bluing is long gone from the grip rail of the guard for the length of my hand just behind the bow. It reappears halfway back, but the nitre blue is gone from the rear screw as well. The nitre-blued triggers are bald on the shoes but bright blue on the sides. The once-rust-blued safety button now sports bright metal, as does the very end of the case-colored top tang. The rest of the tang, from the gold safety forward, has all of the original lacquer and multicolored hues. The tang screw remains nitre blue, but the lollipop of the toplever is shiny on the thumb end.

The barrel bluing is in fine condition, considering the use the gun has seen. Except for a few tiny scratches, the bluing has really protected the tubes. The case colors are great along the top and sides of the action, but you can see how they have fled the bottom, except along the sides of the triggers, which look almost new.

As a comparative visual that works well with most any gun, removing the forend shows me exactly how the barrel blue and forend-iron case colors looked when new—in this case, beautiful. The same can be said of the engraved and nitre-blued forend anchor screw.

Most surprising to me is how nicely the rust bluing of the heel and toe plates has held up; except for the edges, they remain mostly blue (and much to my surprise, the 30-lines-per-inch checkering on the butt looks undamaged as well). I made no attempt to coddle or pamper this gun and have hunted with it extensively for more than a decade. I knew the case colors would go and always have been fond of double-gun actions that have grayed, then silvered, with time and use.

Some might say my Fox, with its mottled tones, looks a bit shabby. However, my springer, Skeeter, is the same age and graying around the muzzle, and I see her as being as pretty as ever.

When all is said and done, the metal finishes of the Fox have held up as I thought they would. In fact, I am delighted that from personal experience I now know what can be expected.

Any new gun should hold up as well as my Fox, because most of these same metal finishes are used today. Good guns deserve great metal finishes.

CHAPTER 18
Hallmark: Signed in Gold

At one time or another, all craftsmen have to come to terms with how to identify their work. Singular creations deserve to be signed for current and future identity and as symbols of pride to anyone who might see them. This speaks to both the craftsman's pride in the result of his work and the owner's pride in the acquisition. The challenge is to be subtle yet definitive.

When I started making custom guns, I used a small die bearing my initials—SDH—that was struck into steel. While researching flintlock guns, I discovered many pieces from as early as the seventeenth century that were hallmarked with insets of precious metal struck with the makers' personal stamps. Silversmiths' hallmarks are well known and well documented, and the fact is that in that era of craftsmanship most tradesmen who worked in metal marked their products with some form of die striking.

If you are lucky enough to own a Paul Revere-hallmarked silver tea service or even a Charles Daly shotgun struck with Lindner's (a Prussian gunmaker) "crown over crossed pistols," you can appreciate the significance of these marks. Understanding the regional jargon of barrel and action makers' die-struck initials as seen on some vintage doubles opens up a whole new world of understanding. For the English gun trade, there are a few contemporary craftsmen who know the names that go with the initials, and there are a few dedicated researchers who have explored the Continental and American gun markings. I don't quite understand how it works, but I know that Italian gunmakers each have their own hallmark and that they are registered and as singular as cattle brands in Montana.

The original SDH hallmark struck in steel seemed a bit too mundane, so my second version was an oval insert of silver struck with the same die. Later, an engraver friend convinced me that raised letters would be a lot classier and that it was easier to make a die with the letters cut into it rather than having raised letters on the die producing inset letters on the gun.

He hand cut a die for me that was approximately $1/4$ by $3/8$ inches. This was fine for the large flats of an octagonal fowler barrel, but when I started creating more cartridge guns a smaller die was in order. The die for my third hallmark measured $3/16$ by $3/8$ inches, but I still found it a bit ostentatious. The current model, which I've been using for about fifteen years, is a mere $1/8$ by $1/4$ inches—small and subtle yet definitive, with raised letters struck in 24-karat gold. For those wishing to do this, the hardest part is finding someone to make the die.

At the gun shows where I display my creations, folks notice the hallmark and frequently ask, "How did you do that?"

For custom rifles, I put the hallmark in the flat of an octagonal barrel or sometimes in the bottom of the action. For all of my custom shotguns, I place the hallmark in the triggerplate just below where the trigger guard return meets the tang.

I use 24-karat sheet gold about .030 inches thick (a bit thicker than a matchbook cover) and lay it on the anvil of my bench vise. Then I place

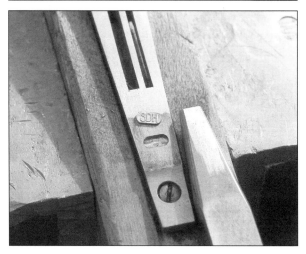

Top: gold and die; center: undercut cavity with chisel; above: gold, with die, ready to be inserted into the cavity.

the die on the gold and strike it with a hammer hard enough to create the letters and define the

perimeter. Care must be taken so the die doesn't bounce or favor one side, resulting in an uneven or double strike. The first strike leaves a clear imprint of the outline and raises the letters to about 3/4 of the finished height.

Using a jeweler's saw, I cut the outline in the gold slightly oversize, then file it to the shape of the oval. That prepares the gold. (Sawing and filing is done over a double sheet of glossy paper to retain all of the minute bits of precious metal.)

With shotguns, I swab the triggerplate with layout bluing and precisely lay out the location of the inlay with calipers and a scribe. In this case, the triggerplate is solidly mounted in a wood block to be held in the milling machine vise. With a 1/8-inch four-fluted end mill ("end cutting") in the machine, the triggerplate is plunge-cut straight down to a depth of .045 inches, then the vise is moved over another 1/8 inch to create the 1/8-inch-by-1/4-inch cavity.

The bottom inside edges of the cavity are slightly undercut with a tiny, specially ground chisel to create a minute dovetail on each side, and a couple of "barbs" are cast up in the bottom center. These will secure the gold in the recess.

The gold is very soft, so with pinched fingers holding the small sheet bearing my hallmark, I hand file the gold until it will barely drop into the cavity. I push it into place with a toothpick so as not to mar the soft metal.

The triggerplate is placed on the anvil, and the die is perfectly aligned on the gold hallmark in the cavity. Because the die and the milled cavity are almost exactly the same size and shape, they are almost self-aligning.

With the hallmark inserted in the cavity, the die is struck for a second time with a hammer to mash the gold into the dovetail and raise the letters to their full height. Because the cavity is a bit deeper than the thickness of the gold, the soft metal is just below the steel surface and is protected from surface abrasions. The triggerplate is finish-polished to a 400-grit glow.

Because this is a mechanical procedure, the gold is permanently affixed and will not fall out. In fact, I once miss struck with the final blow, creating a double-strike, and had a hell of a time digging out the hallmark without damaging the steel around it.

Being a pure metal, gold is impervious to the heat and compounds used in color case-hardening. As a matter of fact, inlaid gold comes out brilliantly clean after case-hardening, though I have had hallmarks tarnish from rust-bluing solutions. When this has happened, I've cleaned the gold with a Q-tip and mild polish, concentrating on the tops of the letters and leaving a bit of attractive patina around them.

All of my custom guns have been hallmarked in this manner. I often have told folks at

A "hallmark" moment: the finished product.

the Firearms Engravers & Gunmakers Exhibition that "I won't need a tombstone when I'm gone; it's already in the guns." And it is forever.

SECTION 5
A Stockmaker's View

CHAPTER 19

Evaluating Shotgun Stock Blanks

"Would you take a look at a stock blank for me?"

I get a couple of such requests each year when I exhibit at the Firearms Engravers & Gunmakers Exhibition (also known as the Custom Gun Show) in Reno, Nevada. At one particular show, there were three major wood merchants in attendance, each with at least one hundred blanks of walnut. Many of the displaying stockmakers also had some choice blanks for sale. I was looking for a few stock blanks for my own inventory. In fact, lots of folks were looking for—and buying—English walnut blanks.

"Sure," I told the man, "Bring it to my display." The blank was Turkish walnut with a red-toned background and a glorious fiddleback figure. "How much are they asking?" I said.

"Twelve hundred dollars," the man answered.

"I wouldn't use it on any gun I stocked," I said.

Although beautiful to look at, the blank had a major S-curve running top to bottom right where the wrist would be. Finished as a slim-wristed, straight-gripped shotgun stock, it might have been snapped in two over a knee.

I'm not going to say any more about why the $1,200 blank wasn't suitable, why it was for sale, or why it was cut into a blank in the first place. Instead, I'm going to describe how an experienced stockmaker goes about choosing wood. I'm going to show some blanks that I have purchased and explain how and why I chose them.

All of the wood shown here, and the only kind from which I make gunstocks, is generically referred to as "English" walnut. In my first book, *Fine Gunmaking: Double Shotguns*, I wrote a lengthy explanation of why I use only English walnut along with virtually everything I know about the wood and the tree, so I won't repeat that here. Suffice it to say that this wood is from *Juglans regia*, a species that is grown all over the world and is commonly referred to by the origin of the individual blank (California English, Australian, Turkish, New Zealand, et cetera.). The tree produces the "thin-shelled" nuts, the ones we love to eat.

I purchased the stock blank featured in Photo Nos. 1 through 5 at the Firearms Engravers & Gunmakers Exhibition: it cost about two-thirds less than the $1,200 Turkish blank. This piece of wood might be called a "baseline" blank because it has all the attributes necessary for making a fine stock and only one minor flaw. This stick is the same grade as, and it shows the same structural characteristics of, stocks on mid- to high-grade British or Continental guns built between the world wars. The only notable difference is that this California-grown blank is probably from a younger tree and is a bit more open-pored than the best French- or Circassian-grown wood used in those times.

The following is a step-by-step evaluation of a stock blank as I would do it at a merchant's display. It usually takes me ten to twenty minutes to judge wood and another fifteen minutes to an hour to talk myself into forking over the money.

Photo No. 1: My first impression of the right side of this blank is that it's exactly what I want to see in a stock. The grain flow—as indicated by the black streaking and confirmed by examining the direction of the tiny pores of the wood—moves straight through the wrist and turns down at the toe. A close look at the pores reveals that they are small and that the cell structure of the wood is relatively dense. I enjoy the reddish-brown background color more than the lighter wood that often comes from California.

Notice the flair of two "pin" knots (tiny knots from twigs eventually covered by the tree's growth) running up the side of the blank about six inches from the front. They look solid to their centers and appear to end on the right side of the blank. The pin knots are near the grip area, so I'll evaluate them on the top and bottom of the blank. I'm confident that I can lay out the blank (place a template for sawing out the stock's actual profile) so the pin knots are slightly behind the nose of the comb, where the mass of wood is greater and stronger.

Photo No. 2: A look at the end grain at the head of the stock reveals more than you might imagine. This critical view is sometimes masked by the wax used to seal the end grain during drying. I believe that a blank should have the sealed ends sawed off, to clearly show the grain, when it

is dry enough to offer for sale, although most wood dealers leave the ends sealed with wax.

In the end view, the black streaking runs side to side, showing the blank to be 100 percent quarter-sawn (my favorite) at the stock head, where it will meet the action. This tells me the pin knots will run through the blank from top to bottom. (Slab-sawn wood has the grain running from top to bottom—or heel to toe—with pin knots running side to side.) Quarter-sawing offers the strongest and stablest cut for a gunstock, especially at the head. It is also most likely to match in appearance from side to side.

Notice that the streaking doesn't appear as straight lines, as it does on the side, but shows some intertwining and wave. This tells me that as wood is removed and the blank is shaped, the black lines will be broader and wavier on the sides of the stock and probably will not appear as the straight lines visible now. As the stock shaping rounds off the square corners, the wave of black streaking will become more pronounced. This blank will likely gain a half to a full grade in appearance during the stockmaking process. Also notice how the black streaking is spread evenly throughout the end grain and doesn't show many open areas of light-colored wood, which means the marbling will be consistent.

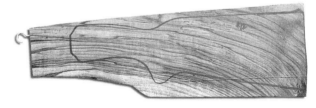

Photo No. 3: The left side of the blank is nearly a mirror image of the right. I like my stocks to look alike on both sides. The pin knots don't show, but a small band of light-colored sap wood does appear at the bottom of the blank. This light wood tends to be softer and more open-pored than the colored heart wood right next to it. The oversized pistol-grip template traced on this side proves there is enough wood for a large stock, but I had it pegged for a straight-gripped stock from the beginning. The grain flow, again, is ideal.

Photo No. 4: The top and bottom of the blank are the hardest parts to gather information from because they are typically rough-cut, unfinished, and dirty. Looking at the top of this baseline blank confirms most of what I've already seen. The black smoke-streaking is a bit wavier than it looks from the sides—good news for appearance. The pin knots have solid centers and should in no way affect the structural integrity of the stock. The reddish-brown background color is handsome and is the same as that on the sides. This view shows that there is no run-out or angular grain.

Photo No. 5: The butt end shows small pores and a slight darkening of the background color. Although it's no longer completely quarter-sawn, there are no flaws, and it's good for checkered butt, heel, and toe plates, or whatever method will be used to cap off the butt end.

Looking over the whole of the blank, it shows no twisting, cupping, warping, or checking. These flaws commonly occur during the drying process and are often associated with slab-sawn or highly figured wood. The square cut of

the blank hasn't changed much from its original sawing, which indicates to me that it isn't likely to release major stresses when shaped.

Photo No. 6: This rifle, which I built for myself, is stocked with a similar stick of California English walnut. This gives a good impression of what our baseline blank eventually will look like. It even has a couple of pin knots in about the same location. Although this blank was not chosen for flash or fancy, it would be difficult to find a stronger or more stable piece of wood. I find this blank exceedingly beautiful as well.

• • •

Generally speaking, there are two types of "fancy" when it comes to describing English walnut stock wood: figure and color. Figure is that luminescence that's usually spread across the prevailing grain flow. It occurs as fiddleback, feather-crotch, or even small pin knots. Figure is much more common in American black and Claro walnut, either of which can have brilliant fiddleback from end to end. Rare is the English blank with that kind of figure.

Color usually refers to the black smoke-streaking and its contrast to the background color. This streaking is perhaps the single most identifying feature of English walnut. When a blank has this heavy swirling smoke, it is referred to as "marbling" or "marble cake," and the background color can range from chocolate brown to yellow, with shades of red, light brown, or honey. I'm not a big fan of high-contrast wood, such as pitch black marbling with a light yellow background color in the same blank. I do like the black well enough; I simply prefer a reddish or brown background color. I often add a bit of red stain as a toning agent during the oil-finishing process to subdue flamboyant wood slightly or add character to plainer sticks. Lately I've seen a few gunstocks made with bright-yellow sapwood showing in the finished stock. English walnut is getting scarcer, but you'll never see sapwood in one of my stocks.

(Author's Note: Photographs 7-10 are in the Color Section, page 8A.)

Photo No. 7: Once in a while a blank turns up with all of the best attributes. This Bertuzzi sidelock's stock was made from an English walnut blank that was quarter-sawn, had nearly perfect wrist grain, lovely contrasting marbling, and flamboyant feather-crotch figure. It is nearly a mirror image, side to side. It has been stained with a red color to give it the look of an early English gun and to tone down the feather-crotch figure. Don't ask me to find another blank like this one—but if you have one for sale, I'm interested.

Photo No. 8: This Fox 16-gauge stock is a wonderful example of marbled English walnut and one of the finest pieces of wood I have ever worked with. Although slab-sawn, it has excellent wrist grain, turning perfectly down to follow the semi-pistol-grip curve. The pattern of the wood's coloration is quite different side to side, but it has equally deep, black marble cake on each side. The stock has an attractive brown background color, to which I've added a bit of red toning.

Marbling is the most common fancy grain found in English walnut. Slab-sawing splashes the black streaking across the width of the blank—as opposed to the thin lines produced with quarter-sawing. Slab-sawing will show the choicest marble cake, but it can also result in one-sidedness.

Photo No. 9: This English walnut blank is quarter-sawn, is well laid out for a straight grip

stock, and is fairly fancy. It has good color contrast and most of its fancy character comes from the feather-crotch grain in the butt. The feather is easy to see on the left side of the blank as it spreads from the comb down toward the toe.

This distinctive wood grain of feather-crotch occurs where a root or large limb meets the trunk of the tree. Although fairly common in black walnut, feather-crotch is relatively rare in English walnut. In either, the root or limb must be very large to spread the feather across both sides of a blank. One-sided feather-crotch is not particularly attractive, at least to my eye.

Photo No. 10: The right side of the same blank shown in Photo No. 9 is a bit light in the feather. I believe it will pick up more character as the stock is shaped, and I'll probably lay the centerline slightly to the left side to allow for cast-off.

Crotch grain doesn't make a stock any stronger and is undesirable in the wrist of the stock. In fact, with figured wood, checks, splits, or cracks are more likely to appear during the drying stage. To lessen the chance of checking, the woodcutter will apply a heavy coat of wax to the top and bottom of the blank wherever the feather comes out. Also note how the feather causes the grain flow to curve upward. Unless a blank is very carefully laid out by the cutter, this will cause upturned grain flow at the toe, which is too fragile for a checkered butt. If the crotch grain is too far forward on the top of the blank, it can result in a fragile comb nose.

Notice how the grain in this blank flows straight and consistently from the wrist through the full length of the toe line. The heel is a different story, as its left side has run out. Clearly, the wood grain is short and fragile at the heel, and in fact the blank has already cracked most of the way across the corner on the left side (circled in the photo), probably during drying. There's not much choice of butt-end capping with this stock. It is destined for a recoil pad in order to spread shock resistance over a larger area of the heel.

The left side of the blank (Photo No. 9) shows a small anomaly a third of the way down from the cracked heel. Feather-crotch wood sometimes has bark pockets, or inclusions, which are a result of limb junctions. I have no idea what's under the skin of the blank, but the flaw could open up. I'll discuss flaws a bit later—especially hidden ones.

This blank is small. Because the woodcutter knew something about stock layout and carefully sealed and dried the wood, it should make a very good gunstock. Layout is critical, and I often spend an hour or more with a Plexiglas template assuring the best possible grain flow for a stock. It is paramount that the template be a close approximation of the future stock's profile and be carefully positioned on both sides of the blank to maximize its good characteristics and minimize its defects. Recently, I have seen photos of domestic and imported blanks with feather-crotch badly laid out by the woodcutter. Several of these blanks have been in a very expensive price range.

This blank shows the classic, or Winchester, layout for a crotch-grain stock. Sometimes a blank can lay out properly in the opposite position, with the feather entering from behind the grip and extending up toward the heel of the stock. I've never seen a proper stock with the feather anywhere in the grip section or entering from the butt end forward. Beware of anyone selling this type of wood; they don't know the attributes of a good gunstock. Without structural integrity in the grip/wrist area, you don't have the makings of a quality gunstock.

So far I've avoided mentioning forend wood. Many times I've heard, "A blank ought to be big enough to provide a forend as well as a butt," or, "The only way to get a good butt-to-forend match is to buy a rifle-size blank." After three decades making gunstocks, I don't believe

either opinion. Two-piece blanks are being cut to minimum size these days, and the last rifle stock blank I used for a two-piece stock had the worst match of forend to butt of any stock I've made in years. (The blank's butt was highly figured and the front end smoky black; I had to put two coats of stain on the forend and one on the butt to match the background color.)

In anticipation of the occasional mismatched forend, I inventory at least twenty-five different forend blanks besides the ones I get with each two-piece stock. Each is different in background color, type of cut, and figure. Rare is the buttstock I can't match to a forend out of that inventory.

If you try to lay out a buttstock to pull a forend out of the same blank, more often than not you'll sacrifice the best layout for the wrist, which is the most important part of the entire stock. The best solution for the one-time buyer is to make sure that the forend blank that comes with a two-piece stock matches the stock in cut, color, figure, and length of drying time. Again, I prefer quarter-sawn wood for forends. Just peek at all the fragile edges, and you'll see that the strongest and stablest wood is best. And if you need wood for a large beavertail forend, you'll need a larger blank than normally supplied with a two-piece set.

Below, I'll show examples of odd blanks that are difficult to evaluate and some of the all-too-common flaws that show up (or are hidden) in walnut blanks. As a prime example, the stock blank shown in Photo Nos. 9 and 10 had a bark inclusion about the size of a walnut in the middle of the wrist grain. I did not discover it until after the action was inlet and fit to the blank and I was in process of band sawing the profile of the stock. I scrapped the wood and started over with another blank, the moral being that no matter how experienced or careful one is in choosing a stock blank, there are no guarantees and always potential problems.

• • •

There are plenty of oddly shaped and oddly cut stock blanks for sale. Trying to squeeze the maximum number of usable blanks from a given walnut plank eliminates any notion of uniformity. Larger bolt-action-rifle blanks are somewhat predictable, but two-piece buttstocks come in all shapes and sizes because they are usually the leftovers after the rifle blanks are determined. The shape and dimensions of a buttstock blank are unimportant. The usable area within them is what counts.

Because shotgun stocks rarely have a cheekpiece, a two-inch-thick blank is all you need. Straight-grip stocks require the least amount of wood of any style of gunstock. Often, as in the case of the feather-crotch blank, a small blank will do nicely.

The woodcutters who saw the boards into blanks are the people who control the layout qualities of the final products. The same folks are usually responsible for wax-sealing the ends and fancy grain of the blanks and have some control over the drying and attendant checking, cracking, or warping. Because of the irregular shape of a gunstock, it is amazing how much a blank can warp, cup, or twist during drying and still make a decent stock.

All these visible flaws that occur during drying—checking, splits, cracks, twisting, warping, and so on—are also associated with fancy-figured wood or slab-sawn blanks that show the greatest color contrast. I tried to find a twisted stock blank to photograph, but the quarter-sawn wood I normally choose shrinks relatively uniformly while drying and isn't prone to warping.

There are two schools of thought on using warped or twisted wood for gunstocks. One is that if the wood is completely dry (at least three years) and well seasoned (another three to five years, or more), all the movement has taken place and the blank should remain stable. The other is

that the mere fact that the wood has twisted suggests that it is full of stresses that will be unleashed when it is pared down to a stock— either that or long-term humidity variations will cause it to move. I believe in holding a blank in the stockmaker's shop for a period of time so that it will "normalize" to those climatic conditions. If a stock is to be machine-inletted and -shaped, it is a good idea to let it sit again, after machining, for the same reason.

The most recent stock I made (with client-supplied wood) had a heck of a warp in the butt when I started on it. A year later I didn't see any change and don't expect to.

I can tell you from experience that when I moved from western Oregon (normal relative humidity 70 percent to 99 percent) to central Montana (20 percent to 40 percent humidity) all my stocks shrank. I'm talking about custom guns that I built from cured blanks. The least affected were the quarter-sawn English walnut stocks. The most drastic change took place in a flintlock fowler with a fifty-six-inch-long full stock of fiddleback sugar maple. The steel buttplate ended up $1/32$ of an inch proud of the wood at the toe.

Each of the following blanks shown here has something odd about it.

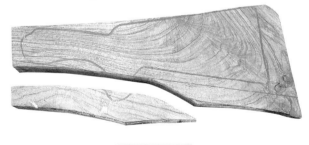

Photo Nos. 11 & 12: This wood looks like a lovely quarter-sawn crotch stick with the bottom of the blank sawed off. There are two visible flaws: a rather large and deep knot that can be seen only on the bottom (Photo No. 12), and a bark pocket at the toe on the left side.

I bought the blank—for a client— from a dealer's photos and wasn't aware of the knot. When it arrived, I decided I wanted to keep it and called the dealer and told him to remember the knot in case I found a major flaw a year later when I band sawed it. The client came through town, looked at the blank and freaked out about the knot. I sawed the bottom of the stock to show him there wouldn't be any problem with his straight-grip stock. But I knew an unseen flaw could remain somewhere in the crotch grain.

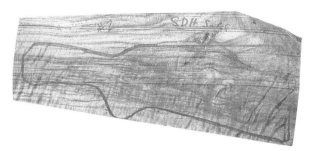

Photo No. 13: The blank shown here is odd because of its orange background and irregular bands of black color. I bought it because of the lovely fiddleback that shows well on both sides, which is typical with quarter-sawn wood. Slab-sawn wood will show the fiddleback better on the top and bottom of the blank. This blank has no visible flaws, although the grain takes a turn and is slab-sawn at the butt end. I bought it for inventory because I have a method of staining and finishing fiddleback that enhances its character.

Photo No. 14: This wood has a reddish background color like that of the genuine French walnut that used to be available. The grain, as seen in the smoke streaks, swirls up and down in the grip area and butt. On the bottom of the left

side, there is a crack (circled) near the butt end. The blank is slab-sawn and barely two inches thick. I bought it because it lays out quite nicely with a certain pistol-grip pattern placed fully forward on the blank, with the heel of the pattern tilted up to the top corner, missing the crack. I also like the rich but subdued color, the figure, and the fact that it has cured for more than a dozen years. I had it in my shop on approval, with plenty of time and templates to help me decide. I doubt that I would have bought it at a show, where I had neither time nor templates for evaluation.

Photo No. 15: The yellowish color of this blank is unusual. It has one pin knot, with the center fallen out, on the right side. The knot is small and far enough back not to cause a problem. There is some open-pored, light-colored wood at the bottom of the blank and at the corner of the heel. The blank also has strong figure on one side of the butt and shows extremely wavy smoke coloration at both quarter-sawn ends. It's another speculation stick that I believed would improve greatly in appearance as it was shaped and, again, after I stained and finished it. The layout wasn't universally applicable and the pores were a bit large, but a few years after I bought it, it became a lovely stock for a single-shot rifle project.

I would not suggest that the uninitiated buy any of these blanks, especially from photos. The feather stick with the big knot (Photo No. 11) caused me some concern, but as with any reputable dealer, the fellow who sold it to me guaranteed replacement if I found a problem inside. As a gunmaker, I can take a calculated risk in buying odd blanks because I have an experienced vision of what they might become. They are often discounted, and, in the case of the twelve-year-old wood, well seasoned simply because no one purchased the ugly duckling.

Now let's look at some inside problems—flaws that could not be seen or judged or worked around before band-sawing the wood. A couple of years ago at the Safari Club International Show, Tony Galazan showed me a beautiful band-sawed stick—a very expensive one—that was rotten to the core, though no problems were evident on the outside. Galazan was looking for the wood merchant, just as I would have been.

Photo No. 16: The blank shows a typical T-shaped bark inclusion in the end grain of a forend block. Nothing shows on the outside of the block, but the pocket goes down a full inch. I usually probe these inclusions, when I can see them, with a small stiff wire.

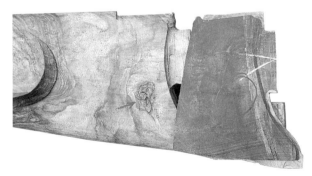

Photo No. 17: This machined rifle stock, with an arrow pointing at a large bark pocket, is extremely fancy English walnut. The fellow who machined the stock thoughtfully saved a slab to show me that the bark pocket wasn't visible from the outside and to give me some matching wood to plug the hole with after I dug out the soft, punky wood. The circle on the slab is the outer location of the bark pocket. The wrist grain of this stock had perfect conformation, and I was aware of the risk of the ornate butt figure. There was no guaranteed replacement because I bought it from a fellow who was passing through town. The stock finished beautifully, and the only time anyone notices the filler plug is when I point it out.

A few years ago I found a nail sticking out of the comb of a stock I was shaping. Hoping it was a finishing nail, I tried to pull it out. Unfortunately, it was a galvanized roofing nail with a $5/8$-inch head buried in the comb. I dug it out and plugged the hole with plain wood that had closely matching grain. During the oil finishing, I "painted in" black smoke-streaks with India ink, which made the repair difficult to see. The stock is 100-percent quarter-sawn, sound, and lovely to look at.

Probably the best place to see a substantial variety of stock blanks is the Firearms Engravers & Gunmakers Exhibition in Reno. Some dealers may warehouse more blanks, but seeing a variety of dealers and literally hundreds of blanks is fantastic. It's also nice, from my personal angle, to have a dozen or more folks to ask, "Will you look at a blank for me?"

I don't recommend that my clients purchase their own wood, and I'll issue the same warning here. But if you insist on buying your own blank, go back and reexamine the baseline blank at the beginning of this chapter. If the batch of blanks you're looking at doesn't have numerous examples of this type of stock layout, perhaps the merchant doesn't know what a stock blank is supposed to look like. I have photos of blanks from wood sellers throughout the country, and some of these people don't have a clue, despite their sky-high prices. Some sellers have oddly shaped blanks that might work if I had them in hand with a template. When they send photos, they tend to show their "best," which often equates more to expense than quality. By the same token, other wood dealers are very knowledgeable, friendly, helpful, honest, and reasonably priced.

SECTION 6
Shotgun Engraving

CHAPTER 20

Custom Shotguns and American Engraving

In the U.S. there has been a long association between custom shotguns and American engraving. By "custom shotguns" I mean, at least for my purpose here, that by and large either the barrels and actions were imported or the guns are elaborations on factory work, largely the products of small-shop custom gunmakers.

For example, in the 1930s the Hoffman Arms Co. built some twenty-five custom shotguns on metalwork reportedly imported from Austria. The guns were engraved by Rudolph Kornbrath, an Austrian import himself. In the 1950s, Griffin & Howe finished out a few Belgian guns that were engraved by Joseph Fugger, at the time the company's house engraver. Fugger was another Austrian-born and -trained engraver who worked with Kornbrath for a time.

Early one-man-shop gunmakers, such as Fred Adolph and R.G. Owen, also built custom shotguns that were engraved by Americans. Perhaps you've seen a Winston Churchill-engraved Parker in a Rolex watch advertisement. (Churchill was a protégé of Fugger's at Griffin & Howe.) That Parker had many metalwork refinements and was custom stocked in the shop of preeminent gunmaker Jerry Fisher. In the thirty-plus years I've been in the trade, I've seen many custom shotguns—mostly Winchester Model 21s, Browning Superposeds, and Parkers—from small-shop custom makers that were embellished by American engravers.

The four shotguns I've chosen to illustrate this chapter are prime examples of how individuals can have guns engraved to suit their tastes. The guns are three custom boxlocks—two from my workshop—and a custom sidelock I recently completed.

There are several ways to own a custom gun embellished by an American engraver. I've been involved with each of these methods, so I speak from experience. The Fox shown (circa 1993) is one of the Hughes/Fox guns I used to build. In fact, the individual who owns this gun became interested in custom guns by way of his love for engraving. After having had a few factory guns engraved in this country, he wanted custom guns created so that the guns themselves would be on par with the quality of the engraving.

I began that Fox project by fully tuning and refining the metalwork inside and out. After the gun had been stocked to the client's dimensions, Eric Gold was commissioned to embellish it. Small English scroll was chosen to suit the client's tastes, the small size of the 20-gauge action, and Gold's ability to produce some of the finest and tightest small scroll one is likely to see. The client requested a healthy amount of coverage but did not want the gun completely covered up. He chose the gold barrel bands, and Eric Gold suggested small golden roses on the fences for a touch more precious metal.

The client lives in Georgia and asked for bobwhite quail on the bottom of the action. He

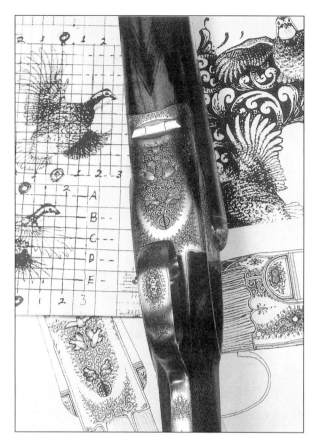

A Hughes/Fox with engraving of quail bursting from small scroll, with engraver Eric Gold's drawings.

did not want a game scene per se, so the engraver designed a covey of quail bursting forth from the small scroll on the bottom of the action. Gold achieved a delightful blend of gamebirds and scroll that I've yet to see matched.

Perhaps the easiest way to obtain custom American engraving is to have an existing gun engraved. An Italian-made Marocchi engraved by Martin Rabeno is a good example. The gun was not restocked, but several steps were taken before engraving. A hardened action had to have the metal annealed—rendered to its softest state—prior to engraving. Because most factory guns are machine-polished, the metal required hand-polishing as well. After engraving, the action had to be rehardened. Often the engraver can handle these steps in his own shop in conjunction with a commercial heat-treating firm.

This is a rewarding way to enhance the personalization of a shotgun, if one is happy with the existing stock.

I currently have a project in my shop offering another avenue. The gun is a Garbi, a 20-gauge two-barrel set ordered from Spain, in-the-white, without engraving or hardening. All of the working parts are fit and functioning; the gun has been proofed, but the action, forend iron, lock-plates, and so on are still soft. The Garbi was ordered with plain wood—the Spanish require a stock on a gun before proofing. As of this writing, and as one of the final steps in the process, I am completing a custom stock for this particular gun, which will feature American engraving.

The Sauer pictured is another example of a custom shotgun. In this case, the client obtained a barely-used 1930s Field Grade ejector gun for the project. Again the metal was annealed, filed up with asymmetric scalloping, and completely hand polished, along with other modifications. The metalwork was custom stocked prior to engraving. All of this work was done in my shop.

Engraver Michael Dubber did a fine job embellishing the gun with modest coverage. Note that the main scroll clusters on the action and fences are not tied to any border but float by themselves. The border work, lever checkering, rosettes, and gold "SAFE" make for complete and attractive decoration. In my opinion, the quality of this engraving is excellent and as fine as one is likely to see on any gun, excepting the most lavish, especially for the amount of coverage.

Another Michael Dubber-engraved shotgun shown is a Bertuzzi sidelock 20-gauge. It had been imported to the U.S. in the 1960s, in-the-white. I located the unfinished gun, and my client purchased it. The stock had a horribly flared pistol grip and an enormous beavertail forend in the style of the times. The stock was scrapped, and the metalwork was chiseled and filed to form. After custom stocking, the sidelock was turned over to Dubber, who treated it to an

A Hughes/Sauer with modest but finely executed rose & scroll by Michael Dubber.

original, yet traditional, version of rose & scroll engraving. The client now has a lovely shotgun, with all the work—except the creation of the barreled action—done in this country.

As a custom gunmaker who loves to create special shotguns, I am always on the lookout for project guns or metalwork that would be adaptable to—and worthy of—extensive custom gunsmithing. As I mentioned in previous chapters—"Arcaded Fences" and "Double Gun Metalwork" —I had an opportunity to buy six Belgian sidelock side-by-side barreled actions, in-the-white. These had been manufactured by the Britte Co. and had been sitting in storage in Belgium since 1937. They are embodiments of old world craftsmanship and pre-World War II quality, and I jumped through some tight hoops to acquire a half dozen. (The first custom gun that I completed using Britte metalwork is shown in the Color Section. Larry Peters engraved it with rose and scroll and my name on the top rib.)

I distinctly remember another shotgun that was perfect for embellishment. An acquaintance wanted to sell a sleek and lovely 28-gauge gun. It was an older Spanish Arrieta sidelock with 28-

A Parker that was customized and engraved by Barry Lee Hands with small scroll and a vignette fashioned from an A.B. Frost etching.

inch barrels, a blued action with minimal engraving, a nice piece of wood, and proper dimensions. It would have been a relatively easy job to polish, engrave, and refinish the metal.

I've seen quite a number of upgraded American guns as well, although these days such projects are undertaken less frequently. For many years, individuals as well as some dealers were taking VH Grade Parkers and upgrading the wood and engraving to DH-and-higher grades. Years ago it was possible to own an upgrade for far less than the cost of an original, but even with the rising cost and diminishing availability of high-quality handwork, upgrades continue to be produced.

The Barry Lee Hands-engraved Parker action pictured is not an upgrade, although the gun was a 12-gauge VH Grade. Hands took on this project for himself, polishing and stocking the gun to fit. He did all of the work except the checkering. The sporting scene is from an A.B. Frost etching—an evocative one, at that. The scroll is Hands's version of small English, with more backgrounding and shading than most British work. I find the layout and execution to be very attractive; the American hunting vignette is perfect for a Parker.

Recently, there have been Japanese-made Parker Reproductions offered as completely finished—stocked, finished, and even checkered—and ready for engraving. I'm sure the future will see many of these guns with embellishments by American engravers.

So what are the drawbacks to having a gun custom built and engraved? If the work is well done, it won't come cheap, and it might take a few years to complete. Since the publication of my book, *Fine Gunmaking: Double Shotguns*, I've seen several examples of custom Fox projects similar to the one I featured. Most have been quite nice, and almost all have been custom-engraved.

If you are interested in commissioning a project, be sure to find a smith familiar with the type of gun you want and an engraver versed in the styles you favor. My clients almost universally enjoy the process as much as the final product. There are many decisions and choices to be made and plenty of discussions to be had. Always remember that the goal is to wind up with a gun built to suit you and embellished to please you.

CHAPTER 21
Firearms Engravers Guild of America

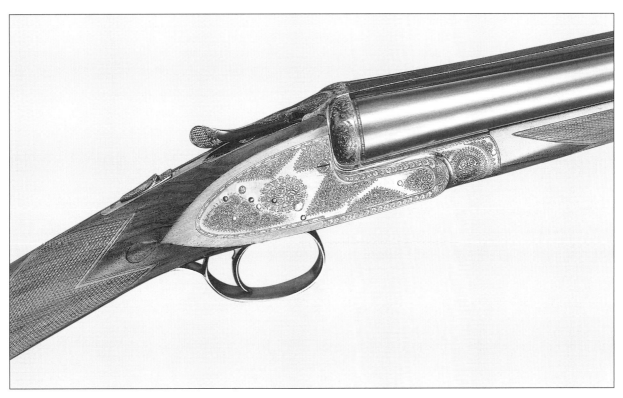

A custom Hughes Bertuzzi with rose & scroll engraving in a negative-space design engraved by Michael Dubber.

At no other time in history has firearms engraving advanced as an applied art form as it has in the past two decades. This is a bold statement, but considering the sheer number of guns available and the depth and breadth of worldwide interest in specialty firearms, it seems quite plausible. I've always contended that contemporary craftsmen have two major advantages over those of yesteryear: the electric light and the printed page. I have heard stories of early-twentieth-century English engravers working at night by lamp light—and they surely did not have available the books we have today. My own firearms library contains perhaps three hundred volumes, and almost all of them include photos of engraved guns.

Recent publications such as Marco E. Nobili's *Il Grande Libro Delle Incisioni* and *Fine*

COURTESY A. GALAZAN

An A. Galazan over-and-under, engraved with English scroll and game scenes by Christian DeCamillis.

European Gunmakers present some of the world's finest engraving, much of it continental. *British Gun Engraving*, by Douglas Tate, and Christopher Austyn's *Gun Engraving* cover more than a century of English artistic development.

Unfortunately, there are few publications documenting the skill and development of contemporary American engravers. The recent reprint of E.C. Prudhomme's *Gun Engraving Review* illustrates a lot of American work prior to 1961, when the book was originally published, with a heavy emphasis on German and Austrian expatriate engravers such as Rudolph Kornbrath and Arnold Griebel. *Steel Canvas*, by R.L.

Wilson, shows American engraving on guns from single-action Colts to Winchester rifles, and a couple of chapters deal with work that's been done since the 1960s. *Custom Firearms Engraving*, by Tom Turpin, is the only book I'm aware of that deals almost exclusively with current American firearms embellishment. Turpin's other book, *Modern Custom Guns*, has a section devoted exclusively to modern American engravers and contains many examples of custom guns. For decades, the annual publication, *Gun Digest*, has included a section titled, "The Art of the Engraver."

Engraver Ron Smith has self-published a

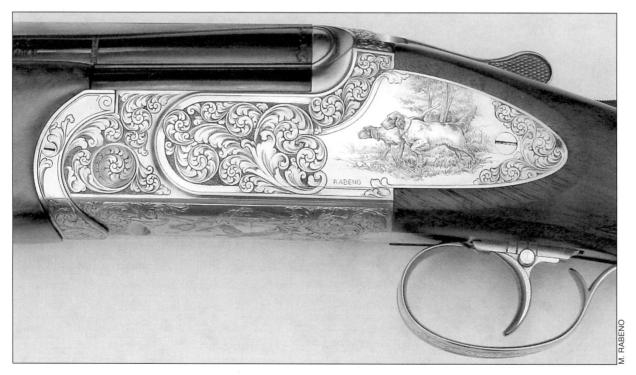

M. RABENO

A Marocchi Conquista with bold scroll and "bank-note" game scene engraved by Martin Rabeno.

ALAN RICHMOND

*A Ruger Red Label with gold wire, scroll, and a lively springer spaniel game scene
engraved by Lee Griffiths.*

couple of books that I find invaluable to the thorough understanding of firearms engraving. While mainly directed towards advancing one's skills as an engraver, both *Drawing & Understanding Scroll Designs* and the more recent *Advanced Drawing of Scrolls* offer a depth of knowledge beyond that of other books. (Both are available through the Firearms Engravers Guild of America, or FEGA.)

Fortunately, FEGA is striving to heighten the awareness of gun engraving by contemporary American artisans. A group of thirty-five engravers met in Houston, Texas, in 1981 and formed the guild. After more than two decades, FEGA boasts a membership of almost four hundred, with over fifty FEGA-certified "Professional" members.

Anyone can become an associate member by simply advancing the membership fee; working engravers can join as regular members for a slightly greater fee. An élite group has earned Professional status by meeting a set of published criteria and receiving the votes of their peers. All FEGA members receive a subscription to the

quarterly journal, *Engraver,* and a how-to notebook with information contributed by members that is quite a treat for engravers and engraving enthusiasts alike. FEGA also offers for sale its Professional Directory, which lists the professional members and showcases their talents in photos. Free admission to FEGA's annual exhibition is another member benefit.

The annual Firearms Engravers & Gunmakers Exhibition is held in January each year in Reno, Nevada. The exhibition provides a wonderful opportunity to see and examine fine engraving firsthand. The exhibition is a joint effort with the American Custom Gunmakers Guild (ACGG), and many of the embellished firearms are examples of the finest custom work being done in the U.S. Visitors may see an eye-catching shotgun at an engraver's exhibit or find an extraordinary example of engraving displayed by a gunmaker. The exhibition is held at the same time as the Safari Club International Show, also in Reno, so those attending either can catch both.

If you attended The Vintage Cup in recent years, you probably saw the FEGA display there.

With a nationwide membership, FEGA is striving to bring American engraving to the public through a variety of venues.

What kind of engraving is one likely to see at such an exhibition? Almost anything imaginable. American engravers have been studying Italian bulino via the books previously mentioned, but some were executing "bank note" before those titles were published. I first saw Robert Swartley's delicate and imaginatively engraved vignettes in a 1970s-vintage *Gun Digest*. Eric Gold has added absolutely marvelous fine English scroll to some of my own creations. Martin Rabeno developed a unique large-scroll style for those who enjoy flamboyant visuals along with technical excellence.

You should know that you're not likely to see a plethora of engraved shotguns at FEGA displays, although each year there seem to be more. Most of the firearms are custom rifles—bolt-actions and single-shots—built by ACGG members. There are also plenty of pistols and knives, as well as many factory guns elaborated solely by engraving. The styles really do run the gamut, and it's great fun to ask individual engravers about their personal interpretations of the various scroll types.

There typically are gold inlays aplenty, and you'll find 24-karat flush and relief-chiseled animals from elephants to woodcock. Some guns contain fine gold wire on blued or case-colored metal—a personal favorite of mine. Gold lettering, barrel bands, and borders accompany other works.

Scroll styles vary wildly and include small, medium, and large sizes; floral, symmetrical, and relief chiseled patterns; and delicate vine scroll. Many of the longtime professionals have advanced scrollwork to the point where their names are associated with particular patterns, such as "Swartley Scroll." The engraver Terry Wallace (now deceased) unabashedly admitted the tremendous influence Swartley had on his work, but he left a large enough body of his own distinctive work that you could call it "Wallace Scroll."

Often a result of attending this joint exhibition is the urge to have work done on your own guns. So study your books, think about your preferences, then wing it to Reno in January for an eyeful of what is sure to get you enthused about engraving.

FEGA has a constantly expanding Web site (www.fega.com) that will please any student of American engraving. The site offers many different views of many different guns engraved by the guild's Professional members.